READING
EXPLORER

5

THIRD EDITION

NANCY DOUGLAS • DAVID BOHLKE

HELEN HUNTLEY • BRUCE ROGERS • PAUL MACINTYRE

NATIONAL
GEOGRAPHIC
LEARNING

Australia • Brazil • Mexico • Singapore • United Kingdom • United States

National Geographic Learning,
a Cengage Company

Reading Explorer 5
Third Edition

Nancy Douglas, David Bohlke, Helen Huntley,
Bruce Rogers, and Paul MacIntyre

Publisher: Andrew Robinson

Executive Editor: Sean Bermingham

Senior Development Editor: Christopher Street

Editorial Assistant: Dawne Law

Director of Global Marketing: Ian Martin

Heads of Regional Marketing:

   Charlotte Ellis (Europe, Middle East and Africa)

   Kiel Hamm (Asia)

   Irina Pereyra (Latin America)

Product Marketing Manager: Tracy Bailie

Senior Production Controller: Tan Jin Hock

Associate Media Researcher: Jeffrey Millies

Art Director: Brenda Carmichael

Operations Support: Hayley Chwazik-Gee

Manufacturing Planner: Mary Beth Hennebury

Composition: MPS North America LLC

For permission to use material from this text or product, submit all requests online at **cengage.com/permissions**
Further permissions questions can be emailed to
permissionrequest@cengage.com

Student Book with Online Workbook:
ISBN-13: 978-0-357-12474-1

Student Book:
ISBN-13: 978-0-357-11630-2

National Geographic Learning
200 Pier Four Blvd
Boston, MA 02210
USA

Locate your local office at **international.cengage.com/region**

Visit National Geographic Learning online at **ELTNGL.com**
Visit our corporate website at **www.cengage.com**

Printed in the United States of America

Print Number: 02   Print Year: 2022

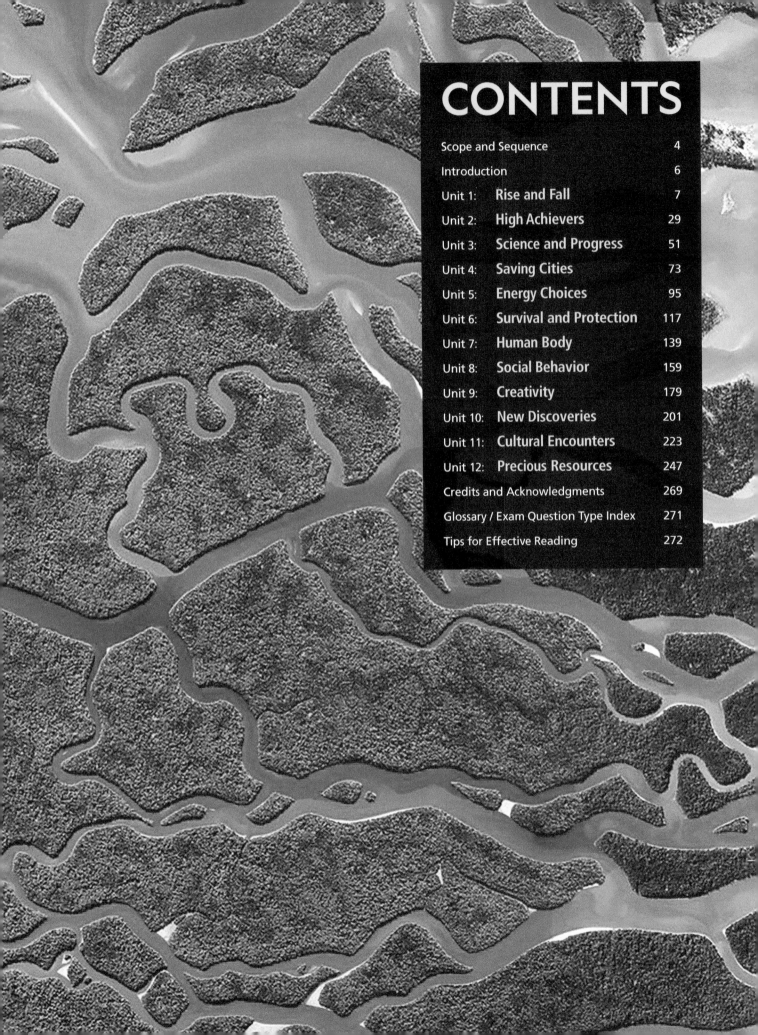

CONTENTS

SCOPE AND SEQUENCE

UNIT	THEME	READING	VIDEO
1	Rise and Fall	**A:** Secrets of the Maya **B:** The Collapse of Angkor	Legacies of the Maya
2	High Achievers	**A:** The Sky Runner **B:** The Free Soloist	Soloing Safely
3	Science and Progress	**A:** The Age of Disbelief **B:** Goalkeepers for the Planet	Energy Entrepreneur
4	Saving Cities	**A:** City Under Siege **B:** Rising Seas	Hurricanes
5	Energy Choices	**A:** Our Energy Diet **B:** Plugging into the Sun	Eco-Detectives
6	Survival and Protection	**A:** Quicksilver **B:** Building the Ark	Life on Ice
7	Human Body	**A:** Secrets of the Brain **B:** Human Bionics	A Giant Step
8	Social Behavior	**A:** The Genius of Swarms **B:** Of Ants and Humans	Crane Migration
9	Creativity	**A:** Decoding Leonardo **B:** The Power of Writing	Infinity Artist
10	New Discoveries	**A:** Cosmic Dawn **B:** Element Hunters	Black Holes
11	Cultural Encounters	**A:** The World of Süleyman the Magnificent **B:** When the Moors Ruled Spain	Crossroads of the World
12	Precious Resources	**A:** Gold Fever **B:** The Rush for White Gold	The Lure of Lithium

ACADEMIC SKILLS

READING SKILL	VOCABULARY BUILDING	CRITICAL THINKING
A: Understanding Complex Infographics (1) **B:** Evaluating Arguments (1)	**A:** Collocations with *grueling* **B:** Word root: *reg*	**A:** Analyzing Evidence **B:** Applying Ideas; Reflecting
A: Guessing Meaning from Context—Idioms and Colloquial Language **B:** Understanding Rhetorical Purpose	**A:** Word usage: *merely* **B:** Collocations with *plummet*	**A:** Applying Ideas **B:** Inferring Reasons; Reflecting
A: Identifying Figurative Language **B:** Making Inferences (1)	**A:** Word usage: *bias, prejudice, discrimination* **B:** Collocations with *initiative*	**A:** Applying Ideas **B:** Evaluating Ideas; Evaluating Problems
A: Recognizing Literal versus Figurative Language **B:** Evaluating Arguments (2)—Reading Critically	**A:** Word usage: *complement* and *compliment* **B:** Expressions with *take*	**A:** Analyzing Arguments **B:** Evaluating Solutions; Applying Ideas
A: Distinguishing Main Ideas and Supporting Information **B:** Determining Similarities and Differences	**A:** Collocations with *obstacle* **B:** Prefixes and Suffixes	**A:** Evaluating Solutions **B:** Analyzing Arguments; Applying Ideas
A: Understanding Words with Multiple Meanings **B:** Determining the Meaning of Root Words	**A:** Word root: *turb* **B:** Synonyms for *imminent*	**A:** Identifying Evidence **B:** Analyzing Arguments; Synthesizing Information
A: Understanding the Use of the Passive Voice **B:** Distinguishing Fact from Opinion	**A:** Collocations with *unprecedented* **B:** Collocations with *valid*	**A:** Reflecting **B:** Justifying Opinions; Applying Ideas
A: Making Inferences (2) **B:** Identifying Multiple Answers to Questions	**A:** Collocations with *coherent* **B:** Collocations with *fatal*	**A:** Identifying Pros and Cons **B:** Analyzing Arguments; Applying Ideas
A: Understanding Complex Infographics (2) **B:** Using Graphic Organizers to Organize Key Ideas	**A:** Collocations with *deny* **B:** Word root: *man*	**A:** Justifying Opinions **B:** Identifying Pros and Cons; Synthesizing Information
A: Increasing Your Reading Speed **B:** Understanding Long Sentences	**A:** Word root: *mit* **B:** Collocations with *quest*	**A:** Justifying Opinions **B:** Identifying Pros and Cons; Inferring Information
A: Creating a Mental Map of a Text **B:** Inferring an Author's Attitude	**A:** Word usage *bias* and *biased* **B:** Collocations with *violate*	**A:** Identifying Evidence **B:** Reflecting; Personalizing
A: Identifying Coherence Devices **B:** Synthesizing Ideas Across Readings	**A:** Suffix: *-ship* **B:** Word root: *vers*	**A:** Evaluating Pros and Cons **B:** Evaluating Arguments; Synthesizing Ideas

READING EXPLORER brings the world to your classroom.

With *Reading Explorer* you learn about real people and places, experience the world, and explore topics that matter.

What you'll see in the Third Edition:

Real-world stories give you a better understanding of the world and your place in it.

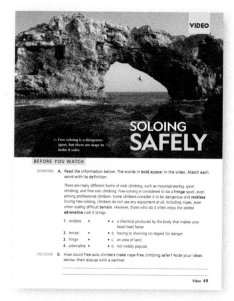

National Geographic Videos expand on the unit topic and give you a chance to apply your language skills.

Reading Skill and **Reading Comprehension** sections provide the tools you need to become an effective reader.

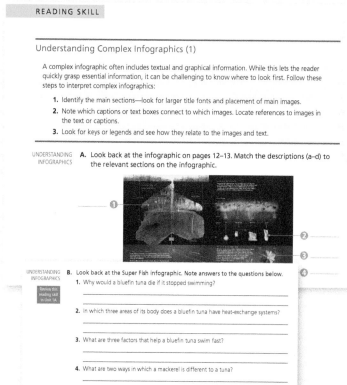

READING SKILL

Understanding Complex Infographics (1)

A complex infographic often includes textual and graphical information. While this lets the reader quickly grasp essential information, it can be challenging to know where to look first. Follow these steps to interpret complex infographics:

1. Identify the main sections—look for larger title fonts and placement of main images.
2. Note which captions or text boxes connect to which images. Locate references to images in the text or captions.
3. Look for keys or legends and see how they relate to the images and text.

UNDERSTANDING INFOGRAPHICS **A.** Look back at the infographic on pages 12–13. Match the descriptions (a–d) to the relevant sections on the infographic.

UNDERSTANDING INFOGRAPHICS **B.** Look back at the Super Fish infographic. Note answers to the questions below.

1. Why would a bluefin tuna die if it stopped swimming?

2. In which three areas of its body does a bluefin tuna have heat-exchange systems?

3. What are three factors that help a bluefin tuna swim fast?

4. What are two ways in which a mackerel is different to a tuna?

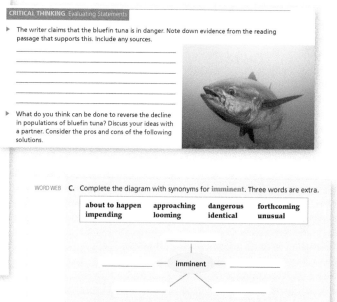

CRITICAL THINKING Evaluating Statements

▶ The writer claims that the bluefin tuna is in danger. Note down evidence from the reading passage that supports this. Include any sources.

▶ What do you think can be done to reverse the decline in populations of bluefin tuna? Discuss your ideas with a partner. Consider the pros and cons of the following solutions.

WORD WEB **C.** Complete the diagram with synonyms for imminent. Three words are extra.

| about to happen impending | approaching looming | dangerous identical | forthcoming unusual |

imminent

Expanded Vocabulary Practice sections teach you the most useful words and phrases needed for academic reading.

RISE AND FALL

A statue of a Maya warrior at the ruins of Chichén Itzá, Mexico

WARM UP

Discuss these questions with a partner.

1. What powerful ancient civilizations no longer exist today?

2. Why do you think these civilizations did not last?

BEFORE YOU READ

DISCUSSION   **A.** Look at the photo and read the caption. What do you know about the Maya civilization? Share your ideas with a partner.

PREDICTING   **B.** Why do you think cenotes were important to the ancient Maya? Discuss your ideas with a partner. Then read the passage to check your answer.

> Archeologist Guillermo de Anda descends into the Holtún cenote in Mexico's Yucatán Peninsula. Experts believe that cenotes—deep holes formed in limestone—were important to the ancient Maya, which ruled this part of the world from around 250 to 900 A.D.

SECRETS
OF THE MAYA

The study of caves and wells in Mexico's Yucatán Peninsula is shining new light on the beliefs of the ancient and modern Maya.

A From deep in a well near the ruins of the Maya city of Chichén Itzá, archeoastronomer[1] Arturo Montero shouts to his colleague on the surface, "I saw it, I saw it! Yes, it's true!" Leaning over the mouth of the well, archeologist Guillermo de Anda hopes to hear what he has suspected for many months. "What is true, Arturo?" he shouts. And Montero yells up again, "The zenith[2] light, it really works! Get down here!"

B The two archeologists are anxious to confirm whether this cenote could have acted as a sacred sundial[3] and timekeeper for the ancient Maya. On two days every year—May 23 and July 19—the sun reaches its zenith over this part of Mexico. At those moments, the sun is vertically overhead and there is no shadow. On the morning of their descent, on May 24, Montero and de Anda see that the sun's rays are nearly vertical. The day before, they realized, a beam of light would have **plunged** straight down into the water.

C Beneath its narrow mouth, the walls of the cenote open up to become a giant dome. It looks like a cathedral, except for the roots of trees that **penetrate** the rock. The beam of sunlight dances like fire on the surrounding stalactites,[4] and it turns the water a beautiful transparent blue. The archeologists were probably the first people in centuries to watch the sun move slowly across the cenote's water.

---

1 An **archeoastronomer** is someone who studies archeological artifacts to determine what ancient people believed and understood about astronomy.

2 The **zenith** is a point directly above a particular location.

3 A **sundial** is a device used for telling the time when the sun is shining. The shadow of a pointer falls onto a surface marked with the hours.

4 **Stalactites** are rock formations hanging from cave ceilings, slowly formed by dripping water.

D   Did Maya priests wait in this well—known as the Holtún cenote—to observe and correct their measurements of the sun's angle when it reached the zenith? Did they come here during times of drought to make offerings to their water god, and at other times to give thanks for a good harvest? These and other questions involving the Maya religion and its extraordinarily accurate calendar are what the two explorers were investigating.

E   In recent years, archeologists have been paying more attention to the meaning of caves, the zenith sun, and cenotes in the beliefs of the ancient and modern Maya. Archeologists already knew that the ancient Maya believed cenotes to be doors to a world inhabited by Chaak, the god of life-giving rain, but the significance of this fact has only recently started to become clear.

F   De Anda began exploring Holtún in 2010. One day, inspecting the walls of the cenote a few meters below the surface, he felt something above his head. He was astonished to find a

⌄ Chichén Itzá is located in Yucatán—a harsh region of Mexico with no rivers. Cenotes are the only permanent sources of fresh water.

natural rock shelf holding human and animal bones, pottery, and a knife—probably used for **sacrifices**—all neatly placed there centuries earlier. Below the water, he saw a number of columns and Maya stone carvings—the well was clearly a sacred site.

Key to Survival

G Three years later, in the cornfield on the surface above the cenote, a crew of Maya farmers is working hard in the **grueling** Yucatán heat to pull the explorers out of the well. "There was a good rain the other day," says the crew's leader, Louis Un Ken, as he wipes the sweat off his face. "The Chaak moved."

H For men like Un Ken, the old gods are still very much alive, and Chaak is among the most important. For the benefit of living things, he pours from the skies the water he keeps in jars. Thunder is the sound of Chaak breaking a jar open and letting the rain fall. The Chaak had moved, Un Ken said, and that meant the planting season would soon arrive.

I Chaak's absence can cause disasters for the Yucatán Maya, possibly the **demise** of the ancient Maya civilization itself. Their land is an endless limestone shelf. Rain sinks through the porous[5] limestone down to groundwater levels, and consequently no river runs through the land. From the air, one sees a green sea of dense jungle, but at ground level, the tropical forest appears very thin. Wherever there is enough **soil**, the Maya plant corn or a *milpa*, a crop-growing system including the corn, beans, and squash that **constitutes** their basic source of protein. But corn is a hungry crop; it sucks lots of nutrients from the soil. For thousands of years, milpa farmers have kept their small fields productive by burning a different area of trees every year and planting in the corn-friendly ashes.

J As for water for the fields, that's where Chaak comes in. Only seasonal rains can make the corn grow, and they must arrive in an exact pattern: no rain in winter so that the fields and forest will be dry enough to burn by March; some rain in early May to soften up the soil for planting; then very gentle rain to allow the seeds to begin to grow; and finally, plenty of rain so the corn can **flourish**.

Pleasing the Rain God

K In the village of Yaxuná, many people still depend on milpa, and an annual ceremony is held there to please the rain god. They walk a long way through the forest to a sacred cave and climb down to its center to bring up the water the ceremony requires. They raise the altar, dig a large cooking pit, and provide 13 fat chickens for the ritual meal. They cook them in the pit so the steam can rise directly to the rain god as an offering.

L One recent such ceremony in Yaxuná was guided by Hipólito Puuc Tamay, a Maya holy man called a *hmem*. He stood in front of an altar praying for the holy **blessing** of rain. On instructions from the hmem, one of the villagers sat on a rock near the altar, blowing from time to time into one of the gourds[6] in which Chaak stores the wind. He was just one of the neighbors, but he was also the rain god, and he sat with his eyes closed so as not to harm the ceremony with his terrible glance. Two other participants brought him to the altar, facing backward, to receive a blessing from the hmem.

M Out of nowhere, a wind came up, and thunder could be heard in the distance. As the ceremonial meal was being distributed, the rain started—a sign, the hmem said, that Chaak had received his offering and was pleased with his people's prayer. Soon, perhaps, the earth would be ready for planting.

---

5 Something that is **porous** has many small holes in it, which water and air can pass through.

6 A **gourd** is a container made from the hard, dry skin of a gourd fruit. Gourds are often used for carrying water or for decoration.

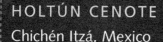

HOLTÚN CENOTE
Chichén Itzá, Mexico

Sun's zenith
May 23, July 19

70 meters (220 feet)

Before and after the sun's zenith, and on many other days, the rays slant into the cenote and are reflected onto the ceiling.

Shelf with offerings

Current water level

Holtún cenote

Additional artifacts

2.5 kilometers (1.6 miles)

LINKS TO THE COSMOS

For the Maya, astronomy was a sacred activity, as were architecture and city planning. De Anda and Montero now think that the Holtún and nearby cenotes may have played an important role in determining where to site buildings.

The El Castillo pyramid at Chichén Itzá is aligned to the March and September equinoxes[7] when the sun's passage makes a snakelike shadow slither down its side. The structure also stands in the middle of four cenotes (where the white lines cross, right), probably symbolizing the sacred mountain at the center of the Maya universe. It was also oriented to the moments when the sun reaches its highest point in the sky (far right), further connecting the cycles of the heavens.

---

7 The **equinoxes** are the two days of the year when the day and night are equal length.

A PLACE OF PRAYER

Desperate for water for their crops, the Maya prayed to the rain god Chaak from deep inside the cenote. They laid out offerings and performed rituals, which may have included human and animal sacrifices. Pots and sculptures found on the cenote's floor suggest that the Maya may have sacrificed objects by breaking them.

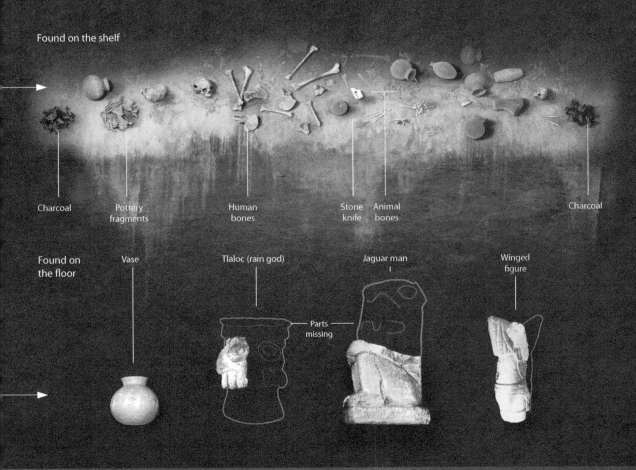

Found on the shelf

Charcoal

Pottery fragments

Human bones

Stone knife

Animal bones

Charcoal

Found on the floor

Vase

Tlaloc (rain god)

Jaguar man

Winged figure

Parts missing

IN LINE WITH THE SUN

Montero and de Anda speculate that Maya astronomers waited inside the Holtún well for the two days in the year when a vertical pillar of sunlight pierces the water without reflecting onto the dome. On these two days, the sun rises directly to the northeast of El Castillo and travels over its peak (right). It then moves in an arc to the northwest (yellow line below), where it passes over the Holtún cenote before sinking to the horizon.

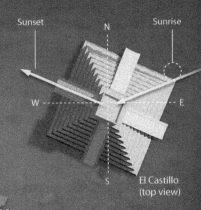

Sunset

Sunrise

N

W   E

S

El Castillo (top view)

Sacred cenote

Chichén Itzá

El Castillo

2.5 kilometers (1.6 miles)

Kanjuyum cenote

Sun's zenith
May 23, July 19

When the sun reaches its highest point in the sky—the solar zenith—its rays fall vertically to the ground.

Xtoloc cenote

A. Choose the best answer for each question.

MAIN IDEA

1. Why were Guillermo de Anda and Arturo Montero excited?

a. They had found the Holtún cenote.
b. They had revealed evidence of an unknown Maya rain god.
c. They had discovered that sunlight enters the cenote at special times.
d. They had seen the cenote's water turn blue.

REFERENCE

2. In paragraph A, what does *it* refer to in *I saw it, I saw it!*?

a. the cenote
b. the zenith light
c. the stone sundial
d. the mouth of the well

DETAIL

3. What are Arturo Montero and Guillermo de Anda NOT investigating in the cenote?

a. whether the ancient Maya had depleted the cenote's water from overuse
b. whether the ancient Maya went there to give thanks and offer sacrifices
c. whether the ancient Maya used the cenote as a sundial and timekeeper
d. whether ancient Maya priests used the cenote to correct their measurements of the sun's angle when it reached the zenith

INFERENCE

4. In paragraph G, what did Luis Un Ken mean when he said, *"The Chaak moved"*?

a. It had rained.
b. It was very hot.
c. Chaak had prayed.
d. Chaak was important.

A diver finds a Maya skull in a sacred cenote in Yucatán, Mexico.

DETAIL

5. Why is farming particularly difficult for the Maya?

a. Rivers flood regularly.
b. Rain does not sink into the ground.
c. Most of the region's land is made of limestone.
d. There are not enough farmers during harvest time.

SEQUENCE

6. To get the best crops, what must happen immediately after the fields are burned?

a. Seeds are planted.
b. The fields dry out.
c. Heavy rain soaks the fields.
d. Some rain softens the ground.

COHESION

7. Where would be the best place to insert this sentence in paragraph K?
The villagers work without rest or sleep to persuade Chaak to come to them.

a. after the first sentence
b. after the second sentence
c. after the third sentence
d. after the last sentence

B. Match each paragraph of the reading with the information it contains (a–g).
Two pieces of information are extra.

1. Paragraph A _____
2. Paragraph C _____
3. Paragraph D _____
4. Paragraph E _____
5. Paragraph F _____

a. what the inside of the cenote looks like
b. a dramatic introduction to the work of the archeologists
c. the reason why archeologists are investigating the cenote
d. the writer's opinion about the importance of the cenote
e. the artifacts found in the cenote
f. a comparison of ancient and modern Mayans
g. something archeologists already knew about cenotes

CRITICAL THINKING Analyzing Evidence

The author suggests that cenotes were of great importance to the ancient Maya. Look back at the reading and infographic and note 5 pieces of evidence the author uses to support this claim.

_____

_____

_____

_____

_____

> **The El Castillo pyramid dominates the center of Chichén Itzá.**

Understanding Complex Infographics (1)

A complex infographic often includes textual and graphical information. While this lets the reader quickly grasp essential information, it can be challenging to know where to look first. Follow these steps to interpret complex infographics:

1. Identify the main sections—look for larger title fonts and placement of main images.

2. Note which captions or text boxes connect to which images. Locate references to images in the text or captions.

3. Look for keys or legends and see how they relate to the images and text.

UNDERSTANDING INFOGRAPHICS

A. Look back at the infographic on pages 12–13. Match the descriptions (a–d) to the relevant sections on the infographic.

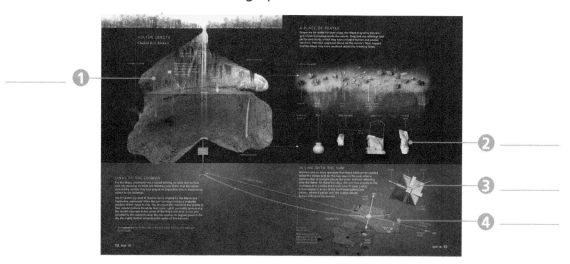

a. There are four cenotes surrounding El Castillo: Holtún cenote, Xtoloc cenote, Sacred cenote, and Kanjuyum cenote.

b. On days other than the sun's zenith, the sun rays reflect onto the cenote's walls.

c. The pyramid at Chichén Itzá is oriented to the moments when the sun reaches its highest point in the sky.

d. A vase and a winged figure were some of the artifacts discovered on the floor of the cenote.

UNDERSTANDING INFOGRAPHICS

B. Are the following statements true or false according to the infographic? Circle **T** (true) or **F** (false).

1. The Holtún cenote and the Kanjuyum cenote are the same distance from Chichén Itzá. **T   F**

2. During the sun's zenith, its rays are reflected onto the cave walls. **T   F**

3. The water surface is 70 meters below the mouth of the Holtún cenote. **T   F**

4. During droughts, the Maya put offerings on an exposed rock shelf. **T   F**

5. A broken Jaguar man was found on the rock shelf. **T   F**

COMPLETION   **A.** Complete the information using the correct form of the words in the box. One word is extra.

demise   flourish   grueling   inspect   plunge   soil

At its peak in the ninth century, the Maya civilization totaled 15 million people and ranged from present-day Mexico to Honduras. Then, the civilization collapsed: People abandoned their homes and left cities in ruins. What caused this society that once ¹_____ to suddenly collapse?

According to one study, three ²_____ droughts led to the ³_____ of the Maya. Researchers who ⁴_____ sediment from the Yucatán Peninsula found that these droughts corresponded with declines in Maya culture. The Maya were particularly at risk because they only had enough supplies of fresh water for 18 months. Without rain, the ⁵_____ couldn't support crops, leading to mass starvation. While the Maya people survived, they continued to suffer from the effects of periodic extreme drought over the next few centuries.

∧ **The ancient Maya kept a remarkably complex and accurate calendar.**

WORDS IN CONTEXT   **B.** Complete the sentences. Circle the correct options.

1. If someone **plunges** into a lake, they *enter slowly / jump in suddenly*.
2. A *religious leader / young child* is likely to give a **blessing** to someone else.
3. The **sacrifice** of an animal involves *killing / decorating* it.
4. If several people **constitute** something, they are the *parts that form it / ones who reject it*.
5. If water **penetrates** a surface, it *enters it / stays on top of it*.

COLLOCATIONS   **C.** The nouns in the box are commonly used with the adjective **grueling**. Complete the sentences using the words in the box.

journey   schedule   training

1. After a grueling _____ through rough terrain, we finally reached our destination.
2. Running a marathon requires months of grueling _____.
3. I have a grueling _____ next week. Eight exams in seven days!

BEFORE YOU READ

PREVIEWING
A. Look at the timeline and read the caption. Complete the notes about the Khmer Empire.

Empire founded by: _____

Location of capital city: _____

Start of empire's decline:_____

SKIMMING AND PREDICTING
B. Skim paragraphs A and B. What reasons for the decline of Angkor are mentioned? What other things might cause a civilization to decline? Discuss with a partner.

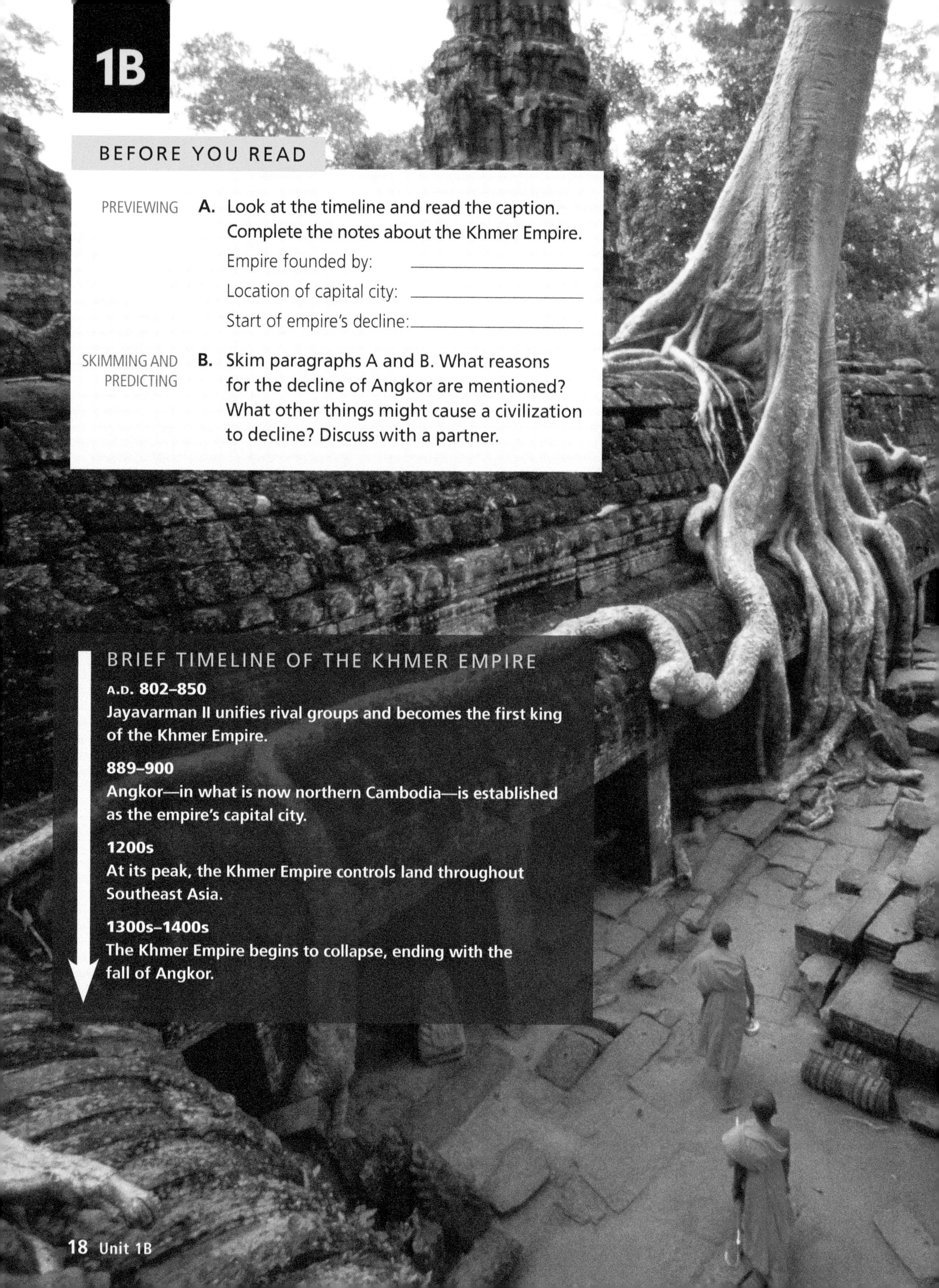

BRIEF TIMELINE OF THE KHMER EMPIRE

A.D. 802–850
Jayavarman II unifies rival groups and becomes the first king of the Khmer Empire.

889–900
Angkor—in what is now northern Cambodia—is established as the empire's capital city.

1200s
At its peak, the Khmer Empire controls land throughout Southeast Asia.

1300s–1400s
The Khmer Empire begins to collapse, ending with the fall of Angkor.

Ruins of more than one thousand temples can be found in the Angkor area. Ta Prohm is one of the best preserved.

THE COLLAPSE OF ANGKOR

After rising to sublime[1] heights, the sacred city may have engineered its own downfall.

An Empire's Fall

A Almost hidden amid the forests of northern Cambodia is the scene of one of the greatest vanishing acts of all time. This was once the heart of the Khmer kingdom. At its height, the Khmer Empire dominated much of Southeast Asia, from Myanmar (Burma) in the west to Vietnam in the east. As many as 750,000 people lived in Angkor, its magnificent capital. The most extensive urban complex of the preindustrial world, Angkor stretched across an area the size of New York City. Its greatest temple, Angkor Wat, is the world's largest religious monument even today.

B Yet when the first Europeans arrived in Angkor in the late 16th century, they found a city that was already dying. Scholars have come up with a list of suspected causes for Angkor's decline, including foreign **invaders**, a religious change of heart, and a shift to maritime trade. But it's mostly guesswork: Roughly 1,300 inscriptions survive on temple doors and monuments, but the people of Angkor left not a single word explaining their kingdom's collapse.

C Some scholars assume that Angkor died the way it lived: by the sword. The historical records of Ayutthaya, a neighboring state, claim that warriors from that kingdom "took" Angkor in 1431. No doubt Angkor would have been a rich prize—inscriptions boast that its temple towers were covered with gold. After its rediscovery by Western travelers just over a century ago, historians deduced from Angkor's ruins that the city had been looted[2] by invaders from Ayutthaya.

---

1 If you say something is **sublime**, you mean it has a wonderful quality.
2 If a store or house is **looted**, people have stolen things from it, for example, during a war or riot.

D Roland Fletcher, co-director of a research effort called the Greater Angkor Project, is not convinced. Some early scholars, he says, viewed Angkor according to the sieges[3] and conquests of European history. "The ruler of Ayutthaya, indeed, says he took Angkor, and he may have taken some formal regalia[4] back to Ayutthaya with him," says Fletcher. But after Angkor was captured, Ayutthaya's ruler placed his son on the throne. "He's not likely to have smashed the place up before giving it to his son."

E A religious shift may also have contributed to the city's decline. Angkor's kings claimed to be the world emperors of Hindu mythology and erected temples to themselves. But in the 13th and 14th centuries, Theravada Buddhism gradually took over from Hinduism, and its principles of social equality may have threatened Angkor's elite. "It was very **subversive**, just like Christianity was subversive to the Roman Empire," says Fletcher.

---

3 A **siege** is a military or police operation in which soldiers or police surround a place in order to force the people there to come out.

4 **Regalia** is the ceremonial jewelry, objects, or clothes that symbolize royalty or high office.

Rows of statues stand outside the stone gate of Angkor Thom—the last capital of the Khmer Empire.

F A new religion that promoted ideas of social equality might have led to a worker rebellion. The city operated on a moneyless economy, relying on tribute[5] and taxation, and the kingdom's main currency was rice. For one temple complex, Ta Prohm, more than 66,000 farmers produced nearly 3,000 tons of rice a year, which was then used to feed the temple's priests, dancers, and workers. Scholars estimate that farm laborers comprised nearly half of Greater Angkor's population.

G Or maybe the royal court simply turned its back on Angkor. Angkor's rulers often erected new temple complexes and let older ones decay. This may have **doomed** the city when sea trade began to develop between Southeast Asia and China. Maybe it was simple economic opportunism that had caused the Khmer center of power to shift: The move to a location closer to the Mekong River, near Cambodia's present-day capital, Phnom Penh, allowed it easier access to the sea.

H Economic and religious changes may have contributed to Angkor's downfall, but its rulers faced another foe. Angkor was powerful largely thanks to an advanced system of canals and **reservoirs**, which enabled the city to keep scarce water in dry months and **disperse** excess water during the rainy season. But forces beyond Angkor's control would eventually bring an end to this carefully constructed system.

I Few ancient sites in southern Asia could compare to Angkor in its ability to guarantee a steady water supply. The first scholar to appreciate the scale of Angkor's waterworks was French archeologist Bernard-Philippe Groslier. In 1979, he argued that the great reservoirs served two purposes: to symbolize the Hindu cosmos[6] and to irrigate the rice fields. Unfortunately, Groslier could not pursue his ideas further. Cambodia's civil war,[7] the brutal **regime** of the Khmer Rouge,[8] and the **subsequent** arrival of Vietnamese forces in 1979 turned Angkor into a no-go zone for two decades.

---

5 A **tribute** is something you give, say, do, or make to show your admiration and respect for someone.

6 The **cosmos** is the universe.

7 A **civil war** is a war fought between different groups of people who live in the same country.

8 The **Khmer Rouge** was a radical communist movement that ruled Cambodia from 1975 to 1979 after winning power through a guerrilla war.

J In the 1990s, Christophe Pottier followed up on Groslier's ideas and discovered that the south part of Angkor was a vast landscape of housing, water tanks, shrines, roads, and canals. Then, in 2000, Roland Fletcher and his colleague Damian Evans—as part of a collaborative study with Pottier—viewed some NASA radar images of Angkor. The researchers marveled at the sophistication of Angkor's infrastructure. "We realized that the entire landscape of Greater Angkor is artificial," Fletcher says. Teams of laborers constructed hundreds of kilometers of canals and dikes[9] that diverted water from the rivers to the reservoirs. Overflow **channels** bled off excess water that accumulated during the summer monsoon months, and after the monsoon, irrigation channels dispensed the stored water. "It was an incredibly clever system," says Fletcher.

K Fletcher was therefore baffled when his team made a surprising discovery. An extraordinary piece of Angkorian workmanship—a vast structure in the waterworks—had been destroyed, apparently by Angkor's own engineers. "The most logical explanation is that the dam failed," Fletcher says. The river may have begun to erode the dam, or perhaps it was washed away by a flood. The Khmer broke apart the remaining stonework and modified the blocks for other purposes.

L Any weakening of the waterworks would have left the city vulnerable to a natural phenomenon that none of Angkor's engineers could have predicted. Starting in the 1300s, it appears that Southeast Asia experienced a period of extreme climate change, which also affected other parts of the world. In Europe, which endured centuries of harsh winters and cool summers, it was known as the Little Ice Age.

M To an already weakened kingdom, extreme weather would have been the final blow. "We don't know why the water system was operating below capacity," says Daniel Penny, co-director of the Greater Angkor Project. "But what it means is that Angkor ... was more exposed to the threat of drought than at any other time in its history." If inhabitants of parts of Angkor were starving while other parts of the city were hoarding a finite quantity of rice, the most likely result was social instability. "When populations in tropical countries exceed the carrying capacity of the land, real trouble begins," says Yale University anthropologist Michael Coe, "and this inevitably leads to cultural collapse." A hungry army weakened by internal problems would have exposed the city to attack. Indeed, Ayutthaya's invasion happened near the end of a long period of drought.

N Add to the climate chaos the political and religious changes already affecting the kingdom, and Angkor's prospects were bleak, says Fletcher. "The world around Angkor was changing; society was moving on. It would have been a surprise if Angkor persisted."

O The Khmer Empire was not the first civilization brought down by climate catastrophe. Centuries earlier, loss of environmental stability likewise brought down another powerful kingdom halfway around the world. Many scholars now believe that the fall of the Maya followed a series of droughts in the ninth century. "Essentially, the same thing happened to Angkor," says Coe.

P In the end, the tale of Angkor is a lesson in the limits of human **ingenuity**. "Angkor's hydraulic[10] system was an amazing machine, a wonderful **mechanism** for regulating the world," Fletcher says. Its engineers managed to keep the civilization's achievement running for six centuries—until a greater force overwhelmed them.

---

9 A **dike** is a wall built to prevent flooding.
10 Something that is **hydraulic** involves the movement or the control of water.

A. Choose the best answer for each question.

MAIN IDEAS

1. What information does the passage NOT include?

    a. The Khmer Empire's conflicts with foreign powers

    b. the history of Angkor before the ninth century

    c. inscriptions left in the temples by the people of Angkor

    d. the purpose of Angkor's irrigation system

DETAIL

2. According to the information in paragraphs A and B, which of the following is NOT true about Angkor?

    a. It once ruled a large part of Southeast Asia.

    b. It was at one time the largest urban center in the world.

    c. It once held as many people as New York City does today.

    d. It was in decline when Europeans arrived in the 16th century.

VOCABULARY

3. In the first sentence of paragraph C, the phrase *by the sword* is closest in meaning to _____.

    a. suddenly   c. violently

    b. unexpectedly   d. secretively

REFERENCE

4. In the last sentence of paragraph D, the word *it* refers to _____.

    a. the kingdom of Ayutthaya

    b. the destruction of Angkor

    c. the formal regalia

    d. the city of Angkor

INFERENCE

5. We can infer from information in paragraph F that the greatest number of people in Angkor worked as _____.

    a. construction workers

    b. dancers

    c. priests

    d. agricultural workers

⌃ **A Buddhist head sculpture at Angkor Thom**

DETAIL

6. How did the climate in Angkor change in the 1300s?

    a. Winters became too cool to grow rice.

    b. Rising temperatures caused great discomfort.

    c. There were terrible storms and constant flooding.

    d. Weather conditions became more extreme.

RHETORICAL PURPOSE

7. Why does the author mention the Little Ice Age in paragraph L?

    a. to show that climate change caused more cultures to fail in Europe than in Asia

    b. to emphasize the extent and significance of climate change in the 1300s

    c. to explain why European cities were not as advanced as Angkor

    d. to show how Angkor's climate in the 1300s was different to Europe's

B. What are Roland Fletcher's views about Angkor? Check (✓) the statements that Fletcher would probably agree with based on information in the reading. Underline the information in the passage that helped you.

1. ☐ The main cause of Angkor's collapse was its conflict with Ayutthaya.
2. ☐ The ruler of Ayutthaya likely destroyed the palace at Angkor.
3. ☐ Theravada Buddhism's principles of social equality threatened Angkor's elite.
4. ☐ Angkor's infrastructure was not very sophisticated.
5. ☐ The dam at Angkor probably failed.
6. ☐ There was little Angkor's rulers could do to avoid its eventual demise.

CRITICAL THINKING Applying Ideas

▶ The reading passage mentions the challenges that Angkor faced. List three of them.

_____

_____

_____

▶ Which of these challenges continue to threaten modern civilizations today? Discuss your ideas with a partner.

⌄ The temple complex Angkor Wat has become a symbol of Cambodia and appears on the country's national flag.

Evaluating Arguments (1)

An argument is a statement put forward by a writer that is supported by reasons or evidence. A writer may present one or more arguments in a text. As a reader, you need to evaluate the arguments to decide which are the strongest. One way to do this is to ask yourself questions as you read.

- Is the evidence a fact, an unproven theory, or an opinion?
- Is the evidence supported by relevant and up-to-date data?
- Are the sources that are cited credible?
- Does the writer provide enough evidence to support the argument?

Pay particular attention to the language the author uses to support any arguments. For instance, an author who uses hedging language (*seems, appears that, may, could, possibly, likely*) may be less confident in their claims.

ANALYZING **A.** Why did Angkor decline? Match each argument (1–6) with the evidence from the reading passage (a–f).

1. _____ Invaders conquered Angkor.

2. _____ A religious shift contributed to the city's decline.

3. _____ The royal court turned its back on Angkor.

4. _____ The water management system broke down.

5. _____ A weakened Angkor was affected by climate change.

6. _____ Angkor began to suffer from social instability.

a. Beginning in the 1300s, Southeast Asia experienced a period of severe drought.

b. A shift to Theravada Buddhism diminished the kings' royal authority.

c. Angkor's own engineers seem to have destroyed a dam.

d. Angkor's army grew hungry from a lack of rice.

e. Angkor's rulers often built new temple complexes and let older ones decay.

f. Historical records of Ayutthaya claim their warriors took Angkor.

ANALYZING **B.** Find the evidence from activity A in the reading passage. Circle any hedging language used to support each argument.

EVALUATING **C.** Which do you think is the strongest argument for why Angkor declined? Note your ideas below, then discuss with a partner.

_____

_____

_____

COMPLETION **A. Complete the information. Circle the correct words.**

During the past century, California has built a sophisticated ¹**mechanism** / **regime** for delivering water to its citizens. Thousands of kilometers of pipes and ²**invaders** / **channels** now crisscross the state, ³**dispersing** / **subsequent** water. However, the state's water resources are now severely stretched—droughts have drained most of the state's ⁴**ingenuity** / **reservoirs** to low levels.

Recently, laws have been introduced to promote water conservation in major cities. However, water experts say that to solve their water problems, Californians should learn to live within the water resources of a dry landscape.

⌃ **Californian communities are dependent on water pumped in from the Colorado River.**

WORDS IN CONTEXT **B. Complete the sentences by circling the correct options.**

1. Someone who shows **ingenuity** shows *cleverness* / *a lack of creativity*.

2. An event that **doomed** a civilization *helped* / *destroyed* it.

3. If you ate **subsequent** to your arrival, you ate *before* / *after* arriving.

4. A **regime** is a system of government, especially one that is *lenient* / *harsh*.

5. Something **subversive** can *weaken* / *strengthen* a political system.

6. An **invader** is someone who enters another country *by force* / *peacefully*.

WORD LINK **C. The word regime includes the root *reg* which means "rule" or "guide of."** Complete the sentences using the words in the box. Use a dictionary to help.

regalia	regimented	regularity	regulations

1. During official ceremonies, kings and queens usually dress in full _____.

2. The life of a prisoner is usually strictly _____.

3. Driving _____ differ throughout the world.

4. In recent years, there has been an increase in the _____ of extreme weather events.

∨ An archeologist inspects a Mayan
carving in a cave in Quintana Roo,
Mexico.

LEGACIES OF
THE MAYA

BEFORE YOU WATCH

DEFINITIONS **A.** Read the excerpts from the video. Match each word in **bold** with its definition.

"Much of what we now know about ancient Maya civilization comes from **deciphering** hieroglyphic characters **inscribed** on pottery, stone slabs, and other ruins."

"Despite the Maya's ingenuity and **agrarian** lifestyle, conflict was **prevalent**."

1. decipher •
2. inscribe •
3. agrarian •
4. prevalent •

• a. (adj) relating to farming and the use of land
• b. (adj) common
• c. (v) to work out the meaning of something
• d. (v) to write or carve words on an object

QUIZ **B.** What do you remember about the ancient Maya from the information in Reading A? Discuss the questions below with a partner.

1. In which part of the world did the Maya civilization develop?
2. Around when was the Maya civilization at its peak?
3. Which crop did the Maya mainly depend on?
4. What do many believe to be the most likely reason for the collapse of the Maya civilization?

GIST **A.** Watch the video. Check your answers in Before You Watch B.

DETAILS **B.** Watch the video again. Complete the notes.

The Maya

Cities

- Civilization consisted of around [1]_____ cities during Classic Period, some with populations of [2]_____

- Built magnificent urban centers which included [3]_____ central to religious practices

Achievements

- Math: invented the concept of [4]_____

- Astronomy: developed [5]_____ based on observations of sun and sky

- Writing: invented a system of writing using hieroglyphs, which can be found today inscribed on [6]_____, stone slabs, and buildings

Decline

- Most cities collapsed by around [7]_____ A.D.

- Theories: warfare, [8]_____, drought

Today

- More than [9]_____ Maya around the world

- Follow many [10]_____ and ceremonial practices of ancestors

CRITICAL THINKING Reflecting   According to the video, many Maya people today follow some of the "ceremonial practices" of their ancestors. What traditions or practices do you follow that have been passed down from your ancestors? Discuss with a partner.

VOCABULARY REVIEW

Do you remember the meanings of these words? Check (✓) the ones you know. Look back at the unit and review any words you're not sure of.

Reading A

☐ blessing   ☐ constitute*   ☐ demise   ☐ flourish   ☐ grueling

☐ inspect*   ☐ penetrate   ☐ plunge   ☐ sacrifice   ☐ soil

Reading B

☐ channel*   ☐ disperse   ☐ doomed   ☐ ingenuity   ☐ invader

☐ mechanism*   ☐ regime*   ☐ reservoir   ☐ subsequent*   ☐ subversive

*Academic word list

HIGH ACHIEVERS

With no ropes or climbing equipment, Alex Honnold scales the sheer rock face of El Capitan in California's Yosemite Valley.

WARM UP

Discuss these questions with a partner.

1. What are some sporting activities people mainly do on or near mountains?

2. Why are some of these activities difficult to do?

29

BEFORE YOU READ

DISCUSSION **A.** Look at the photo and read the caption. What kind of physical and personal characteristics might make a person successful at this sport? Discuss with a partner.

PREDICTING **B.** Read the first paragraph of the reading. What challenges do you think Mira Rai had to overcome in order to become a trail runner? Discuss your ideas with a partner. Then read and check your answers.

THE
SKY RUNNER

A Growing up in a village in eastern Nepal's Bhojpur Mountains, Mira Rai had dreams that went far beyond the conventional expectations for Nepali women. The eldest daughter of five children, she was expected to fetch water, tend crops and livestock, and help out at home. By age 12, she no longer regularly attended school, and instead hauled heavy bags of rice up and down steep trails—often barefoot—to trade at the market. It was hard work—but great training for a future trail runner.

B "As a girl," Rai recalls, "I would constantly be told to know my place, suppress my voice, and act in a certain manner. For me, breaking free from these traditions itself was a big dream."

C Several years ago, Rai's dream became reality. She was running outside Kathmandu when two male trail runners invited her to enter her first trail race, the Kathmandu West Valley Rim 50K. She had never run 50 kilometers before, had no special **gear** or training for such a distance, and was also the only woman in the competition. But against all **odds**, she beat everyone—even the men. From there, a community of supporters came together to give her a chance to compete in international trail running competitions.

Mira Rai—a trail and ultramarathon runner—trains on mountain paths in Nepal. Ultramarathons can be up to 160 kilometers long and are often held in remote places—such as deserts—and on tough terrain—such as steep mountains.

D Today, the running world recognizes Rai as a high-elevation trail racing phenomenon. Now she is on a mission to help both women and men of Nepal through sports. Rai believes her work to empower others has just begun. "We have realized that Nepal has tremendous potential to develop competitive athletes," she says.

E Wasfia Nazreen, a mountain climber from Bangladesh, knows first-hand the impact Rai has had on the young women of Nepal. "For someone who has left school so early and missed the learning we take for granted, Mira has been able to turn back time and set a rare example by being the change herself," she says.

F "It's hard to find good role models[1] for young women in our region, especially one coming from the same **rural** village background as most of the young generation," Nazreen says. Mira is blazing a trail, not just in terms of being able to speak nationally on gender equality, but also by getting young people into running through the new Kathmandu Trail Race Series. "The grit[2] and joy she embodies **throughout** all her hardships and victories is an inspiration to all of us!"

G Rai, however, remains **humble**. "I have been able to do the things I did because so many people believed in me and took chances, and I want to give back so others can have a chance just the way I did," she says. "We have a saying in Nepal, '*Khana pugyos, dina pugos,*' which means, 'Let there be enough to eat, let there be enough to give.'"

H **Interviewer: Which is more difficult: running a hard, steep trail race or breaking gender stereotypes?**

Mira Rai: Running is no issue, but breaking gender **stereotypes** is. For the society we live in, it's difficult for women and men alike because doing anything out of convention means a lot of struggle—especially for women. As women, we are expected to help out with

---

1 A **role model** is someone who is a good example for young people to follow.
2 If you show **grit**, you have courage.

⌄ **Eastern Nepal is home to several different Nepali ethnic groups, many living in isolated villages.**

chores at home from childhood and then get married and raise a family, so it becomes a struggle, not **merely** a challenge. You get called a rebel, and for an adventure sport that involves risks, nobody encourages you. "You'll end up breaking your bones!" they'd say. Though the mindset[3] seems to be changing, it's still at a snail's **pace** and has a long way to go before women are seen as equivalent to men.

What advice do you have for someone who wants to be a stronger runner like you?

MR: It was a matter of chance and luck that I became a runner. Back in the village we had to walk hours on end—up and down grueling terrain, often barefoot, with a heavy weight on our backs—and this definitely contributed. I started running, I got professional training that taught me techniques, and gradually I became more determined, motivated, and **persistent** to chase my dreams. However, I've also learned that proper diet, enough rest, confidence, yoga, and mental well-being—as well as having good support from my mentor Richard Bull and my coach Dhruba Bikram Malla—are just as important as being in shape.

You stopped going to school regularly when you were 12. Do you wish you'd had more school?

MR: I feel that if I'd finished more school, I would have been able to communicate with more confidence and have a better insight into world affairs. In many cases when I first started racing abroad, I couldn't even be a part of conversations because of my poor English skills. I used to just sit there and listen, but I didn't feel uncomfortable being there as everybody was very supportive. However, with media and sponsors, it would've definitely been more helpful had I obtained more education back home. Even today when I try to read newspapers, I fail to understand quite a few words, so I am taking English classes these days, and it's certainly helping.

---

3 Your **mindset** is your way of thinking.

K **Running has helped you see the world. What is it like to return to your village now that you have been to China, Italy, and other places?**

MR: I return once a year during the Dashain, the largest festival of the year, and the people there are living the same sort of lives as I saw when I was a kid. We used to have kerosene lanterns, but now there are bulbs that run on solar power. The village had no access by road back in the day; now there are dirt tracks that connect to big towns. But the mud houses are the same. There's phone connection, but it doesn't work well. When I go back, I meet a lot of youngsters that ask me how they can live differently. They definitely seem motivated, but sadly their folks do not agree with such ambition. While the physical infrastructure in my village has improved, the mindset has not. I remain hopeful that the future generation will break the mold.

L **What work are you doing now with communities in Nepal?**

MR: While recovering from knee surgery, I have been providing guidance to men and women alike in running and encouraging them to **pursue** a career as professional athletes. Every so often, I visit schools and children's homes to share my knowledge about running, particularly training, diet, and more importantly, an active lifestyle.

M We have realized that Nepal has tremendous potential to develop competitive athletes, so we're organizing a series of trail races in Kathmandu. These are short races aimed for both beginners and experienced runners. I also organized a small race back in my hometown of Sano Dumma last October, to introduce the sport to the young crowd and get them interested in running. In the coming days, I plan to organize races that aim to identify and promote promising runners.

N **Is there a personal challenge that you still want to achieve?**

MR: I have always dreamed of running in the Ultra-Trail du Mont Blanc in France. It's a challenging race for elite runners from all over the world—166 kilometers! I would love to see where I stand in this race.

> Rai competes in the Manaslu Trail Race in Nepal with the world's eighth highest mountain, Mount Manaslu, as a backdrop.

A. Choose the best answer for each question.

GIST

1. Which of the following would be the best alternative title for the passage?

    a. The World's Most Difficult Race

    b. The Village Girl Who Took On the World

    c. Trail Running: A Growing Phenomenon

    d. Changing Attitudes Toward Gender in Nepal

DETAIL

2. Which of the following is NOT true about Mira Rai's life as a child?

    a. She had to work on a farm.

    b. She only started school when she was 12.

    c. She didn't like being told how to behave.

    d. She had four younger siblings.

DETAIL

3. In paragraph F, what is NOT given as a reason that Rai is a good role model?

    a. She works to promote gender equality in her country.

    b. She encourages youngsters to take up running.

    c. She has worked to improve housing in her village.

    d. Her determination to overcome hardships inspires others.

REFERENCE

4. In paragraph H, what is Rai referring to when she says, "it becomes a struggle, not merely a challenge"?

    a. doing anything unconventional

    b. running a trail race

    c. raising a family

    d. going to school

VOCABULARY

5. The word *grueling* in paragraph I is closest in meaning to _____.

    a. unknown

    b. risky

    c. endless

    d. tiring

COHESION

6. Where would be the best place in paragraph I to insert this sentence?
It wasn't much fun, but it definitely helped me develop my stamina.

    a. after the first sentence

    b. after the second sentence

    c. before the last sentence

    d. after the last sentence

DETAIL

7. Which of these questions about Rai's home village cannot be answered by information in the passage?

    a. How did people light their homes there in the past?

    b. When does Mira Rai make her annual visit there?

    c. Has education in the village improved?

    d. How can people living there now get to other towns?

B. **Complete the summary of paragraphs A–G. Use no more than three words from the reading passage for each answer.**

Born and raised in Nepal, Mira Rai was expected to be a [1]_____ Nepalese woman. As a child, she had to fetch water for her family and carry large [2]_____ to market. But these challenging tasks provided good [3]_____ for her future career.

Rai got her big break when she participated in her [4]_____—the Kathmandu West Valley Rim 50K. Incredibly, she beat everyone. Her victory propelled her to international fame.

One of Rai's goals is to help both male and female athletes in her native country. She believes that Nepal has a lot of [5]_____ to produce world-class athletes. A famous climber from Bangladesh said that Rai has had a very positive influence on young female athletes. She said that it was not easy for young women from the countryside to find good [6]_____. She said that Rai also gives talks to promote [7]_____ in her home country.

CRITICAL THINKING Applying Ideas | **Think of someone who, like Mira Rai, became successful after overcoming hardships in their life. Note your ideas below, then describe the person to your partner.**

_____

_____

> **A trail runner in Chugach State Park, Alaska, United States**

Guessing Meaning from Context—Idioms and Colloquial Language

The language found in interviews often contains colloquial language and idiomatic expressions. As with other vocabulary, the context can be helpful in determining meaning. If the context doesn't help and you have no idea what an idiom means, consult a dictionary.

INFERRING
MEANING

A. Find the expressions in bold in the reading passage. Choose the correct meaning.

1. **breaking free** (paragraph B)

   a. escaping
   b. learning

2. **against all odds** (paragraph C)

   a. in opposition to others
   b. despite the challenges

3. **take for granted** (paragraph E)

   a. need to work hard for
   b. fail to properly appreciate

4. **blazing a trail** (paragraph F)

   a. running at a very fast speed
   b. being the first to do something new

5. **break the mold** (paragraph K)

   a. follow old traditions
   b. do something in a new way

INFERRING
MEANING

B. Find and note expressions in the reading passage that have the same meaning as the definitions below.

1. accept one's position in society (paragraph B) _____

2. involved in an important task (paragraph D) _____

3. extremely slowly (paragraph H) _____

RELATING

C. Choose three of the expressions in Activity A or B. Write sentences about yourself or people you know using each one.

1. _____

_____

2. _____

_____

3. _____

_____

COMPLETION **A.** Complete the information using the correct form of the words in the box. Five words are extra.

gear	humble	merely	odds	pace
persistent	pursue	rural	stereotype	throughout

The Ultra-Trail du Mont Blanc isn't ¹_____ a trail race through a pretty part of the Alps: It's also a grueling test of endurance. Each summer around 10,000 athletes run through ²_____ countryside, up steep hills, and down deep valleys.

Some ultramarathons are broken up into stages, allowing runners to take rests ³_____ the race. But the Ultra-Trail du Mont Blanc is non-stop—and lasts through

▲ **French ultra trailer Xavier Thevenard competes in the 170 km Ultra-Trail of Mont-Blanc.**

the night. Runners are required to bring appropriate ⁴_____ for such a long race, including flashlights and a security blanket. The best runners aim to keep a steady ⁵_____ in order to finish the race in 20 to 24 hours. In recent years, more than a third of participants did not cross the finish line.

DEFINITIONS **B.** Complete the definitions using the unused words from the box in Activity A.

1. If you are _____, you are quiet about your accomplishments.

2. If you _____ something, you try and get it.

3. The _____ of something happening refers to how likely it is.

4. A _____ is a fixed, but often mistaken, idea about what a group of people are typically like.

5. If you are _____ at something, you continue to do it.

WORD USAGE **C.** The adverb **merely** can be used to emphasize that you mean exactly what you are saying and nothing more. Mark where it should be placed in each sentence.

1. He didn't quit the ultramarathon; he stopped to take a rest.

2. They didn't mean to cause a problem—they were trying to help.

3. He didn't talk much about his motivation, mentioning that he did it for his family.

Experienced climbers using ropes normally take several days to ascend El Capitan, a steep vertical rock face in California's Yosemite Valley.

BEFORE YOU READ

DISCUSSION **A.** Look at the photo and read the caption. Then read the first paragraph of the reading passage. What challenges might Alex Honnold face making this climb? Discuss your ideas with a partner.

PREDICTING **B.** What kind of physical and mental characteristics do you think someone would need to successfully complete this climb? Note some ideas and then compare with a partner.

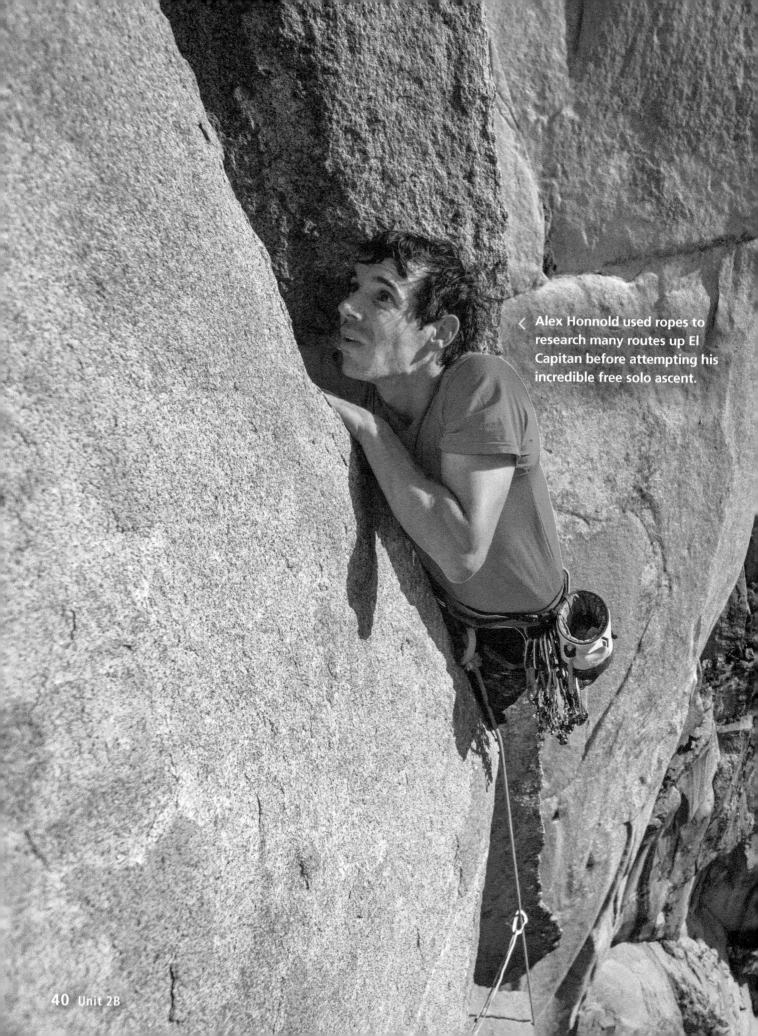

Alex Honnold used ropes to research many routes up El Capitan before attempting his incredible free solo ascent.

THE FREE SOLOIST

A In June 2017, Alex Honnold completed a stunning scramble up El Capitan, a 3,000-foot granite wall in Yosemite National Park. Mark Synnott recounts how Honnold's meticulous planning and training prepared him for "the ultimate climb"—a four-hour vertical ascent without a rope.

B It's 4:54 a.m. on a chilly November morning in 2016 in Yosemite National Park. A full moon casts an eerie glow onto the southwest face of El Capitan, where Alex Honnold clings to the side of the granite wall with nothing more than the tips of his fingers and two thin edges of shoe rubber. He's attempting to do something that professional rock climbers have long thought impossible—a free solo ascent of the world's most famous cliff. That means he is alone and climbing without a rope as he inches his way up more than half a mile of vertical rock.

C A light breeze rustles his hair as he shines his headlamp on the cold, smooth patch of granite where he must next place his foot. Above him, the stone is blank for several feet, **devoid of** any holds. Unlike parts of the climb higher up, which feature shallow divots, pebble-size nubs, and tiny cracks that Alex can cling onto with his amazingly strong fingers, this part—a barely less than vertical slab on a section called the Freeblast—must be mastered with a **delicate** balance of fine skills and poise.[1] Climbers call it friction climbing. "It's like walking up glass," Alex once said.

D He wiggles his toes; they're numb. His right ankle is stiff and swollen from a severe sprain he sustained two months earlier when he fell while practicing this part of the route. That time he was attached to a rope, but now, falling isn't an option. Free soloing isn't like other dangerous sports. There is no "maybe" when you're 60 stories up without a rope: If you make a mistake, you die.

---

1 If someone has **poise**, they have calm self-confidence.

E Six hundred feet below, I sit on a fallen tree watching the tiny circle of Alex's light. It hasn't moved in what feels like an eternity, but is probably less than a minute. And I know why: he's facing the move that has haunted him ever since he first dreamed up this **scheme** seven years ago. I've climbed this slab myself, and the thought of doing it free solo makes me nauseated. The log on which I'm sitting lies less than a hundred yards from where Alex will land if he slips.

F A sudden noise jolts me back to the present; my heart skips. A cameraman, part of the crew recording the feat, hustles up the trail toward the base of the wall. I can hear the static of his walkie-talkie. "Alex is bailing," he says. Thank God, I think, Alex will live.

*   *   *

G Some in the climbing world view free soloing as something that isn't meant to be. Critics regard it as reckless showmanship that gives the sport a bad name, noting the long list of those who've died attempting it. Others, myself included, recognize it as the sport's purest expression. Such was the attitude of Austrian alpinist Paul Preuss, considered by climbing historians to be the father of free soloing. He proclaimed that the very essence of alpinism[2] was to master a mountain with superior physical and mental skill—not "**artificial** aid." By age 27, Preuss had made some 150 ropeless first ascents, and was celebrated throughout Europe. Then, on October 3, 1913, while free soloing the North Ridge of the Mandlkogel in the Austrian Alps, he fell to his death.

H But Preuss's ideas would live on, influencing **successive** generations of climbers and inspiring the "free climbing" movement of the 1960s and '70s, which espoused using ropes and other gear only as safety devices, never to assist a climber's upward progress. The

---

2 **Alpinism** refers to mountain climbing in the Alps and also other mountains.

next serious free soloist of note appeared in 1973, when "Hot" Henry Barber shocked the climbing community by scaling the 1,500-foot north face of Yosemite's Sentinel Rock without a rope. In 1987, Canadian Peter Croft free soloed two of Yosemite's most celebrated routes—Astroman and Rostrum—back-to-back in the same day.

I Croft's achievement stood until 2007, when Alex Honnold, a shy 22-year-old from Sacramento, showed up in Yosemite Valley. He stunned the climbing world by repeating Croft's Astroman-Rostrum masterpiece. The next year he free soloed two famously tough routes—Zion National Park's Moonlight Buttress and the Regular Northwest Face of Yosemite's Half Dome—climbs so long and technically difficult that no serious climber had imagined they could be scaled without a rope. As sponsorship offers poured in and journalists and fans hailed his achievements, Alex was secretly **contemplating** a much bigger goal.

J It's important to note that Alex's quest to free solo El Capitan wasn't some adrenaline-fueled stunt that he'd come up with on a whim. In 2009, during our first climbing expedition together, he had mentioned the idea to me. There was something about his supreme confidence, though, and the way he effortlessly moved up incredibly difficult rock faces that made the comment seem like more than just an idle boast.

K Alex researched several El Capitan routes, finally settling on Freerider, a popular test piece for veteran climbers and one that usually requires multiple days to **ascend**. Its 30 or so pitches—or rope lengths—challenge a climber in practically every possible way: the strength of fingers, forearms, shoulders, calves, toes, back, and abdomen, not to mention balance, flexibility, problem solving, and emotional **stamina**. Certain times of the day the sun heats the rock so much that it burns to touch it; hours later the temperature can **plummet**

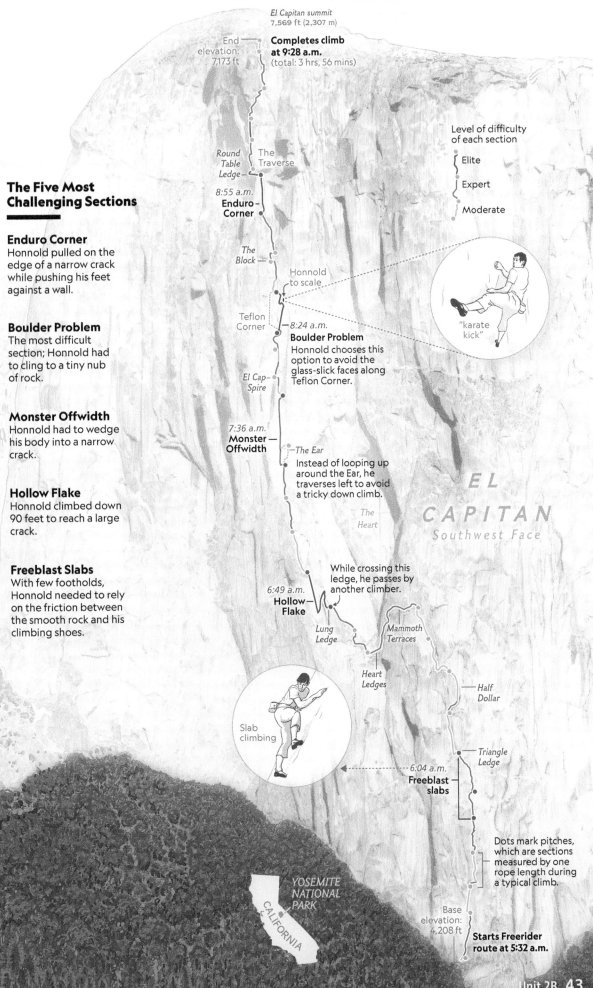

The Five Most Challenging Sections

Enduro Corner
Honnold pulled on the edge of a narrow crack while pushing his feet against a wall.

Boulder Problem
The most difficult section; Honnold had to cling to a tiny nub of rock.

Monster Offwidth
Honnold had to wedge his body into a narrow crack.

Hollow Flake
Honnold climbed down 90 feet to reach a large crack.

Freeblast Slabs
With few footholds, Honnold needed to rely on the friction between the smooth rock and his climbing shoes.

El Capitan summit
7,569 ft (2,307 m)

End elevation:
7,173 ft

Completes climb at 9:28 a.m.
(total: 3 hrs, 56 mins)

Level of difficulty of each section

Elite

Expert

Moderate

Round Table Ledge

The Traverse

8:55 a.m.
Enduro Corner

The Block

Honnold to scale

"karate kick"

Teflon Corner

8:24 a.m.
Boulder Problem
Honnold chooses this option to avoid the glass-slick faces along Teflon Corner.

El Cap Spire

7:36 a.m.
Monster Offwidth

The Ear
Instead of looping up around the Ear, he traverses left to avoid a tricky down climb.

The Heart

*E L
C A P I T A N*
Southwest Face

While crossing this ledge, he passes by another climber.

6:49 a.m.
Hollow Flake

Lung Ledge

Mammoth Terraces

Heart Ledges

Half Dollar

Slab climbing

Triangle Ledge

6:04 a.m.
Freeblast slabs

Dots mark pitches, which are sections measured by one rope length during a typical climb.

Base elevation:
4,208 ft

Starts Freerider route at 5:32 a.m.

YOSEMITE NATIONAL PARK

CALIFORNIA

below freezing. Storms blow in, powerful winds lash the wall, water leaks out of cracks. Bees, frogs, and birds can burst from crevices during crucial moves. Rocks of all sizes can suddenly give way and tumble down.

L The Freeblast may be the scariest part, but more physically demanding sections await higher up: a chimney-like crack he'll have to climb through; a wide gap where he'll have to perform almost a full split, pressing the rock with his feet and hands to inch his way up. And then 2,300 feet above the valley floor is the Boulder Problem—a blank face that requires some of the most technically challenging moves of the climb.

M But before he could **tackle** the Boulder Problem, he would have to get over the Freeblast. In 2016, the vertical slab proved to be an insurmountable[3] obstacle and he was forced to give up his attempt. But Alex knew he would try again.

---

3 If something is **insurmountable**, it is a problem too great to be overcome.

*   *   *

N **Saturday morning, June 3, 2017.** Seven months after Alex's failed attempt, I am in a meadow near the foot of El Capitan. The tall grass is covered with dew, and the sky is gray, as it always is just before dawn. I squint through a telescope, and there is Alex, 600 feet above the valley floor, moving up onto the Freeblast, the glassy slab that has frustrated him for nearly a decade.

O Alex's movements, normally so smooth, are worrisomely jerky. His foot tap-tap-taps against the wall as if he's feeling his way tentatively into the slab. And then, just like that, he's standing on a ledge several feet above the move that has been hanging over his head for years.

P I realize I've been holding my breath, so I consciously exhale. Thousands of moves are still to come, and the Boulder Problem looms far above, but he won't be turning back this time. Alex Honnold is on his way to completing the greatest rock climb in history.

∨ Alex Honnold inspects his hands after completing a practice session on El Capitan.

A. Choose the best answer for each question.

INFERENCE

1. The divots, nubs, and cracks mentioned in paragraph C _____.

  a. are dangerous features of the mountain
  b. occur in all parts of the mountain
  c. occur only in the lowest part of the mountain
  d. are helpful to a free solo climber

AUTHOR TONE

2. In paragraph E, the author's tone is _____.

  a. optimistic
  b. technical
  c. anxious
  d. humorous

VOCABULARY

3. When the cameraman says, "Alex is bailing" in paragraph F, he means that Honnold _____.

  a. nearly fell
  b. is climbing slowly
  c. has reached the summit
  d. is giving up for now

AUTHOR ATTITUDE

4. According to the information in paragraph G, the author _____.

  a. feels free soloing is too dangerous
  b. agrees with the ideas of Paul Preuss
  c. believes climbers need artificial aids
  d. disapproves of Honnold's plans

DETAIL

5. Who was the second free soloist to become well known?

  a. Paul Preuss
  b. Henry Barber
  c. Peter Croft
  d. Alex Honnold

COHESION

6. Where would be the best place in paragraph J to insert this sentence?
At first, I thought he was totally crazy.

  a. before the first sentence
  b. after the first sentence
  c. after the second sentence
  d. after the last sentence

DETAIL

7. Which of the following was NOT given as one of the challenges involved in climbing the Freerider route?

  a. ice
  b. heat
  c. animals
  d. wind

B. Scan the reading passage for the words in **bold** below. Study the context around each word or phrase and then match it to its definition.

_____ **1. meticulous** (paragraph A)

_____ **2. cling** (paragraph B)

_____ **3. slab** (paragraph C)

_____ **4. eternity** (paragraph E)

_____ **5. nauseated** (paragraph E)

_____ **6. reckless** (paragraph G)

_____ **7. espoused** (paragraph H)

_____ **8. on a whim** (paragraph J)

a. feeling sick

b. based on a sudden decision

c. a large flat piece of stone

d. adopted or supported

e. infinite or never ending time

f. to hold on tightly to

g. careless of risks or consequences

h. careful and detailed

C. Find and underline the words or phrases in the reading passage that mean the same as the definitions below.

1. to praise and show approval (paragraph I)

2. to hit with a lot of force (paragraph K)

3. to partly close eyes when looking (paragraph N)

4. quick and sudden (paragraph O)

CRITICAL THINKING Inferring Reasons   What do you think Honnold's main motivation was for doing the climb? Is it an example of "reckless showmanship" or could there be other reasons? Note your ideas below, then discuss with a partner.

_____

_____

_____

Alex Honnold strengthens his fingers by hangboarding for 90 minutes every day.

Understanding Rhetorical Purpose

An author's rhetorical purpose refers to either their overall reason for writing a text, or their reason for including certain information in it. Identifying an author's purpose is a key part of engaging critically with any reading passage. It is also an important skill for taking exams. Examples of this type of question might include:

What is the author's purpose in mentioning …?
Why does the author mention/include …?
The author includes the information … in order to …
The author uses … as an example of …
The author mentions … for which of the following reasons?

RHETORICAL
PURPOSE

A. 1. What is the main purpose of the passage?

  a. to persuade the reader to take up rock climbing
  b. to describe Alex Honnold's personality
  c. to give an account of Honnold's most difficult climb
  d. to give an overview of the sport of free soloing

2. Why does the author include the quote "It's like walking up glass" in paragraph C?

  a. to help the reader visualize how shiny the wall as
  b. to show how confident Honnold was in this part of the climb
  c. to emphasize how challenging this part of the climb was
  d. to explain why this part of the climb was relatively easy

3. Why does the author mention Paul Preuss's exploits in paragraph G?

  a. to explain why he was a better climber than Honnold
  b. to warn of the dangers of climbing for the untrained
  c. to refute the idea that climbing is still dangerous
  d. to show how influential his free solo climbs were

4. Why does the author include information about the temperature, weather, and animals in paragraph K?

  a. to illustrate how challenging this climbing route is
  b. to explain why Honnold nearly ended his climb there
  c. to show how dangerous a climb can be if you are unprepared
  d. to support the idea that free solo climbing is the purest form

RHETORICAL
PURPOSE

B. Why do you think the author mentions that Honnold completed his climb successfully in the first paragraph rather than leaving this for the final paragraph? Discuss your ideas with a partner.

COMPLETION **A. Complete the information using the correct form of the words in the box. Four words are extra.**

artificial	ascend	contemplate	delicate	devoid of
plummet	scheme	stamina	successive	tackle

When Honnold first began to seriously ¹_____ a free solo climb of El Capitan, he spoke with friend and fellow climber Jimmy Chin to discuss filming the event. This eventually resulted in the movie *Free Solo*—which won the 2018 Academy Award for best documentary film.

To film the event, Chin hired a team of climbers who would climb an easy route up El Capitan ahead of Honnold, lugging up cameras, ropes, and supplies. Then they'd rappel down on ropes to keep pace with Honnold as he ²_____ the near vertical cliff. Honnold of course used no ³_____ aids.

Filming was ⁴_____ work. No one was allowed to make any noise that might distract Honnold—distractions that could cause him to ⁵_____ to his death.

Chin wanted his film to be about Honnold's process. The final movie showcases Honnold's incredible focus, ⁶_____, and determination. "Whether it ended with him summiting El Cap or deciding not to go for it didn't matter," Chin says.

DEFINITIONS **B. Match each unused word from the box in Activity A with its definition.**

1. _____: an organized plan for doing something

2. _____: entirely lacking or free from

3. _____: happening one after another

4. _____: to try and deal with something or someone

COLLOCATIONS **C. The nouns in the box are frequently used with the word plummet. Complete the sentences with the correct words.**

popularity	price	temperatures

1. The _____ of oil plummets when there's too much supply.

2. Typically, a politician's _____ plummets after a scandal.

3. In the middle of winter, _____ can plummet to record lows at night.

SOLOING
SAFELY

∧ Free soloing is a dangerous sport, but there are ways to make it safer.

BEFORE YOU WATCH

DEFINITIONS **A.** Read the information below. The words in **bold** appear in the video. Match each word with its definition.

There are many different forms of rock climbing, such as mountaineering, sport climbing, and free soloing. Free soloing is considered to be a **fringe** sport, even among professional climbers. Some climbers consider it to be dangerous and **reckless**. During free soloing, climbers do not use any equipment at all, including ropes, even when scaling difficult **terrain**. However, those who do it often enjoy the added **adrenaline** rush it brings.

1. reckless •   • a. a chemical produced by the body that makes your heart beat faster

2. terrain •   • b. having or showing no regard for danger

3. fringe •   • c. an area of land

4. adrenaline •   • d. not widely popular

DISCUSSION **B.** How could free solo climbers make rope-free climbing safer? Note your ideas below, then discuss with a partner.

_____

_____

GIST **A.** Watch the video. What are two ways Matt Maddaloni uses to make free soloing safer?

DETAILS **B.** Watch the video. Note answers to the questions.

1. Why does Maddaloni mention *sneezing*?

_____

2. What does *grade* mean when Maddaloni says, "I wanted to get that grade as difficult as it could be"?

_____

3. How does Maddaloni take "a page from the circus"?

_____

4. What does Maddaloni mean when he says he's "a bit of an oddball"?

_____

CRITICAL THINKING Reflecting Free soloing has become more popular following the 2018 documentary *Free Solo*. Note answers to the questions below, then discuss with a partner.

▶ Do you think such documentaries or films encourage more climbers to free solo? What might be some positive and negative consequences of this?

_____

▶ Are there any ethical issues with promoting extreme sports like free soloing?

_____

VOCABULARY REVIEW

Do you remember the meanings of these words? Check (✓) the ones you know. Look back at the unit and review any words you're not sure of.

Reading A

☐ gear   ☐ humble   ☐ merely   ☐ odds*   ☐ pace

☐ persistent*   ☐ pursue*   ☐ rural   ☐ stereotype   ☐ throughout

Reading B

☐ artificial   ☐ ascend   ☐ contemplate   ☐ delicate   ☐ devoid of

☐ plummet   ☐ scheme*   ☐ stamina   ☐ successive*   ☐ tackle

*Academic Word List

SCIENCE AND PROGRESS

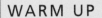
Discuss these questions with a partner.

1. In what ways does science help us understand the world better?

2. What issues has science not yet found an answer for?

Drone delivery systems such as Zipline aim to provide people in remote areas of the world with instant access to vital medical supplies.

BEFORE YOU READ

DISCUSSION **A.** Look at the photo and read the caption. What are these people concerned about? Why do you think they are concerned? Discuss your ideas with a partner.

PREDICTING **B.** Read the first two paragraphs of the reading passage. Why do you think many people are skeptical about science? What are some examples of this kind of skepticism? Discuss your ideas with a partner. Then read the passage to check your ideas.

Demonstrators in Washington D.C., United States, express concerns about the alleged effects of vaccines on children.

THE AGE OF DISBELIEF

We are surrounded by science and technology like never before, yet increasing numbers of people doubt the claims of scientists. Writer Joel Achenbach investigates the reasons for a rising tide of skepticism.[1]

A We live in an age when all manner of scientific knowledge—from the safety of vaccines[2] to the reality of climate change—faces organized and often angry opposition. Doubters have declared war on the **consensus** of experts. There are so many of these controversies[3] these days, you'd think an evil villain had put something in the water to make people argumentative.

B In a sense all this is not surprising; our lives are affected by science and technology as never before. For many of us this new world is comfortable and rich in rewards—but also more complicated and sometimes unnerving. We now face risks we can't easily analyze.

C We're asked to accept, for example, that it's safe to eat food containing genetically modified organisms. Experts say there's no evidence that it isn't safe, and no reason to believe that altering genes in a lab is more dangerous than altering them through traditional breeding. But to some people the very idea of transferring genes between species brings up images of mad scientists running wild.

D The world seems full of real and imaginary hazards, and **distinguishing** the former from the latter isn't easy. Should we be afraid that the Ebola virus, which is spread only by direct contact with bodily fluids, will mutate into an airborne super-plague? The scientific consensus says that's extremely unlikely: No virus has ever been observed to completely change its mode of transmission in humans. But if you type "airborne Ebola" into an Internet search engine, you'll find that some people believe that this virus has almost supernatural powers.

E In this often confusing world we have to decide what to believe and how to act accordingly. In principle, that is what science is for. "Science is not a body of facts," says geophysicist Marcia McNutt, who once headed the U.S. Geological Survey and is now editor of the journal *Science*. "Science is a method for deciding whether what we choose to believe has a basis in the laws of nature or not." But that method doesn't come naturally to most of us.

---

1 **Skepticism** refers to having doubts or not believing in something.
2 A **vaccine** is a medication taken to prevent a disease, such as the measles.
3 A **controversy** is an argument about an issue that is important to many people.

Making Sense of the World

F The trouble goes way back, of course. The scientific method has led us to truths that are less than self-evident, often mind-blowing, and sometimes hard to accept. For example, both the sun and moon appear to cross the sky above the Earth, but while the moon does indeed circle our world, the Earth circles the sun. Although the roundness of the Earth has been known for thousands of years, alternative geographies persisted even after trips around the world had become common. Nineteenth-century flat-Earthers, for example, believed that the planet was centered on the North Pole and bounded by a wall of ice, with the sun and moon traveling only a few hundred kilometers about the Earth.

G Even when we intellectually accept the precepts[4] of science, we cling to our intuitions—what researchers call our naive beliefs. As we become scientifically literate, we repress our naive beliefs, but never eliminate them entirely. They remain hidden in our brains as we try to make sense of the world.

H Most of us do that by relying on personal experience, anecdotes, or stories rather than statistics. If we hear about a cluster of cancer cases in a town with a hazardous waste dump, we assume pollution caused the cancers. Yet just because two things happened together doesn't mean one caused the other, and just because events are clustered doesn't mean they're not still random.

I We have trouble comprehending randomness; our brains crave pattern and meaning. Science warns us, however, that we can deceive ourselves. To be confident there's a causal connection between the dump and the cancers, you need statistical analysis showing that there are many more cancers than would be expected randomly, evidence that the victims were **exposed to** chemicals from the dump, and evidence that the chemicals really can cause cancer.

J Even for scientists, the scientific method is a hard **discipline**. Like the rest of us, they're vulnerable to confirmation **bias**—the tendency to look for and see only evidence that confirms what they already believe. But unlike the rest of us, they submit their ideas to formal peer review[5] before publishing them. Once their results are published, other scientists will try to reproduce them—and, being skeptical and competitive, will be very happy to announce that they don't hold up.

Struggling for Truth

K Sometimes scientists fall short of the ideals of the scientific method. Especially in biomedical research, there's a disturbing trend toward results that can't be reproduced outside the lab that found them. Francis Collins, the director of the National Institutes of Health, worries about the "secret sauce"—specialized procedures and customized software—that researchers don't share with their colleagues. But he still has faith in science.

L "Science will find the truth," Collins says. "It may get it wrong the first time and maybe the second time, but ultimately it will find the truth." That aspect of science is another thing a lot of people have trouble with. To some climate change skeptics, for

---

4 A **precept** is a rule for action.
5 A research paper that is **peer reviewed** is checked by another scientist before it is published.

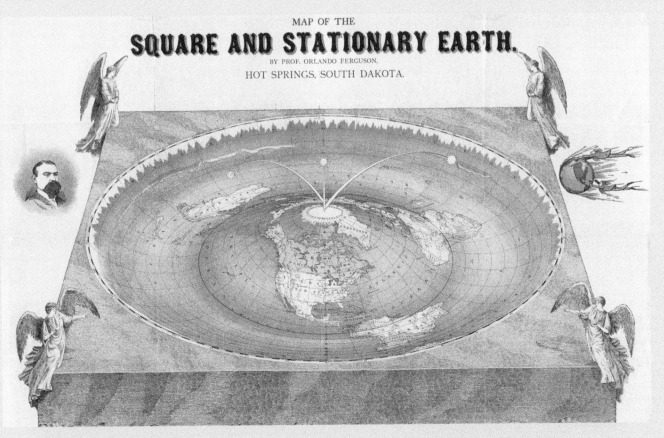

That the Earth is round has been known since antiquity—but alternative geographies have persisted. This 1893 map by Orlando Ferguson, a South Dakota businessman, is a variation on 19th-century flat-Earth beliefs.

example, the fact that a few scientists in the 1970s were worried (quite reasonably, it seemed at the time) about the possibility of a coming ice age is enough to discredit the concern about global warming now.

M In 2014, the United Nations' Intergovernmental Panel on Climate Change, which consists of hundreds of scientists, released its fifth report in the past 25 years. This one repeated louder and clearer than ever the consensus of the world's scientists: The planet's surface temperature has risen by about 1.5 degrees Fahrenheit in the past 130 years. Moreover, human actions—including the burning of fossil fuels—are extremely likely to have been the dominant cause of the warming since the mid-20th century. Many people, however, **retain** doubts about that consensus.

N Americans, for example, fall into two basic camps, says Dan Kahan of Yale University. Those who are more egalitarian[6] and community-minded are generally suspicious of industry. They tend to think it's up to something dangerous that calls for government regulation; they're likely to see the risks of climate change. In contrast, people with a hierarchical[7] and individualistic mindset respect leaders of industry and don't like government interfering in their affairs. They tend to reject warnings about climate change because they know that accepting them could lead to some kind of tax or regulation to limit emissions.

---

6 If someone is described as **egalitarian**, they believe in equal opportunities and rights for all.

7 If someone is described as having a **hierarchical** mindset, they believe that certain people in society are more important than others.

▲ Freckles, a genetically modified goat, is one of several preserved specimens at the Center for Postnatural History in Pittsburgh, a museum dedicated to the study of genetic alteration by humans.

O In the United States, an individual's view on climate change tends to identify them as belonging to one or the other of these two opposing tribes. When we argue about it, Kahan says, we're actually arguing about who we are, what our crowd is. We're thinking: People like us believe this. People like that do not believe this. For a hierarchical individualist, Kahan says, it's not irrational to reject established climate science. This is because accepting it wouldn't change the world, but it might get them thrown out of their tribe. Science appeals to our **rational** brain, but our beliefs are motivated largely by emotion—and the biggest motivation is remaining tight with our peers.

The Implications of Doubt

P Doubting science has consequences. The anti-vaccine movement, for example, has been going strong since the respected British

immunity. Increasing vaccine skepticism threatens to undermine the herd immunity of communities against diseases such as whooping cough and measles.

Q Investigations into the "science communication problem" have given us insights into how people decide what to believe—and why they so often don't accept the scientific consensus. It's not that they can't grasp it, says Kahan; it's because of confirmation bias—the tendency of people to use scientific knowledge to reinforce beliefs that have already been shaped by their worldview. Meanwhile the Internet has made it easier than ever for climate skeptics and doubters of all kinds to find their own information and experts. Gone are the days when a small number of powerful **institutions**—elite universities, encyclopedias, major news organizations— served as gatekeepers of scientific information. The Internet has democratized information, which is a good thing, but along with cable TV, it has made it possible to live in a "filter bubble" that lets in only the information you agree with.

R How to penetrate this bubble? How can scientists convince skeptics? Throwing more facts at people may not be enough. Liz Neeley, who helps train scientists to be better communicators, says that people need to hear from believers they can trust, who share their **fundamental** values. She has personal experience with this: Her father is a climate change skeptic and gets most of his information on the issue from conservative media. One day she confronted him: "Do you believe them or me?" She told him she believes the scientists who research climate change, and knows many of them personally. "If you think I'm wrong," she said, "then you're telling me that you don't trust me." Her father's position on the issue softened—but it wasn't the facts that did it.

medical journal the *Lancet* published a study in 1998 linking a vaccine to autism. Although the article was discredited, the notion of a vaccine-autism connection has been endorsed by celebrities and reinforced through Internet sources. This has **implications** for the "herd immunity" of populations. When a significant portion of a population is vaccinated, it provides a measure of protection for individuals who have not developed

A. Choose the best answer for each question.

GIST **1.** Which of the following would be the best alternative title for the passage?

　　a. The Danger of Vaccines: A New Perspective
　　b. The Scientific Method
　　c. Naive Beliefs
　　d. Scientific Facts under Fire

INFERENCE **2.** Which of these beliefs would the author probably agree with?

　　a. Airborne Ebola virus may cause a huge epidemic.
　　b. Eating foods made with GMOs may make people sick.
　　c. Vaccines may cause autism in some people.
　　d. Climate change may pose a serious threat.

INFERENCE **3.** What does the author imply about "naive beliefs"?

　　a. They typically become stronger as people age.
　　b. They persist even in people with a scientific education.
　　c. They are much less common than they once were.
　　d. They are not present in prominent scientists.

INFERENCE **4.** What would the author probably tell the people in a town with a waste dump and a high rate of cancer?

　　a. You should move to another community as soon as possible.
　　b. You should no longer permit the dumping of toxic wastes in your town.
　　c. You should perform tests to determine if there is cause and effect.
　　d. You should remove the dump to a safer, more remote location.

DETAIL **5.** What does the author NOT say about the scientists who review the work of other scientists?

　　a. They enjoy finding flaws in the works of their fellow scientists.
　　b. They try to duplicate the results of the other scientists' experiments.
　　c. They tend to be supportive of the scientists who publish their findings.
　　d. They will publish their review of the findings of these other scientists.

COHESION **6.** Where would be the best place in paragraph P to insert this sentence?
The journal later retracted the study because of inaccuracies in the findings.

　　a. after the first sentence　　　　　c. after the third sentence
　　b. after the second sentence　　　　d. after the fourth sentence

CAUSE AND EFFECT **7.** According to the author, the "science communication problem" mentioned in paragraph Q is caused by the fact that _____ .

　　a. the majority of scientists don't explain their research well
　　b. most people don't have the background to understand scientific research
　　c. there are fewer and fewer outlets for scientific research studies
　　d. people tend to believe only findings that fit into their belief systems

B. Look back at Dan Kahan's description of two groups of Americans in paragraph N. Complete the Venn diagram with the descriptions a–g. Compare your ideas with a partner.

**Egalitarian /
Community-minded
people are likely to …**

**Hierarchical /
Individualistic people
are likely to …**

a. distrust government intervention
b. question the motivations of the energy industry
c. access information online that reinforces their beliefs
d. believe that accepting climate change could lead to more regulations
e. be against higher taxes
f. support government regulations on industry
g. accept the findings of climate scientists

CRITICAL THINKING Applying Ideas   Discuss the following questions with a partner.

▶ Look at the Venn diagram in Activity B. Which of the examples listed do you believe in?

▶ Do you think you are more of an egalitarian/community-minded person or a hierarchical/individualistic person?

▶ Do you think people can be easily into these two groups? Why or why not?

⌃ Opponents argue about politics at a
2018 demonstration in London, UK.

Identifying Figurative Language

Writers often use figurative language to create vivid images in their reader's minds. This creative language engages the reader—often emotionally—and can be thought-provoking and, occasionally, humorous. As you read, make a mental note of the kinds of figurative language used and consider why the author is using them.

Besides similes and metaphors, here are some additional types of figurative language:

personification = the giving of humanlike qualities to something nonhuman
allusion = a brief reference to a person or idea
hyperbole = an exaggeration of an idea for the purpose of emphasis
imagery = a device by which a rich picture is created in the reader's mind
anecdote = a short personal story often used to illustrate a point
alliteration = a device in which words with the same consonant appear in a series

IDENTIFYING FIGURATIVE LANGUAGE

A. Read the sentences. What type of figurative language is used in each case? Choose the correct option.

1. He told so many lies he became known as "the Pinocchio of Politics."

   a. alliteration   b. allusion   c. personification

2. The view from the stage was daunting—a sea of wide-eyed faces waiting silently in anticipation.

   a. allusion   b. imagery   c. personification

3. When it comes to distinguishing fake from real news, a trustworthy news source can be your best friend.

   a. allusion   b. anecdote   c. personification

4. I don't think you could find a single person in the world who would agree with you on this.

   a. hyperbole   b. alliteration   c. personification

5. Some people will find fault in the most fundamental facts if it doesn't fit with their world view.

   a. personification   b. imagery   c. alliteration

IDENTIFYING FIGURATIVE LANGUAGE

B. Look back at the reading passage. Find the examples below.

1. two examples of hyperbole in paragraph A
2. an example of imagery in paragraph C
3. an example of alliteration in paragraph H
4. an anecdote in paragraph R

INTERPRETING

C. Work with a partner. Look again at the examples in Activity B. Why do you think the author chose to use these examples? How do they help support the author's ideas?

COMPLETION **A.** Complete the information by circling the correct words.

Astronaut Neil Armstrong, the first man on the moon, said "Knowledge is ¹**biased** / **fundamental** to all human achievements and progress." Yet, some people believe that the 1969 moon landing never actually happened and was, instead, filmed in a TV studio on Earth. Why do people believe this?

∧ **Astronaut Edwin E. Aldrin Jr. poses for a photograph on the lunar surface.**

- TV footage of the landing appears to show a flag flapping, as if ²**retained** / **exposed** to a studio fan. Yet, the flag flaps because the astronauts just put it there, and the effect of when they let go kept it moving.

- In some photos where the two astronauts are visible, it appears that neither of them is holding a camera. According to some, the ³**consensus** / **implication** of this is that someone else must have taken the photos. Actually, the camera used by the astronauts was mounted to Neil Armstrong's chest.

- Skeptics say the shadows in the photos were caused by light coming from multiple studio cameras. There are, in fact, multiple light sources on the moon: from the sun, the Earth's reflected light, and light reflecting off the astronauts and capsule.

- Some people think the astronauts' footprints look as if they were made in wet sand. However, prints made on the moon's super-fine dust ⁴**retain** / **imply** their original form thanks to the airless atmosphere.

The overwhelming ⁵**bias** / **consensus** among experts is that the moon landing actually happened—it's not fake news.

DEFINITIONS **B.** Complete the sentences. Circle the correct options.

1. A **discipline** is an activity that *has strict rules* / *is widely popular*.

2. **Institutions** include *banks and universities* / *lawyers and politicians*.

3. If you **distinguish** one thing from another, you see how they are *different than* / *similar to* each other.

4. If an argument is **rational**, it is based on *confused* / *clear* thinking.

WORD USAGE **C.** The words **prejudice** and **discrimination** are synonyms for **bias**. Their meanings, however, are slightly different. Match each word with its definition. Use a dictionary to check your answers.

1. bias   •   • a. the unfair treatment of a specific group of people

2. prejudice   •   • b. a tendency to favor one thing over another

3. discrimination •   • c. an unreasonable negative feeling towards a group of people

3B

∨ Bill and Melinda Gates speak on stage about their Goalkeepers campaign—a multiyear project dedicated to tracking and accelerating progress towards the UN Sustainable Development Goals

BEFORE YOU READ

DISCUSSION **A.** Read the first paragraph of the reading passage. Then look at the Sustainable Development Goals infographic on page 66. Answer the questions with a partner.

1. Which of these goals do you think are most important?

2. Which goals do you think will be the easiest to achieve by 2030? Which will be the hardest to achieve?

PREDICTING **B.** Which goals do you think the Goalkeeper's report will show we're making the most progress on? Discuss with a partner. Then read and check your answers.

GOALKEEPERS
FOR THE PLANET

A   In 2015 at the United Nations, world leaders adopted 17 Sustainable Development Goals aimed at reducing poverty, inequality, and other global problems by 2030. Such objectives have long been championed by philanthropists[1] Bill and Melinda Gates. In 2017, the Gates Foundation launched Goalkeepers, an **initiative** to spur action[2] and track progress toward the UN goals. Its 2018 status report says there have been "mind-blowing improvements in the human condition." The report also calls for more **investment** and **innovation** to ensure this progress continues.

B   Susan Goldberg, editor-in-chief of *National Geographic Magazine*, met with Bill and Melinda Gates for a joint interview on the report, which was released to the public on September 18, 2018.

C   **I've just read the Goalkeepers report. Why did you decide to start doing this?**

Melinda Gates: Because we think that the news isn't really out there—the news that the world has made this incredible progress, this increase in lives saved, the reduction in poverty. The UN set these amazing goals for the future to help us continue to reduce poverty, and we want to make sure that we hold people **accountable** for that progress and really inspire the next generation of leaders who are going to take these tasks on.

D   **What are you seeing in different countries? Who's doing a great job?**

Bill Gates: Even a very poor country can do a good job on health, can do a good job on agriculture, on education, and that provides a lot of hope because you can copy what's being done there. Rwanda has been a big **outlier** in the quality of health services. Ethiopia, on agriculture, is growing over 5 percent a year. In education, Vietnam is one we talk about because they're so far ahead of where you'd expect given their wealth. But it's when you get those three things together— health, education, agriculture—that eventually these countries can become self-sufficient.

E   **MG:** One of the things that's also encouraging: Rwanda is a very small country [in population], Ethiopia is the second largest on the continent of Africa—but they have learned the lessons of what has helped people make progress from around the world. So they're looking at what happened in Asia in agriculture, how did Brazil decrease the stunting[3] rate [among malnourished children] so phenomenally across a very large country with lots of poverty.

---

1   A **philanthropist** is someone who freely gives money and help to people in need.

2   If something **spurs** you into **action**, it causes you to do something.

3   The word **stunting** refers to the impaired growth and development that children experience from poor nutrition and poor health.

ACADEMIC ACHIEVEMENT

While more children are attending school in every region of the world, there is still work to be done in many countries to improve the quality of education.

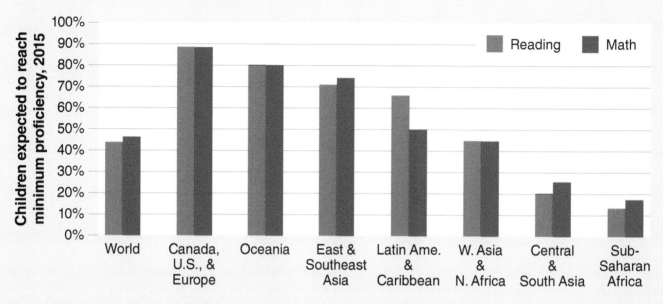

Sources: Bill & Melinda Gates Foundation

F **When you think about learning from one another, I was struck by the example from Vietnam, where you've got 15-year-olds who are doing as well on international tests in school as people from the United Kingdom or from the United States. What are the lessons from Vietnam that can translate across other countries?**

BG: It's a really new thing to try and get into the amount of learning. The agenda for poor countries up until now has largely been to get the kids into school—and attendance rates have gone up a lot, for girls and boys. The biggest missing piece still is how much knowledge they're gaining. A few countries, by training the teachers the right way and bringing the right material into the classroom, have really achieved learning way beyond what you might expect.

G **MG:** When you look back at the UN goals that were **initially** set in 2000, one of the goals was to get kids into school, and that has essentially been achieved, particularly at the primary level and quite a bit at the secondary level. So it's neat to see a goal achieved, but now with this next set of goals, it's about how to get the depth of learning and the education right.

H **Thinking about Africa: How young it is, how many young people there are, is both a huge challenge and a great opportunity. Can you talk a little bit about that?**

BG: The African continent today is about a billion people out of the seven billion on Earth, and as this century goes forward, over half the young people in the entire world will be there. With those people moving into the job market, if the right investments are made—stability, education, health—Africa will have growth and innovation, far more than lots of other places. If, on the other hand, we don't take care of the HIV crisis, then you'll just have more people who will get

POVERTY

Around the world, the percentage of people living in extreme poverty has fallen significantly since 1990. However, in sub-Saharan Africa, the figure remains relatively high, especially in the fastest-growing countries.

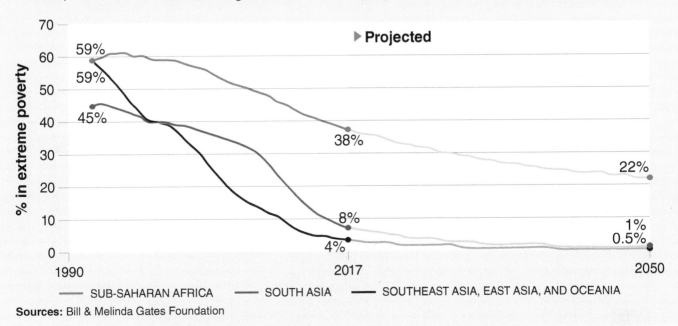

Sources: Bill & Melinda Gates Foundation

infected. If you don't have the right conditions, then the young people, particularly the men, can add to that **instability**. So Africa definitely hangs in the balance.[4]

Melinda, family planning has been one of the issues that you're most involved in. Can you talk to me a little about that?

MG: Family planning is crucial anywhere, in any community around the world, because if a woman can decide if and when to have a child, she's going to be healthier and her child is going to be healthier. That's one of the longest-standing pieces of global health research we have … [If parents] can space the births of those children, they can then feed them, they can educate them, the woman can work and contribute her income to the family. It changes everything in the family **dynamic**, and it changes the community, and ultimately you get these country-level effects where it's good for everybody.

You've gone all over the world and seen the problems up close. If you could wave a magic wand[5] and fix just one thing, what would it be?

BG: The development of children. Today more than half the kids in Africa never fully develop physically or mentally because of malnutrition, their diet, and the diseases they face. With research on the human gut microbiome,[6] we're gaining an understanding of stunting, why they don't grow. I'm super excited that by the end of the decade we expect to have cheap **interventions** so those kids will fully develop. That means all the investments you make in their education, wanting to benefit from their **productivity**, will work far better. So if there was just one thing, it's the intervention to stop malnutrition.

---

4 If something **hangs in the balance**, no one is sure what will happen to it in the future.

5 A **magic wand** is a long thin rod that magicians or fairies wave when they perform tricks, sometimes to make a wish come true.

6 The **human gut microbiome** refers to the beneficial microbes that live in the human digestive system.

SUSTAINABLE DEVELOPMENT GOALS

End poverty in all its forms everywhere

End hunger, promote improved nutrition and sustainable agriculture

Ensure healthy lives and promote well-being for all at all ages

Ensure inclusive and quality education and promote lifelong learning

Achieve gender equality and empower all women and girls

Ensure availability and sustainable management of water and sanitation for all

Ensure access to affordable, reliable, sustainable, and modern energy for all

Promote inclusive and sustainable economic growth, and decent work for all

Build resilient infrastructure, and foster innovation

Reduce inequality within and among countries

Make cities and human settlements inclusive, safe, and sustainable

Ensure sustainable consumption and production patterns

Take urgent action to combat climate change and its impacts

Conserve and sustainably use the oceans, seas, and marine resources

Sustainably manage forests, combat desertification, and halt biodiversity loss

Promote peaceful and inclusive societies for sustainable development, and access to justice for all

Revitalize the global partnership for sustainable development

The UN Sustainable Development Goals provide a blueprint for achieving a better and more sustainable future for all by 2030. They aim to tackle global challenges, including poverty, inequality, and environmental degradation

A. Choose the best answer for each question.

GIST

1. The Goalkeepers report was _____.

    a. mostly optimistic
    b. somewhat pessimistic
    c. extremely pessimistic
    d. mostly inconclusive

REFERENCE

2. In the third sentence of paragraph D, what does *that* refer to?

    a. the fact that new generations of leaders are being inspired
    b. the fact that even very poor countries are making progress
    c. the fact that many countries are becoming totally self-sufficient
    d. the fact that the UN set extremely difficult goals

DETAIL

3. Bill Gates indicates that there has been a significant improvement in all three areas of health, agriculture, and education in _____.

    a. Rwanda
    b. Ethiopia
    c. Vietnam
    d. none of these three countries

UNDERSTANDING INFOGRAPHICS

4. What does the Poverty infographic tell us about Sub-Saharan Africa?

    a. Poverty is steadily rising.
    b. Poverty is falling more slowly than in other regions.
    c. Poverty has remained about the same as in the past.
    d. Poverty is at about the same level as Southeast Asia.

VOCABULARY

5. The word *phenomenally* in paragraph E is closest in meaning to _____.

    a. gradually
    b. effortlessly
    c. amazingly
    d. deliberately

DETAIL

6. According to Bill Gates, countries wanting to improve their educational system should focus on _____.

    a. getting more and more students into the classroom
    b. expanding the size of schools and building more schools
    c. training teachers and getting better classroom materials
    d. preparing students to take international tests

SYNTHESIZING

7. Which of the goals from the list of sustainable development goals is Bill Gates most concerned with?

    a. Goal 2
    b. Goal 5
    c. Goal 7
    d. Goal 9

B. Look back at the reading passage and charts. Circle **T** (true), **F** (false), or **NG** (not given).

1. The Goalkeepers report was produced by the UN.   **T F NG**

2. The stunting rate among malnourished kids in Africa has decreased since 2000.   **T F NG**

3. Nearly half of the world's young people currently live in Africa.   **T F NG**

4. East Asia and Southeast Asia have better reading and math proficiency than the world average.   **T F NG**

5. Poverty in South Asia has increased since 2017.   **T F NG**

6. Math proficiency in Central and South Asia is above the world average.   **T F NG**

7. The UN's Sustainable Development Goals are listed in order of importance.   **T F NG**

CRITICAL THINKING Evaluating Ideas

Work in a group. Look again at the Sustainable Development Goals. Which three do you think are the most important for furthering development in your country? What are some steps that people could take to help meet each goal? Note your ideas below.

∧ **A nutrition clinic for mothers in south-eastern Rwanda**

Goal 1: _____

_____

_____

_____

_____

Goal 2: _____

_____

_____

_____

_____

Goal 3: _____

_____

_____

_____

_____

Making Inferences (1)

When reading a text, it is often possible to infer information that is not stated directly. We can draw upon information and arguments in the text, together with our own background knowledge, to infer things that are *probably* true. When you make inferences, think about what evidence or information led you to make the inference.

MAKING
INFERENCES

A. Look back at Reading B. Choose the best answer for each question.

1. In paragraph A, what can we infer about the UN Sustainable Development Goals?
   a. Member countries agreed to them.
   b. The Gates Foundation wrote them.
   c. They are not officially approved yet.
   d. They only apply to developing countries.

2. In paragraph C, we can infer that Bill and Melinda Gates produced the Goalkeepers report because _____.
   a. not enough progress was being made
   b. a lot of people aren't aware of the UN's progress
   c. the news media is not good at producing reports
   d. the UN didn't want to do it

3. Based on information in paragraph E, which of these opinions do you think Melinda Gates would likely agree with?
   a. It's easier to make progress towards the sustainable goals if a country is large.
   b. Most African countries should copy Brazil's model for reducing stunting.
   c. Rwanda and Ethiopia are the best places to live in Africa.
   d. Countries should consider adopting successful ideas from around the world.

4. According to the information in paragraph I, which of the following statements would Melinda Gates most likely agree with?
   a. The importance of family planning has only recently been fully understood.
   b. There is no evidence that family planning has any effect upon a family's overall health.
   c. It has been known for a long time that family planning is extremely important.
   d. It's important that governments restrict the number of children families can have.

B. For each item in Activity A, underline the evidence or information in the reading passage that helped you infer the correct answer. Share your ideas with a partner.

VOCABULARY PRACTICE

COMPLETION **A.** Complete the information using the correct form of the words in the box. One word is extra.

dynamics initiative instability investment outlier productive

Today, 3 in 10 people are still not able to access safe drinking water. But progress is being made. With the aid of the UN, local communities are making ¹_____ in better freshwater and sanitation facilities.

One such success story is in Sierra Leone. Wracked by years of political ²_____ and conflict, the country's infrastructure was in ruins. Students at the Harry C. Primary School in Masorie, for example, were not able to use their broken well for over a decade. But a(n) ³_____ between UNICEF and a local organization fixed the well, meaning students no longer had to spend time fetching water from outside the school grounds. Now students can spend time on more ⁴_____ educational tasks.

The fixed well in Masorie is not a(n) ⁵_____—over the past 25 years Sierra Leone says access to safe drinking water has nearly doubled.

DEFINITIONS **B.** Complete the definitions using the words in the box.

accountable dynamics initially innovation intervention

1. If you are _____ to someone for something, you are responsible for it.
2. The word _____ refers to the beginning of a process or situation.
3. A(n) _____ is a situation in which you become involved with and try and change.
4. A(n) _____ is a new thing or a new method of doing something.
5. _____ are the factors that shape a personal relationship.

COLLOCATIONS **C.** The word **initiative** is part of several common expressions. Complete the sentences using the correct form of the phrases in the box.

global initiatives   a lack of initiative   take the initiative

1. It's important that local people _____ and pressure politicians to act quickly.
2. The UN's Sustainable Development Goals are _____ aimed at improving the lives of people around the world.
3. I think both countries are showing _____ in solving the dispute.

> **Entrepreneur Sanga Moses developed a fuel that has improved the lives of many people in Uganda.**

ENERGY ENTREPRENEUR

BEFORE YOU WATCH

PREVIEWING **A.** You are going to watch a video about a company that created an alternate source of fuel in Uganda. Read the information below and answer the questions.

Uganda currently loses about 2% of its forest cover annually, use of wood for fuel being the second driver after land-clearing. Around 95% of Ugandan households use wood as a primary energy source for cooking. The demand for wood puts Uganda's forests under tremendous pressure. In addition, smoke from indoor cooking causes respiratory diseases, particularly among women and children. Globally, the World Health Organization attributes approximately 4.3 million premature deaths per year to indoor air pollution.

1. What are the problems with fuel use in Uganda?

_____

_____

2. What might be some ways to address the problem?

_____

_____

GIST **A.** Watch the video. What does Sanga Moses's company do? How do his products reduce deforestation and help local people? Note your answers below.

_____

_____

_____

DETAILS **B.** Watch the video again. Note answers to the questions.

1. Why was Sanga Moses inspired to start his company?

_____

2. Who was supportive of Sanga Moses's initial plan and why?

_____

3. How many households does Eco-fuel Africa hope to reach in the next ten years?

_____

4. What environmental, economic, and educational benefits does Eco-fuel Africa have?

_____

CRITICAL THINKING Evaluating Problems

▶ What challenges did Sanga Moses face as he tried to solve Uganda's energy crisis? Note your ideas below.

_____

_____

▶ Which challenge do you think was the most difficult to overcome? Why? Discuss with a partner.

VOCABULARY REVIEW

Do you remember the meanings of these words? Check (✓) the ones you know. Look back at the unit and review any words you're not sure of.

Reading A

☐ bias*   ☐ consensus*   ☐ discipline   ☐ distinguish   ☐ exposed to*

☐ fundamental* ☐ implication*   ☐ institution*   ☐ rational*   ☐ retain*

Reading B

☐ accountable   ☐ dynamics*   ☐ initially*   ☐ initiative*   ☐ innovation*

☐ instability* ☐ intervention*   ☐ investment*   ☐ outlier   ☐ productivity

*Academic Word List

4

SAVING CITIES

In 2005, large areas of New Orleans, United States, were left flooded following Hurricane Katrina.

WARM UP

Discuss these questions with a partner.

1. Can you think of any places that have recently experienced floods?

2. What impact does flooding have on coastal communities?

73

4A

BEFORE YOU READ

QUIZ **A.** How much do you know about Venice? Complete the quiz. Check your answers on page 94.

1. Approximately *2,000,000 / 20,000,000* people visit Venice each year.
2. Over the last century, Venice has sunk by around *25 cm / 150 cm*.
3. Recently, the city banned people from *feeding pigeons / selling T-shirts* in the main square.

SKIMMING **B.** Skim the reading. What problem facing Venice do you think the reading is mainly about? Circle one option, then read the passage to check your ideas.

a. Venice's rising tides

b. problems caused by tourism

c. the city's declining birthrate

d. rising levels of pollution

∧ The popularity of gondola rides in Venice often leads to "traffic jams" on the city's canals.

CITY UNDER SIEGE

The city Thomas Mann[1] called "half fairy tale and half tourist trap" finds itself threatened by more than just the rising tide. Cathy Newman investigates the trouble with Venice.

A Nowhere in Italy is there a crisis more beautifully **framed** than in Venice. Neither land nor water, the city lifts like a mirage from a lagoon[2] at the head of the Adriatic Sea. For centuries it has threatened to vanish beneath the waves of the *acqua alta*, the relentlessly regular flooding caused by rising tides and sinking foundations—but that is the least of its problems.

B Just ask Massimo Cacciari, former mayor of Venice and professor of philosophy, a man who raises the level of political intellect to just short of the stratosphere.[3] Ask him about the *acqua alta* and Venice sinking, and he says, "So go get boots." Boots are fine for water, but useless against the flood that causes more concern for Venetians than any lagoon spillover: the flood of tourists. In 2016, there were around 55,000 residents living in the historic city center. The number of visiting tourists that year was over 20 million.

C In May 2008, for example, on a holiday weekend, 80,000 tourists descended on the city. Public parking lots in Mestre, where people board a bus or train to the historic center, filled with floodwater and were closed. Those who managed to get to Venice surged through the streets like schools of bluefish, snapping up pizza and gelato, leaving paper and plastic bottles in their wake.[4]

D "Beauty is difficult," says Cacciari, sounding as if he were addressing a graduate seminar. The black of Cacciari's dark hair and luxuriant beard **complement** his current mood. The preceding day, heavy rains had flooded Mestre again.

---

1 **Thomas Mann** (1875–1955) was the author of the 1912 novella *Death in Venice*.
2 A **lagoon** is a body of water cut off from the open sea by coral reefs or sand bars.
3 The **stratosphere** is the atmospheric layer between 15 and 50 km above the Earth.
4 Something that is left in someone's **wake** remains behind after the person has left.

Rain caused the flood, not *acqua alta*, Cacciari says. "High tide is not a problem for me; it's a problem for you foreigners."

E The problems, he stresses, lie elsewhere. The cost of maintaining Venice: "There is not enough money from the state to cover it all—the cleaning of canals, restoration of buildings, raising of foundations." The cost of living: "It's three times as costly to live here as in Mogliano, 20 kilometers away. It's affordable only for the rich or elderly who already own houses because they have been passed down. The young can't afford it."

F Finally, there is tourism, of which, Cacciari says: "Venice is not a **sentimental** place of honeymoon; it's a strong, contradictory, overpowering place. It is not a city for tourists; it cannot be reduced to a postcard."

G If you are a Venetian, the city is a different place altogether—the abnormal is normal, and a flood is routine. The alarm sounds, protective steel doors come down, and boots, essential to any Venetian wardrobe, are pulled on. The four kilometers of *passerelle*—an **elevated** boardwalk[5] supported on metal legs—are set up, and life goes on.

H When Silvia Zanon goes to Campo San Provolo, where she teaches middle school, she knows it will take 23 minutes to walk there from her apartment on the Calle delle Carrozze. On the way she crosses the Piazza San Marco, blissfully[6] empty in early morning. "I step on the paving stones and fall in love with the city all over again," she says.

I Gherardo Ortalli, a professor of medieval history, finds his path less poetic. "When I go out in the *campo* with my friends, I have to stop because someone is taking a photograph of us," he says. For Ortalli, it almost feels like local people are becoming an endangered species. "Perhaps one day we will be. You will go and see a sign on a cage: 'Feed the Venetians.' When I arrived 30 years ago, the population was 120,000."

---

5 A **boardwalk** is a footpath made of wooden boards.

6 Somewhere that is **blissfully** empty is a place that is happy and peaceful because it is empty.

"Now, Venice gets giant cruise ships. You can't understand Venice from 10 stories up; you might as well be in a helicopter."

J The decline seems inevitable, and Ortalli thinks Venice will end up as simply a theme park for the rich, who will jet in to spend a day or two in their palazzo, then leave. It is 10 a.m., and he is headed toward a kiosk to buy a newspaper before going to his office, though you can hardly find the papers for all the tourist kitsch: miniature masks, gondola pins, jester[7] caps. "Everything is for sale," he sighs, "even Venice."

K Augusto Salvadori was once in charge of managing the impact of tourism in Venice. *Love* is an **inadequate** word to describe how Salvadori feels about Venice. He was not just the city's director of tourism and promoter of tradition; he was its defender. "The city is consumed by tourism," says Salvadori. "What do Venetians get in exchange? During part of the year, Venetians cannot elbow their way onto public transportation. The cost of garbage collection increases; so does the price of living."

L "Perhaps to help," Salvadori says, "we put a city tax on hotels and restaurants. [Then] they said tourists would not come—but I say, tourists won't come for a few euros? I could not worry about hotels; I had to think of the Venetians. My battle was for the city because Venice is my heart."

M Tourism has been part of the Venetian landscape since the 14th century, when pilgrims stopped en route to the Holy Land. I ask Ortalli what is so different about tourism now. "Now, Venice gets giant cruise ships. The ship is 10 stories high. You can't understand Venice from 10 stories up; you might as well be in a helicopter. But it's not important. You arrive in Venice, write a postcard, and remember what a wonderful evening you had."

N "There goes another piece of Venice," Silvia Zanon, the teacher, said sadly when Camiceria San Marco, a 60-year-old clothing store, had to move to a smaller, less prime spot because the rent had tripled. Susanna Cestari worked there for 32 years. "It's like leaving the house where you were born," she said, while packing boxes for the move. At least 10 hardware stores have recently gone out of business. In the Rialto market, souvenir sellers have replaced vendors who sold sausages, bread, or vegetables. Tourists will not notice; they do not visit Venice to buy an eggplant.

O Some people suggest that Venice's wounds are self-**inflicted**. "They don't want tourists," observes a former resident, "but they want their money." There is talk about **implementing** new policies to limit the number of tourists, **imposing** additional taxes, and urging visitors to avoid the high seasons of Easter and Carnevale. But tourism—together with the loss of resident population, and combined with the interests of hotel owners, gondoliers, and water taxi drivers who all have an interest in **maximizing** the influx of visitors—defies simple solutions.

P "Let me remind you, the loss of population ... is not only a problem in Venice but in all historical towns, not only Italy," cautions former Mayor Cacciari. "The **so-called** exodus, which dates back very far in time, is deep-rooted with the lodging[8] issue." For some, a solution to Venice's troubles already seems out of reach. "It is too late," Gherardo Ortalli, the historian, says. "The stones will remain, but the people won't."

Q But, for now, there is still life as well as death in Venice. Silvia Zanon, on her way to school, still crosses San Marco only to fall in love with the city again. And, assuming it is in season, you can still manage to buy an eggplant. The city's beauty, difficult and bruised, somehow survives.

---

7 A **jester** was a professional clown employed by the nobility during the Middle Ages. Jesters' hats are known for being colorful with pointed tips.

8 **Lodging** is temporary, often rented, accommodations.

VENICE

— VERSUS —

THE SEA

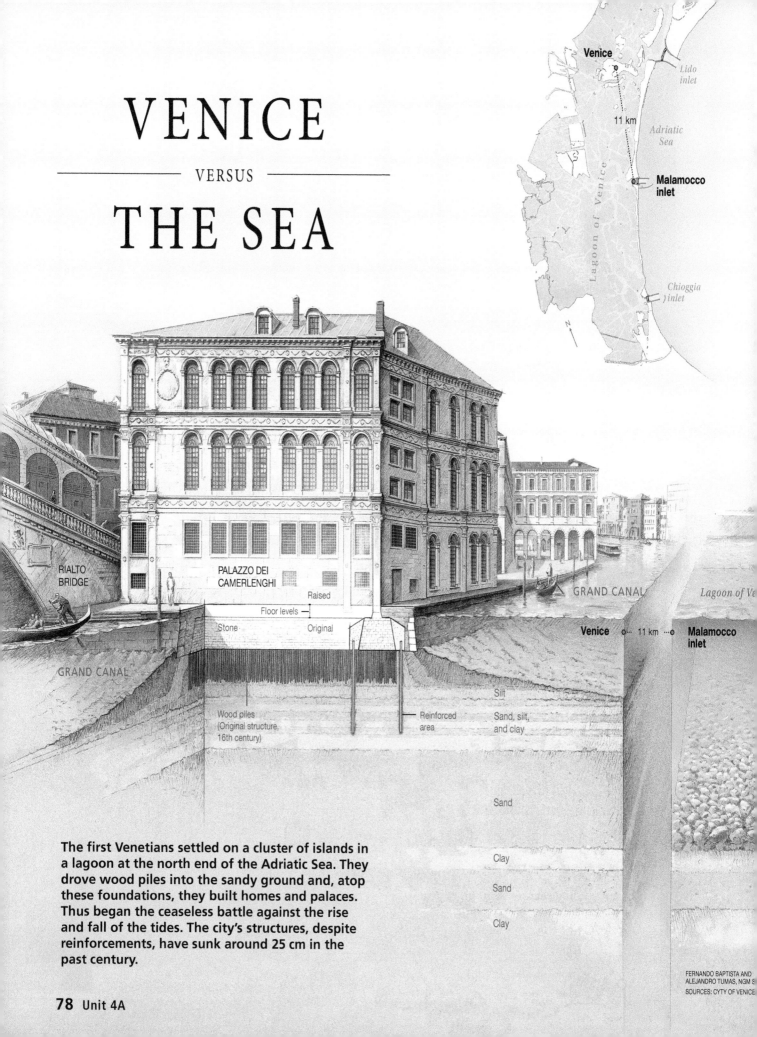

Venice

11 km

Adriatic Sea

Lido inlet

Malamocco inlet

Lagoon of Venice

Chioggia inlet

N

RIALTO BRIDGE

PALAZZO DEI CAMERLENGHI

Raised

Floor levels

Stone   Original

GRAND CANAL

Wood piles
(Original structure,
16th century)

Reinforced area

GRAND CANAL   Lagoon of Ve

Venice   11 km   Malamocco inlet

Silt

Sand, silt, and clay

Sand

Clay

Sand

Clay

The first Venetians settled on a cluster of islands in a lagoon at the north end of the Adriatic Sea. They drove wood piles into the sandy ground and, atop these foundations, they built homes and palaces. Thus began the ceaseless battle against the rise and fall of the tides. The city's structures, despite reinforcements, have sunk around 25 cm in the past century.

FERNANDO BAPTISTA AND
ALEJANDRO TUMAS, NGM S
SOURCES: CYTY OF VENICE

STEMMING THE TIDE

The $6 billion MOSE project, begun in 2003 and projected to be completed in 2022, strings four barriers made up of 78 floodgates across three inlets (left) to Venice's lagoon. The gates, raised when unusually high tides threaten flooding, block seawater from pouring into the lagoon

BEYOND THE BRINK

Number of times water rose one meter or higher

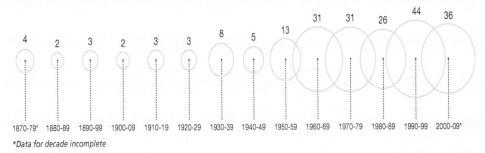

4	2	3	2	3	3	8	5	13	31	31	26	44	36
1870-79*	1880-89	1890-99	1900-09	1910-19	1920-29	1930-39	1940-49	1950-59	1960-69	1970-79	1980-89	1990-99	2000-09*

Data for decade incomplete

① Hollow steel gates filled with water lie flat in chambers built into the lagoon bed at each inlet.

② When flooding is predicted, air is pumped into the gates to displace water, allowing them to rise within half an hour.

③ Fully elevated, the gates separate the sea from the lagoon. When the tide recedes, water flows back into the gates to lower them.

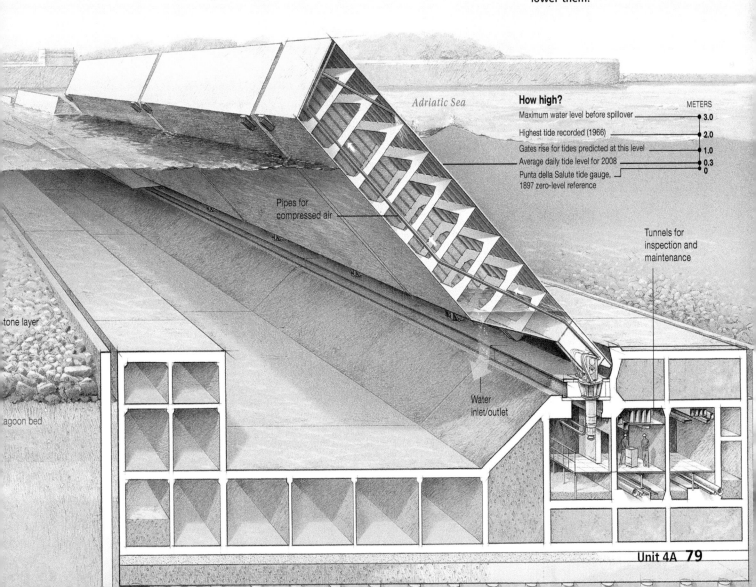

Adriatic Sea

How high?

	METERS
Maximum water level before spillover	3.0
Highest tide recorded (1966)	2.0
Gates rise for tides predicted at this level	1.0
Average daily tide level for 2008	0.3
Punta della Salute tide gauge, 1897 zero-level reference	0

Pipes for compressed air

Tunnels for inspection and maintenance

tone layer

agoon bed

Water inlet/outlet

A. Choose the best answer for each question.

INFERENCE

1. In paragraph B, what does Massimo Cacciari imply when he says, "So go get boots."

    a. Tourists shouldn't complain about the floods.

    b. Nothing can be done about the increase in tourism.

    c. The *acqua alta* is not a big problem.

    d. Venetians are well-prepared for the regular flooding.

RHETORICAL PURPOSE

2. Why does the author present the statistics in paragraph B?

    a. to indicate that more tourists are coming to Venice than before

    b. to emphasize the population decline in Venice

    c. to contrast the number of tourists with the number of residents

    d. to point out the dangers of serious flooding

INFERENCE

3. What can be inferred about the holiday weekend in May 2008, mentioned in the article?

    a. There were more tourists than residents in the city.

    b. Many residents left the city because of the floods.

    c. All of the city center's parking lots were full of cars.

    d. Vendors ran out of snacks, such as pizza and gelato, for tourists.

DETAIL

4. What does Massimo Cacciari say about the young people of Venice in paragraph E?

    a. Most of them have moved to the nearby town of Mogliano.

    b. They find it is too expensive to live in Venice these days.

    c. They are involved in cleaning canals, restoring buildings, and raising foundations.

    d. Many of them live in houses that have been passed down from their parents.

DETAIL

5. Which of the following is given as an example of an ordinary resident of Venice?

    a. Massimo Cacciari

    b. Silvia Zanon

    c. Thomas Mann

    d. Augusto Salvadori

DETAIL

6. How has the population of Venice changed in the last 30 years?

    a. It has increased slightly.

    b. It has declined sharply.

    c. It has stayed about the same.

    d. It goes up and down depending on the flooding.

REFERENCE

7. The word *they* in the second sentence of paragraph O refers to the _____.

    a. people who live in Venice

    b. International Center of Studies on the Tourist Economy

    c. people who say that Venice's wounds are self-inflicted

    d. tourists who visit Venice

B. Look again at the infographic Venice Versus the Sea. Choose the correct answer for each question.

1. What is the main purpose of the MOSE project?
   a. to stop Venice sinking further
   b. to prevent sea water from flooding the city
   c. to make the lagoons larger

2. Which decade had the most instances of water rising over a meter?
   a. 1930s   b. 1960s   c. 1990s

3. How high does the tide need to be before the gates rise?
   a. 1 meter   b. 2 meters   c. 3 meters

4. How high does the tide need to be before it floods Venice?
   a. 0.3 meters   b. 3 meters   c. 14 meters

5. How is the water removed from the gates, allowing them to rise?
   a. air is pumped into them
   b. the steel gates are lifted up
   c. workers in tunnels underneath empty them

CRITICAL THINKING Analyzing Arguments

▶ The author states that tourism is "the heart and soul of the Venetian economy—good and bad." List the positive and negative effects of tourism the author mentions in the passage.

Positive effects of tourism
Negative effects of tourism

▶ Overall, do you think positive effects of tourism in Venice outweigh the negative effects? Discuss with a partner.

˅ **Tourists ride a gondola along Venice's grand canal.**

Recognizing Literal versus Figurative Language

It is important to be able to recognize when words and phrases are being used figuratively instead of literally. Figurative language—such as similes, metaphors, and personification—uses words with a meaning that is different from the literal interpretation.

The farmers plowed their fields. (*Plow* is used literally—farmers had real plows)
The ship plowed through the sea. (*Plow* is used as a metaphor—the ship moved like a plow)

CLASSIFICATION **A. Find these words or phrases in Reading A. Write L if they are used literally or F if they are used figuratively.**

1. _____ flooding (paragraph A)   **5.** _____ defender (paragraph K)

2. _____ flood (paragraph B)   **6.** _____ eggplant (paragraph N)

3. _____ foundations (paragraph E)   **7.** _____ wounds (paragraph O)

4. _____ elevated (paragraph G)   **8.** _____ bruised (paragraph Q)

INTERPRETING **B. Read the excerpts from Reading A. Underline any figurative language, then choose the sentence that best describes what the author means.**

1. Neither land nor water, the city lifts like a mirage from a lagoon at the head of the Adriatic Sea.

   a. The city rises in a way that almost seems unreal.
   b. The city looks like something you might see in a desert.

2. Just ask Massimo Cacciari, former mayor of Venice and professor of philosophy, a man who raises the level of political intellect to just short of the stratosphere.

   a. Cacciari is the highest-ranking politician in Venice.
   b. Cacciari is one of the smartest politicians in Venice.

3. Those who managed to get to Venice surged through the streets like schools of bluefish, snapping up pizza and gelato, leaving paper and plastic bottles in their wake.

   a. The tourists moved in large, hungry groups.
   b. The tourists raced through quickly and carelessly.

4. Ortalli thinks Venice will end up as simply a theme park for the rich, who will jet in to spend a day or two in their palazzo, then leave.

   a. In the future, Venice will not be a real, functioning city.
   b. In the future, Venice will be a really fun place.

VOCABULARY PRACTICE

COMPLETION **A. Complete the information. Circle the correct words.**

A popular image of the European Alps consists of cowbells, cheese-making, and quiet villages [1]**framed** / **imposed** against a background of snow-capped mountains. But that picture must also include the millions of trucks and cars that cross the mountains each year.

△ **The Gotthard Base Tunnel while under construction**

Transporting millions of tons of goods annually [2]**implements** / **inflicts** significant damage on the local environment. Carbon dioxide from vehicle emissions becomes trapped in the narrow valleys. The steep valley walls also amplify the sounds generated by the traffic. The [3]**inadequate** / **elevated** levels of noise and pollution are even thought to have affected the health of Alpine residents.

Laws have been [4]**elevated** / **implemented** to lower the number of vehicles in residential areas, but they have so far proved [5]**inadequate** / **maximized** at reducing traffic. There are hopeful signs, however. June 2016 saw the completion of the Gotthard Base Tunnel—the GBT—which is the world's longest rail tunnel. It is hoped that the tunnel will lessen the environmental strain on one of the world's most famous landscapes.

DEFINITIONS **B. Match each word in the box with its definition.**

complement	impose	maximize	sentimental	so-called

1. _____: commonly referred to by the specified name
2. _____: to increase as much as possible
3. _____: related to emotions rather than reason
4. _____: to form a good combination
5. _____: to force something on someone

WORD USAGE **C. The words complement and *compliment* are sometimes confused. *Compliment* means "to say something nice to or about someone." Circle the correct word in these sentences.**

1. It's nice to get *complemented* / *complimented* on a great essay.
2. A pink tie can *complement* / *compliment* a light gray suit.
3. Peanut butter is the perfect *complement* / *compliment* to jam.
4. Some diners like to send their *complements* / *compliments* to the chef after dinner.

BEFORE YOU READ

DISCUSSION **A.** Look at the photo and read the caption. Why might rising sea levels be an issue for coastal communities? Discuss your ideas with a partner.

SKIMMING AND PREDICTING **B.** The reading passage discusses some of the challenges of rising sea levels. Read the headings and captions, and skim the passage. In your own words, write what you think these sections are mainly about. Then read the article to check your ideas.

Storm of the Century _____

Coastlines at Risk _____

Retreat from the Coast _____

Dutch Lessons _____

A roller coaster in New Jersey, United States, lies damaged and partially submerged in water following Hurricane Sandy.

RISING SEAS

As the planet warms, the sea rises, and coastlines flood, how will we face the danger of rising seas?

Storm of the Century

A By the time Hurricane Sandy veered toward the northeast coast of the United States on October 29, 2012, it had mauled[1] several countries in the Caribbean and left dozens dead. Faced with the largest storm the Atlantic had ever produced, New York and other cities ordered mandatory **evacuations** of low-lying areas, but not everyone **complied**. Those who chose to ride out Sandy got a preview of the future, in which a warmer world will lead to rising seas.

B Brandon d'Leo, a sculptor and surfer, rented a second-floor apartment across the street from the beach on New York City's Rockaway Peninsula. At about 3:30 in the afternoon, he

went outside and saw waves crashing against the nine-kilometer-long boardwalk. A short time later, d'Leo and a neighbor were watching the sea through the glass door of his living room when his neighbor saw something alarming. "I think the boardwalk just moved," she said. Within minutes, another **surge** of water lifted the boardwalk, and it began to break apart.

C Three large sections of the boardwalk smashed against two pine trees in front of d'Leo's apartment. The street had become a river 1.2 meters deep; cars began to float. After the storm, d'Leo said, "I have six surfboards in my apartment, and I was thinking, if anything comes through that wall, I'll try to get everyone on those boards and try to get up the block."

D After a difficult night's sleep, d'Leo went outside and saw that while the water had **retreated**, thigh-deep pools still filled parts of some streets. "Everything was covered with sand," he said. "It looked like another planet."

---

1 If someone is **mauled** (e.g., by a wild animal), they are attacked fiercely and aggressively.

Coastlines at Risk

E By the end of the century, a hundred-year storm surge like Sandy's might occur every decade, with coastal cities like New York now facing a double threat: rising oceans and more severe storm surges. By 2070, experts estimate, 150 million people and $35 trillion in property in the world's large port cities will be at risk from coastal flooding. How will the cities cope?

F Malcolm Bowman, a researcher at the State University of New York, believes that storm-surge barriers must be built across New York City's harbor. Compared with some other leading ports, New York is essentially defenseless in the face of hurricanes and floods. London, Rotterdam, St. Petersburg, New Orleans, and Shanghai have all built levees[2] and storm barriers in the past few decades. When Hurricane Sandy struck, New York paid a high price for not having such protection. The storm left 43 dead and cost the city about $19 billion, and according to Bowman, storm-surge barriers could have prevented it. He says, "It might take five years of study and another ten years to get the political **will** to do it. By then, there might have been another disaster. We need to start planning immediately."

G Mayor Michael Bloomberg outlined a $19.5 billion plan to defend New York City against rising seas. His proposal called for the construction of levees, local storm-surge barriers, sand dunes, and more than two hundred other measures. It went far beyond anything planned by any other U.S. city, but the mayor dismissed the idea of a harbor barrier. "A giant barrier across our harbor is neither practical nor affordable," Bloomberg said.

Retreat from the Coast

H With the threat of sea-level rise everywhere, cities around the world have turned to the

---

2 A **levee** is a raised structure of earth or other material built to hold back water.

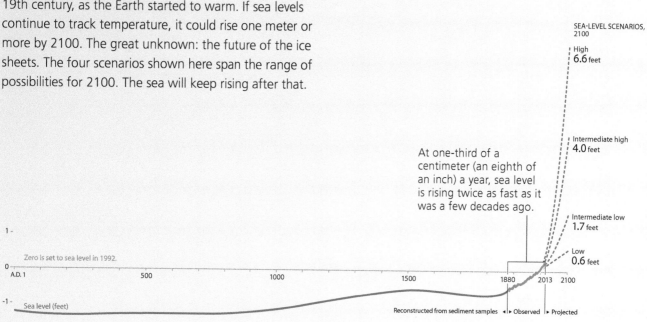

Rising Seas

Sea level didn't change much for nearly 2,000 years, judging from sediment cores. It began to rise in the late 19th century, as the Earth started to warm. If sea levels continue to track temperature, it could rise one meter or more by 2100. The great unknown: the future of the ice sheets. The four scenarios shown here span the range of possibilities for 2100. The sea will keep rising after that.

SEA-LEVEL SCENARIOS, 2100

High 6.6 feet

Intermediate high 4.0 feet

At one-third of a centimeter (an eighth of an inch) a year, sea level is rising twice as fast as it was a few decades ago.

Intermediate low 1.7 feet

Low 0.6 feet

1

Zero is set to sea level in 1992.

0

A.D. 1   500   1000   1500   1880 2013 2100

-1   Sea level (feet)

Reconstructed from sediment samples ◄|► Observed |► Projected

Netherlands for guidance—a country that has faced and overcome the problem of rising seas. One Dutch firm, Arcadis, has prepared a design for a storm-surge barrier to protect New York City. The same company helped design a barrier 3.2 kilometers long that protected New Orleans from Hurricane Isaac's four-meter storm surge in 2012. "Isaac was a tremendous victory for New Orleans," said Piet Dircke, an Arcadis executive. "All the barriers were closed; all the levees held; all the pumps worked. You didn't hear about it because nothing happened."

New Orleans may be safe for a few decades, but the long-term prospects for it and other low-lying cities look **dire**. Even if we begin reducing our emissions of heat-trapping gases tomorrow, oceans will likely rise as Earth slowly adjusts to the amount already in the atmosphere. Among the most **vulnerable** cities is Miami. "I cannot **envision** southeastern Florida having many people at the end of this century," says Hal Wanless,

of the University of Miami's Department of Geological Science. "We think Miami has always been here and will always be here. How do you get people to realize that Miami—or London—will not always be there?"

Unless we change course dramatically, our carbon emissions will drastically change the geography of many shorelines by the next century, if not sooner, and large numbers of people will have to abandon many coastal areas of the world. "From the Bahamas to Bangladesh and a major amount of Florida, we'll have to move, and we may have to move at the same time," says Wanless. Columbia University geophysicist Klaus Jacob sees most of Manhattan's population fleeing to higher ground and the island becoming a kind of Venice, subject to periodic flooding, perhaps with canals and yellow water cabs. At different times in different countries, engineering solutions will no longer be enough. Then the retreat from the coast will begin.

Uneven Impacts

If sea level rises an average of one meter by 2100, winds, currents, and melting ice sheets will distribute the rise unevenly. Certain coastal cities will be especially vulnerable.

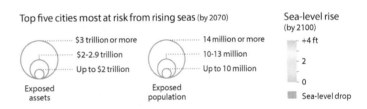

Top five cities most at risk from rising seas (by 2070)

Exposed assets
- $3 trillion or more
- $2–2.9 trillion
- Up to $2 trillion

Exposed population
- 14 million or more
- 10–13 million
- Up to 10 million

Sea-level rise (by 2100)
- +4 ft
- 2
- 0
- Sea-level drop

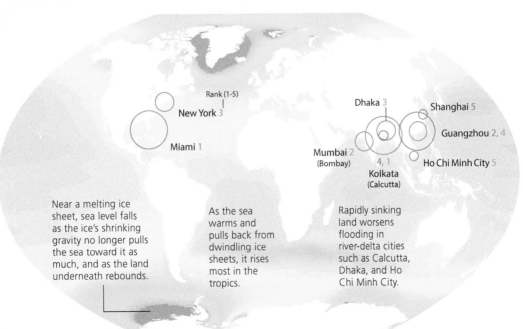

Rank (1–5)

New York 3

Miami 1

Dhaka 3

Shanghai 5

Guangzhou 2, 4

Mumbai 2 (Bombay)

Kolkata (Calcutta) 4, 1

Ho Chi Minh City 5

Near a melting ice sheet, sea level falls as the ice's shrinking gravity no longer pulls the sea toward it as much, and as the land underneath rebounds.

As the sea warms and pulls back from dwindling ice sheets, it rises most in the tropics.

Rapidly sinking land worsens flooding in river-delta cities such as Calcutta, Dhaka, and Ho Chi Minh City.

Dutch Lessons

K Can a single storm change not just a city's but a nation's policy? It has happened before. The Netherlands experienced its own coastal catastrophe nearly 70 years ago, and it transformed the country.

L The storm roared in from the North Sea on the night of January 31, 1953. Ria Geluk was six years old at the time and living on an island in the Dutch province of Zeeland. She remembers a neighbor knocking on her family's door in the middle of the night to tell them that the dike[3] had failed. Later that day, the whole family climbed to the roof. Geluk's grandparents lived just across the road, but water poured into the village with such force that they were trapped in their home, and they died when it collapsed. The disaster killed 1,836 in all, including a baby born on the night of the storm.

M Afterwards the Dutch began an ambitious program of dike and barrier construction called the Delta Works, which lasted more than four decades and cost more than $6 billion. One crucial project was the eight-kilometer barrier built to defend Zeeland from the sea. The final component of the Delta Works—a movable barrier protecting Rotterdam Harbor and some 1.5 million people—was finished in 1997. Like other sea barriers in the Netherlands, it's built to **withstand** a 1-in-10,000-year storm—the strictest standard in the world.

N The transparent domes of Rotterdam's Floating Pavilion represent an even more innovative approach to taming[4] the sea. The three domes—each about three stories tall—are made of a plastic that is a hundred times as light as glass. Though the domes are used for meetings and exhibitions, their main purpose is to demonstrate the potential of floating urban architecture. The city anticipates that as many as 1,200 homes will float in the harbor by 2040. "We think these structures will be important not just for Rotterdam but for many cities around the world," says Bart Roeffen, the architect who designed the pavilion.

O An inscription[5] on the side of a storm-surge barrier in Zeeland says "*Hier gaan over het tij, de maan, de wind, en wij*"—Here the tide is ruled by the moon, the wind, and us. It reflects the confidence of a generation that **took for granted**—as we no longer can—a reasonably stable world. "We have to understand that we are not ruling the world," says Jan Mulder of Deltares, a Dutch coastal management firm. "We need to adapt."

---

3 A **dike** is a long wall that prevents water from flooding a place.

4 If you **tame** something dangerous, you bring it under control.

5 An **inscription** is writing carved into something made of stone or metal.

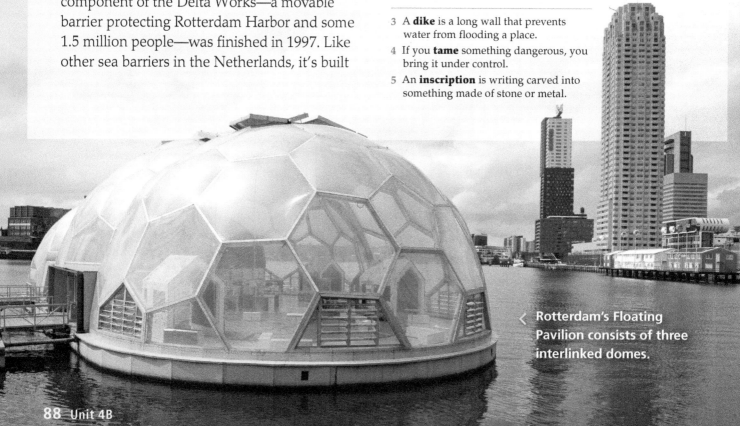

< Rotterdam's Floating Pavilion consists of three interlinked domes.

READING COMPREHENSION

A. Choose the best answer for each question.

GIST
1. What would be another good title for this reading?
   a. Can Our Coasts Be Saved?
   b. The Devastation of Hurricane Sandy
   c. How the Netherlands Beat Back the Sea
   d. How to Slow Global Warming

DETAIL
2. What helped save lives when Hurricane Sandy struck New York?
   a. Levees and storm barriers held most of the water back.
   b. Boardwalks helped slow the surge of water.
   c. The storm had weakened after leaving the Caribbean.
   d. Low-lying areas had already been evacuated.

FIGURATIVE LANGUAGE
> Review this reading skill in Unit 4A

3. Find the sentences below in the passage. Which one does NOT include an example of figurative language?
   a. By the time Hurricane Sandy ... left dozens dead. (paragraph A)
   b. "Everything was covered ... like another planet." (paragraph D)
   c. Columbia University ... yellow water cabs. (paragraph J)
   d. Then the retreat from the coast will begin. (paragraph J)

UNDERSTANDING INFOGRAPHICS
4. Which city is at risk of losing up to $3 trillion in assets due to rising sea levels?
   a. Miami
   b. Dhaka
   c. Ho Chi Minh City
   d. Shanghai

RHETORICAL PURPOSE
5. What is the author's tone in paragraph J?
   a. Optimistic: We have the capacity to fix the problem.
   b. Pessimistic: Unless we change course, we will have to move inland.
   c. Neutral: We don't know how the author feels.
   d. Humorous: Mentioning that New York will be like Venice with water cabs takes away the seriousness of the issue.

DETAIL
6. What is Rotterdam's Floating Pavilion?
   a. temporary shelters for flood victims
   b. an example of possible future living spaces
   c. domes that convert wave energy into power
   d. meeting spaces that also act as surge barriers

PURPOSE
7. What is the main purpose of the section on page 88?
   a. to describe the event that caused the Netherlands to begin their dike- and barrier-building program
   b. to show how dangerous coastal communities like Zeeland can be, even when they are well protected
   c. to make a case for expanding the Dutch success story in Zeeland to other parts of the country
   d. to illustrate that storms 70 years ago were just as dangerous as the storms of today

B. Match each paragraph with its purpose.

1. Paragraph A _____

2. Paragraph B _____

3. Paragraph D _____

4. Paragraph F _____

5. Paragraph G _____

6. Paragraph H _____

7. Paragraph I _____

8. Paragraph J _____

a. to describe the aftermath of a storm

b. to discuss a proposal put forth by one city to be better prepared for major storms

c. to warn the reader what could happen in the future if we don't deal with rising seas

d. to explain how one Dutch company helped prepare New Orleans for a destructive storm

e. to show why others cities are better prepared for storms than New York City

f. to introduce two local residents who were affected by a huge storm

g. to predict how one U.S. city will be affected by rising seas at the end of the century

h. to explain why New York City ordered evacuations of certain coastal areas of the city

CRITICAL THINKING Evaluating Solutions   Imagine you are mayor of New York City. How would you prevent another catastrophic sea surge? Discuss your ideas with a partner. Consider the costs and practicality of the following options:

- Create a series of dams, dikes, and levees
- Build a storm-surge barrier
- Move at-risk communities away from the coast

- Invest in floating buildings
- Increase the height of current sea walls
- Build a chain of barrier islands along the coast

> **A man watches the waves in New York Harbor as Hurricane Sandy approaches.**

Evaluating Arguments (2)—Reading Critically

In order to evaluate a writer's arguments, it is important to read critically. Critical reading involves analyzing, interpreting, and evaluating the text as you read through it, and reflecting on it afterward.

A useful technique is to read a text twice. On the first reading, identify the main arguments that the author is making and highlight them in the text. Then underline any details that support the author's argument. The second time, read the text critically. Scrutinize each argument. Look for poorly supported or exaggerated claims. See if you can find bias, faulty reasoning, or other weaknesses. Then reflect on what you have read and decide where you stand.

READING
CRITICALLY

A. **Read this excerpt from the reading passage. Highlight the sentence that gives the author's main argument. Underline any supporting details.**

Unless we change course dramatically, our carbon emissions will drastically change the geography of many shorelines by the next century, if not sooner, and large numbers of people will have to abandon many coastal areas of the world. "From the Bahamas to Bangladesh and a major amount of Florida, we'll have to move, and we may have to move at the same time," says Wanless. Columbia University geophysicist Klaus Jacob sees most of Manhattan's population fleeing to higher ground and the island becoming a kind of Venice, subject to periodic flooding, perhaps with canals and yellow water cabs. At different times in different countries, engineering solutions will no longer be enough. Then the retreat from the coast will begin.

REFLECTING

B. **Read the excerpt again. Note answers to the questions below, then discuss with a partner.**

1. How important does the author think the issue of carbon emissions is? Underline the persuasive language the author uses.

_____

_____

2. Look at the first sentence of the excerpt. How reliable is this information? What additional information would you like to know?

_____

_____

3. The author's view is supported by the opinions of two other people. Who are they? How valid are their opinions?

_____

_____

4. Do you think the author might be biased? Give reasons for your answer.

_____

_____

COMPLETION **A.** Complete the information by circling the correct words.

Imagine Boston's Faneuil Hall, the U.S. Naval Academy, and Jamestown—lost forever due to rising seas. It's a future many Americans cannot ¹**comply / envision**, but these—and other cultural sites—are ²**vulnerable / surging**. Amid all the ³**dire / complied** warnings regarding climate change, little attention has been paid to how it may affect cultural resources.

∧ **Cultural landmarks such as Jamestown in Virginia could be at risk of the effects of rising seas.**

In Virginia—home to Jamestown, the first permanent English settlement in the Americas—sea level rises are a big problem. Residents may ⁴**take for granted / retreat** that low-lying coastal areas will always be as they remember it, but the delicate seashore would not be able to ⁵**retreat / withstand** sea levels rising by a meter or more. It's likely that some residents will have to ⁶**comply / retreat** from the coast and move inland.

WORDS IN CONTEXT **B.** Complete the sentences. Circle the correct words.

1. If you **comply** with an order, you *follow / ignore* it.
2. Someone with a strong **will** is very *determined / experienced*.
3. The **evacuation** of a place involves people moving *toward / away from* it.
4. A **surge** is a sudden *decrease / increase* in the amount of something.

WORD LINK **C.** The expression **take for granted** includes the verb *take*, which is part of many other common expressions. Complete the sentences with the correct expression from the box.

take sides	take advantage of	take it seriously	take for granted

1. Many shoppers _____ low prices during sales events. People love a bargain!
2. Homeowners living on the coast should not _____ that their properties will be safe from storm surges.
3. Rising sea levels are a huge problem, but some politicians don't _____.
4. My two best friends were having an argument. I didn't want to _____, so I kept quiet.

VIDEO

Hurricane Irma strikes
the Florida coast.

HURRICANES

BEFORE YOU WATCH

DEFINITIONS **A.** Read the excerpts from the video. Match each word in **bold** with its definition.

"Scientists have a **thorough** understanding of how hurricanes form and **sustain** their power."

"Hurricanes form from a **cluster** of thunderstorms."

"Hurricanes can cause mass **devastation**."

1. sustain   •   • a. (n) extreme damage or destruction

2. cluster   •   • b. (adj) complete; including the finest details

3. thorough   •   • c. (v) to continue or maintain

4. devastation •   • d. (n) a group of things that are close together

QUIZ **B.** What do you know about hurricanes? Complete the sentences by circling the best options.

1. Hurricanes form over *cold / warm* waters.

2. The very center of a hurricane is called the *"eye" / "heart"*.

3. A storm is classed as a hurricane when wind speeds reach *74 / 174* mph.

4. Most deaths caused by hurricanes are a result of *storm surges / falling trees*.

GIST **A.** Watch the video. Check your answers in Before You Watch B.

DETAILS **B.** Watch the video again. Complete the sentences.

1. In the Atlantic Ocean, most hurricanes occur during _____.

2. Hurricanes form from groups of _____.

3. The "eyewall" is the _____ around the center of a hurricane.

4. The Saffir-Simpson scale ranks hurricanes on a scale of 1 to 5 based on wind speed and _____.

5. Hurricanes benefit our climate as they move heat from _____ to the poles, keeping the Earth's temperature stable.

6. As scientists learn more about hurricanes, they will be able to improve _____ systems and help cities build better infrastructure.

CRITICAL THINKING Applying Ideas

▶ In addition to hurricanes, what are some other natural disasters? Note your ideas below.

_____

_____

▶ Look back at your list. Which natural disaster do you think is the deadliest? Why? Note your ideas below, then discuss with a partner.

_____

_____

VOCABULARY REVIEW

Do you remember the meanings of these words? Check (✓) the ones you know. Look back at the unit and review any words you're not sure of.

Reading A

☐ complement* ☐ elevate ☐ frame ☐ implement* ☐ impose*

☐ inadequate* ☐ inflict ☐ maximize* ☐ sentimental ☐ so-called

Reading B

☐ comply ☐ dire ☐ envision ☐ evacuation ☐ retreat

☐ surge ☐ take for granted ☐ vulnerable ☐ will ☐ withstand

*Academic Word List

Answers to Before You Read A, page 74: 1. 20,000,000, **2.** 25 cm., **3.** feeding pigeons

ENERGY CHOICES

5

Visitors ride Segways
through a wind
park in Feldheim,
Germany.

WARM UP

Discuss these questions with a partner.

1. What are the world's main sources of energy? Which are the most important in your country?

2. What are some of the advantages and disadvantages of using renewable energy sources?

> The New York skyline viewed via thermal imaging.
> Red and yellow patches indicate escaping heat. Heating,
> cooling, and powering of these buildings account for
> almost three-quarters of New York City's emissions.

BEFORE YOU READ

DISCUSSION **A.** What are some different ways you use energy in your daily
life? Discuss with a partner. Consider the following areas:

on your commute   at home   at work   socializing

SKIMMING AND **B.** Skim the first part of the reading (paragraphs A–C). Discuss
PREDICTING the questions below with a partner. Then read the passage to
check your ideas.

1. What kind of experiment is the author participating in?

2. What do you think he found out?

OUR ENERGY DIET

With a little effort, and not much money, most of us could reduce our energy diets by 25 percent or more. So, what's holding us back? Writer Peter Miller goes on a strict low-carbon diet to find out.

A Not long ago, my wife and I tried a new diet—not to lose weight but to answer a question about climate change. Scientists have reported that the world is heating up even faster than they predicted just a few years ago. The consequences, they say, could be severe if we don't keep reducing emissions of carbon dioxide (CO_2) and other greenhouse gases that are trapping heat in our atmosphere. But what can we do about it as individuals? And will our efforts really make any difference?

The Experiment

B We decided to try an experiment: For one month we would track our personal emissions of CO_2 as if we were counting calories. We wanted to see how much we could cut back.

C The average U.S. household produces about 80 kilos[1] of CO_2 a day by doing **commonplace** things like turning on air conditioning or driving cars. This is more than twice the European average and almost five times the global average. But how much should we try to reduce?

D I checked with Tim Flannery, author of *The Weather Makers: How Man Is Changing the Climate and What It Means for Life on Earth*. In his book, he challenged readers to make deep cuts in personal emissions to keep the world from reaching critical tipping points,[2] such as the melting of the ice sheets in Greenland or West

---

1 **Kilo** is an abbreviation of the word *kilogram*.
2 A **tipping point** is a stage of a process when a significant change takes place, after which the process cannot be turned back.

Antarctica. "To stay below that **threshold**, we need to reduce CO_2 emissions by 80 percent," he said. "That sounds like a lot," my wife said. "Can we really do that?"

E   It seemed unlikely to me, too. Still, the point was to answer a simple question: How close could we come to a lifestyle the planet could handle? Finally, we agreed to aim for roughly 80 percent less than the U.S. average: a daily diet of about 13 kilograms of CO_2. Our first challenge was to find ways to convert our daily activities into kilos of CO_2. We wanted to track our progress as we went so that we could change our habits if necessary.

F   To get a rough idea of our current carbon footprint, I put numbers from recent **utility** bills into several calculators on websites. The results that came out were not very flattering.[3] The Environmental Protection Agency (EPA) website figured our annual CO_2 emissions at 24,618 kilos, 30 percent higher than the average U.S. family with two people. The main culprit was the energy we were using to heat and cool our house. Clearly we had further to go than I thought.

The Diagnosis

G   We got some help in Week Two from a professional "house doctor," Ed Minch of Energy Services Group in Wilmington, Delaware, who we asked to do an energy **audit** of our house. The first thing he did was to walk around the outside of the house to see if the architect and builder had created any opportunities for air to seep[4] in or out, such as overhanging floors. Next, he went inside and used an infrared scanner to look at our interior walls. Finally, his assistants set up a powerful fan in our front door to lower air pressure inside the house and force air through whatever leaks there might be in the shell of the house.

H   Our house, his instruments showed, was 50 percent leakier than it should be. Addressing this became a priority, as heating represents up to half of a house's energy costs, and cooling can account for a tenth. Minch also gave us tips about lighting and **appliances**. "A typical kitchen these days has ten 75-watt spots[5] on all day," he said, "and that's a huge waste of money." Replacing them with **compact** fluorescents could save a homeowner $200 a year. Refrigerators, washing machines, dishwashers, and other appliances, in fact, may represent half of a household's electric bill.

I   Everywhere I looked, I saw things sucking up energy. One night I sat up in bed and counted ten little lights in the darkness: cell phone charger, desktop calculator, laptop computer, printer, clock radio, cable TV box, camera battery recharger, carbon monoxide detector, cordless phone base, smoke detector. What were they all doing? One study found that "vampire" power sucked up by electronics in standby **mode** can add up to 25 percent of a house's electric bill.

J   "You can go nuts[6] thinking about everything in your house that uses power," said Jennifer Thorne Amann, author of *Consumer Guide to Home Energy Savings*. "You have to use common sense and prioritize. Don't agonize[7] too much, and think about what you'll be able to sustain after the experiment is over. If you have trouble reaching your goal in one area, remember there's always something else you can do."

---

3 Something that is **flattering** makes you look good.

4 If something **seeps** in or through, it leaks slowly.

5 The word **spots** is short for *spotlights*, or strong, focused lights.

6 If someone **goes nuts**, he or she goes crazy.

7 When people **agonize** about something, they are very worried about it.

Thermal photography can give clues to where a house's heat is escaping. By addressing these leakages, large amounts of energy can be saved.

The Results

K   By the last week in July, we were finally getting into the flow of the reduced carbon lifestyle. We walked to the neighborhood pool instead of driving, biked to the local farmers market on Saturday morning, and sat out on the deck until dark, chatting over the sound of the crickets. Whenever possible I worked from home, and when I **commuted**, I took the bus and subway.

L   Our numbers were looking pretty good, in fact, when we crossed the finish line on August 1. Compared with the previous July, we had cut electricity use by 70 percent, natural gas by 40 percent, and reduced our driving to half the national average. In terms of CO_2, we trimmed our emissions to an average of 32 kilograms a day, which, though twice as much as we'd targeted as our goal, was still about half the national average.

M   We can do more, of course. We can sign up with our utility company for power from regional wind farms. We can purchase locally grown foods instead of winter raspberries from Chile and bottled water from Fiji. We can join a carbon-reduction club, or set up one of our own.

The Future

N   What we really wanted to know was whether it would make any difference. Our low-carbon diet had shown us that, with little or no hardship and no major cash outlays,[8] we could cut day-to-day emissions of CO_2 in half—mainly by using less energy at home and on the highway. Similar efforts in office buildings, shopping malls, and factories throughout the nation, combined with **incentives** and efficiency standards, could halt further increases in U.S. emissions.

O   Yet efficiency, in the end, can only take us so far. To get the deeper reductions we need, as Tim Flannery advised, we must replace fossil fuels faster with energy from wind farms, solar plants, geothermal facilities, and biofuels. We must slow deforestation, which contributes to the buildup of greenhouse gases, and we must develop technologies to capture and bury carbon dioxide from existing power plants. Efficiency can buy us time—perhaps as much as two decades—to figure out how to remove carbon from the world's diet.

P   Not that there won't still be **obstacles**. Every sector of our economy faces challenges, says energy-efficiency guru[9] Amory Lovins of the Rocky Mountain Institute. "But they all have huge potential. I don't know anyone who has failed to make money at energy efficiency. There's so much low-hanging fruit, it's falling off the trees and mushing up[10] around our ankles."

Q   The rest of the world isn't waiting for the United States to show the way. Sweden has pioneered carbon-neutral houses, Germany affordable solar power, Japan fuel-efficient cars, China wind-power installations, the Netherlands prosperous cities filled with bicycles. Does the United States have the will to match such efforts?

R   Change starts at home with the replacement of a light bulb, the opening of a window, a walk to the bus, or a bike ride to the post office. My wife and I did it for only a month, but I can see the low-carbon diet becoming a habit. As my wife said, "What do we have to lose?"

---

8   A **cash outlay** is the amount of money that has to be spent, often at the beginning of a project, for the project or business to get started.

9   A **guru** is a religious teacher or leader, or an expert in a particular field.

10   If a fruit is **mushing up**, it is becoming a soft mass, a process caused by rotting.

A TRAVELER'S FOOTPRINT

When it comes to choosing the best mode of transportation for a trip, we typically weigh speed, cost, and comfort. What if fuel efficiency was factored in too? Below are the results of a case study for the journey from Toronto to New York City.

JOURNEY LENGTH

Fuel efficiency and carbon emissions are impacted by journey length. Flying is the quickest way to get from Toronto to New York, but the relatively short distance means that a traveler could also choose to go by car, bus, or train.

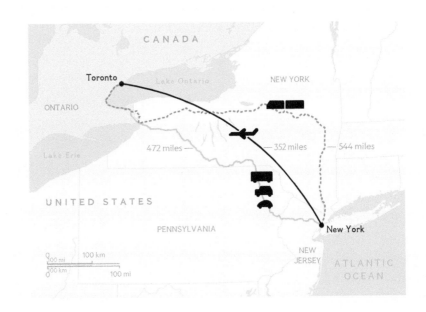

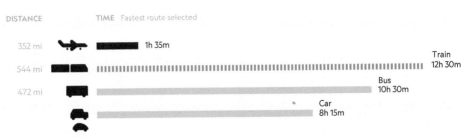

DISTANCE   TIME   Fastest route selected

352 mi — 1h 35m

544 mi — Train 12h 30m

472 mi — Bus 10h 30m

Car 8h 15m

ENERGY EFFICIENCY

Aside from electric cars, the bus is the most energy-efficient way to travel between Toronto and New York. The energy efficiency of the train for this journey is relatively low due to the longer distance and type of fuel used.

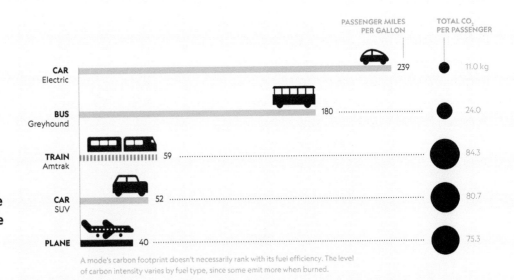

PASSENGER MILES PER GALLON   TOTAL CO$_2$ PER PASSENGER

CAR Electric — 239   11.0 kg

BUS Greyhound — 180   24.0

TRAIN Amtrak — 59   84.3

CAR SUV — 52   80.7

PLANE — 40   75.3

A mode's carbon footprint doesn't necessarily rank with its fuel efficiency. The level of carbon intensity varies by fuel type, since some emit more when burned.

A. Choose the best answer for each question.

GIST

1. The best alternative title for this reading would be _____.

    a. Replacing Fossil Fuels

    b. One Family's Energy Diet

    c. Our Current Carbon Footprint

    d. How People Are Changing the Climate

REFERENCE

2. The word *it* in paragraph A refers to _____.

    a. a new diet   c. climate change

    b. an effort   d. the world

DETAIL

3. About how much CO_2 does the average family in Europe produce a day?

    a. 40 kilos   c. 160 kilos

    b. 80 kilos   d. 300 kilos

INFERENCE

4. The author is initially _____ reducing his family's CO_2 production by 80 percent.

    a. fairly agreeable to   c. not very interested in

    b. enthusiastic about   d. not confident about

DETAIL

5. In paragraph I, what does the author say about the standby mode on electronic devices?

    a. Using it is an efficient way to save energy and money.

    b. It uses as much energy as leaving the device turned on.

    c. It uses 25 percent less energy than turning a device off and then on again.

    d. Using it can account for up to 25 percent of a household's electricity.

PARAPHRASE

6. Which of the following is closest in meaning to this sentence (paragraph L)?
In terms of CO_2, we trimmed our emissions to an average of 32 kilograms a day, which, though twice as much as we'd targeted as our goal, was still half the national average.

    a. The author and his wife were not able to cut their CO_2 output to the national average, but they still met their goal.

    b. The author's family reduced their CO_2 emissions to half the national average, but only reached half their targeted goal.

    c. The author's family reduced their CO_2 output to 70.5 percent of the national average, but not as much as they had targeted.

    d. The author's family planned to reduce their CO_2 emissions to half the national average, but they were able to reduce emissions by twice that much.

INTERPRETING INFOGRAPHICS

7. According to the information in the infographic A Traveler's Footprint, which of the following is NOT true about the journey from Toronto to New York?

    a. The longest journey is by train.

    b. The passenger miles per gallon is higher for a train than an SUV.

    c. Driving an electric car is the most fuel efficient mode of transport.

    d. The total CO_2 per passenger is highest on a plane.

B. Complete the summary using numbers from the reading passage.

Peter Miller and his wife started an experiment to see how much they could reduce their personal CO_2 emissions over the course of [1]_____ month. The average U.S. household produces about [2]_____ kg of CO_2 per day. Miller and his wife decided to aim to reduce their CO_2 to just [3]_____ kg per day.

After calculating their current carbon footprint, the Millers discovered that they were producing [4]_____ percent more CO_2 than the average [5]_____ -person family. The main reason was the energy they were using to heat and cool their homes. They asked professional "house doctor," Ed Minch to do an energy audit of their home. Minch suggested many ways in which the Millers could save energy. The Millers also started walking and cycling more often.

At the end of the month, the Millers had reduced their carbon emissions to an average of [6]_____ kg per day. Though they hadn't quite reached their target, the amount was still [7]_____ percent of the national average.

CRITICAL THINKING Evaluating Solutions   Which of these ideas for reducing the carbon footprint of your school or college would be easy to implement? Which ideas would be more challenging? Which would have the greatest impact? Discuss your ideas with a partner.

- Require recycling of all paper, plastic, glass, and electronics.
- Provide incentives to students who walk or cycle to school.
- Reduce the amount of heating and cooling used.
- Allow only the purchase of "green" products.
- Stop using fossil fuels.
- Require that all food and drink be locally sourced.

Students at a school in Albuquerque, United States, learn about recycling.

Distinguishing Main Ideas and Supporting Information

Most articles have a single, unifying idea (also called the thesis). In addition, each section of an article will normally have its own main idea, and so may individual paragraphs. The author develops these main ideas by supplying details, reasons, and explanations that strengthen the most important points. To clearly understand an article, it's important to identify main ideas and to distinguish between them and supporting information.

MAIN IDEA **A.** Complete the main idea of the whole reading in your own words.

The author performed an experiment to see _____

_____.

MAIN AND SUPPORTING IDEAS **B.** Read the sentences below (**a–h**). Complete the chart with four sentences that summarize the main ideas of the sections and four sentences that provide supporting information.

	Main idea	**Supporting information**
Section 1: The Experiment		
Section 2: The Diagnosis		
Section 3: The Results		
Section 4: The Future		

a. According to the EPA website, the author's annual household CO_2 emissions totaled 24,618 kilos.

b. Increasing household energy efficiency is a first step, but other measures are needed to tackle global warming.

c. With some outside advice, the author learned his home was losing a lot of energy through heat leakage and household appliances.

d. Although there was more he could do, the author was pleased that he was able to significantly lower his carbon footprint.

e. To help reduce his carbon emissions, the author walked and cycled whenever possible.

f. The author investigated his household carbon footprint and found it was surprisingly high.

g. The author learned that compact fluorescents can save home owners about $200 a year.

h. Countries such as Germany and Japan have developed some innovative ways to reduce carbon emissions.

COMPLETION **A.** Complete the information using the correct form of the words in the box. One word is extra.

audit	commonplace	incentive
mode	obstacle	threshold

On Marathon Monday half a million people line the streets of Boston to watch the oldest annual marathon in the world. For thousands of amateur runners, the main objective is to keep below their pain [1]_____ and just try to finish the race. For other runners, raising money for charity is the main [2]_____.

∧ **Each year, discarded drinking cups litter Boston's roads following the city's annual marathon.**

As with other large outdoor events, trash is a problem—discarded cups, bottles, and wrappers are [3]_____ along the course. In recent years, race organizers have taken steps toward making the Boston Marathon more sustainable. Teams of volunteers now collect, sort, and recycle all the trash. Organizers also use energy-efficient electric scooters to support the race. But is it enough?

An "eco-friendliness" [4]_____ indicated that the Boston Marathon still has [5]_____ to overcome, such as its reliance on plastic bottles and water cups, before it can claim to be a truly sustainable race.

COMPLETION **B.** Complete the sentences by circling the correct words.

1. Reducing energy use can save customers money on their **utility** / **compact** bills.
2. Household **obstacles** / **appliances** can use a lot of electricity.
3. Putting your laptop on standby **audit** / **mode** can be a waste of energy.
4. Compared to SUVs, **mode** / **compact** cars are a more energy-efficient way to **commute** / **audit** to work.

COLLOCATIONS **C.** The words in the box are frequently used with the noun **obstacle**. Complete the sentences using the correct words. One word is extra.

hit	overcome	major	present

1. Current economic conditions _____ a huge obstacle to hitting our financial targets.
2. A(n) _____ obstacle to achieving one's goal is lack of money.
3. To be successful, a professional athlete must learn to _____ obstacles.

BEFORE YOU READ

UNDERSTANDING INFOGRAPHICS

A. Look at the infographic on page 110. Note answers to the questions below.

1. How much of Germany's electricity comes from renewable sources? Around how much comes from solar power?

_____

2. How does this compare with the United States and China?

_____

PREDICTING

B. What factors do you think influence the amount of solar power a country produces? Discuss with a partner and note some ideas below. Check your ideas as you read the passage.

_____

_____

⌄ **A truck drives through the huge array of mirrors at the Nevada Solar One power plant in the United States.**

PLUGGING
INTO THE SUN

A   *Early on a clear November morning in the Mojave Desert, a full moon is sinking over the gigawatt[1] glare of Las Vegas. Nevada Solar One is sleeping. But the day's work is about to begin.*

B   It is hard to imagine that a power plant could be so beautiful: 400 hectares of gently curved mirrors lined up like canals of light. Parked facing the ground overnight, they are starting to awaken—more than 182,000 of them—and follow the sun.

C   "Looks like this will be a 700-degree day," says one of the operators in the control room. His job is to monitor the rows of mirrors as they concentrate sunlight on long steel pipes filled with **circulating** oil, heating it as high as 400 degrees Celsius. The heat produces steam, driving a turbine and dynamo, pushing as much as 64 megawatts onto the grid—enough to electrify 14,000 households, or a few Las Vegas casinos.

D   When Nevada Solar One came online in 2007, it was the first large solar plant to be built in the United States in more than 17 years. During that time, solar technology blossomed[2] elsewhere. The owner of Nevada Solar One, Acciona, is a Spanish company, and the mirrors were made in Germany. Putting on hard hats and dark glasses, plant manager Robert Cable and I drive out to take a closer look at the mirrors. Men with a water truck are hosing some down. "Any kind of dust affects them," Cable says. On a clear summer day with the sun directly overhead, Nevada Solar One can convert about 20 percent of the sun's rays into electricity. Gas plants are more efficient, but this fuel is free.

E   "If we talk about geothermal or wind, all these other sources of **renewable** energy are limited in their quantity," says Eicke Weber, director of the Fraunhofer Institute for Solar Energy Systems, in Freiburg, Germany. "The total power needs of the humans on Earth is approximately 16 terawatts," he adds. (A terawatt is a trillion—1,000,000,000,000—watts.) In a few years, that number is expected to grow to 20 terawatts. "The sunshine on the solid part of the Earth is 120,000 terawatts," says Weber. "From this perspective, energy from the sun is virtually unlimited."

Tapping the Sun

F   Solar energy may be unlimited, but its potential is barely tapped. Today, solar power accounts for a tiny fraction of U.S. electricity production—just over 2 percent. "But," said Robert Hawsey, an associate director of the National Renewable Energy Laboratory (NREL) in Golden, Colorado, "that's expected to grow. Ten to 20 percent of the nation's peak electricity demand could be provided by solar energy by 2030."

---

1 One **gigawatt** is a billion (10^9) watts.
2 If something has **blossomed**, it has grown and developed well.

In Bavaria, Germany, many houses are equipped with their own solar panels.

G Achieving that level will require government help. Nevada Solar One was built because the state had set a **deadline** requiring utilities to generate 20 percent of their power from renewable sources by 2015. During peak demand, the solar plant's electricity is almost as cheap as that of its gas-fired neighbor—but that's only because a 30 percent federal tax credit helped **offset** its construction costs.

H The aim now is to bring down costs and reduce the need for **subsidies** and incentives. To achieve this, NREL's engineers are studying mirrors made from lightweight polymers instead of glass, and tubes that will absorb more sunlight and lose less heat. They're also working on solar power's biggest problem: how to store some of the heat produced during daylight hours for release later on.

I Nevada Solar One use solar thermal energy (STE) technology, which collects the sun's rays via mirrors to produce thermal energy (heat). Another method is to convert sunlight directly into electricity with photovoltaic (PV) **panels** made of semiconductors such as silicon. Back in the 1980s, an engineer named Roland Hulstrom calculated that if PV panels covered just three-tenths of a percent of the United States, they could electrify the entire country.

J Years later, PV panels contribute a small—but growing—amount to the nation's electricity supply. On rooftops in California, Nevada, and other states with good sunshine and tax incentives, they are increasingly common—almost as familiar as air conditioners.

K For years, PV power was not as developed as solar thermal, but today it is the dominant solar power technology. Massive investment, government incentives, and technological breakthroughs have caused prices for PV panels to fall dramatically. In 2009, the U.S. company First Solar became the first to manufacture thin-film solar cells at a cost of under a dollar a watt—close to what's needed to compete with fossil fuels.

Germany's Solar Solution

L   On a cold December morning west of Frankfurt, Germany, fog hangs frozen in the trees, and clouds block the sun. In the town of Morbach, the blades of a 100-meter-high wind turbine appear and disappear in the gloom,[3] while down below, a field of photovoltaic panels struggle for light. Considering its unpredictable weather, who would have thought that Germany would transform itself into one of the top producers of photovoltaic power in the world?

M   A fraction of Germany's five-gigawatt photovoltaic power comes from centralized plants like the one at Morbach. With land at a **premium** in Germany, solar panels can be found mounted on rooftops, farmhouses, even on soccer stadiums and along the autobahn.[4] The panels, dispersed across the German countryside, are all connected to the national grid.

N   The solar boom has completely transformed towns like "sunny Freiburg," as the tourist brochures call it. The town sits at the edge of the Black Forest in the southern part of the country. Towering walls of photovoltaics greet visitors as they arrive at Freiburg's train station. Across the street from a school covered with photovoltaic panels is Solarsiedlung ("solar settlement"), one of the town's condominium complexes.[5]

O   "We are being paid for living in this house," said Wolfgang Schnürer, one of Solarsiedlung's residents. The day before, when snow covered the roof, Schnürer's system produced only 5.8 kilowatt-hours, not enough power for a German household. But on a sunny day in May, it **yielded** more than seven times that much.

P   In Germany, regulations require utility companies to pay even the smallest PV producers a premium of about 50 euro-cents a kilowatt-hour. In 2008, Schnürer's personal power plant yielded over 6,000 kilowatt-hours, more than double the amount the family consumed. When they **subtracted** their usage from the amount they produced, the family found they were more than 2,500 euros (nearly $3,000) in profit.

Q   Anybody who installs a PV system is guaranteed above-market rates for 20 years—the equivalent of an 8 percent annual return on the initial investment. "It is an **ingenious** mechanism," Eicke Weber said. "I always say the United States addresses the idealists, those who want to save the planet. In Germany, the law addresses anyone who wants to get 8 percent return on his investment for 20 years."

R   In total, Germany now generates over 6.5 percent of its electricity annually from solar energy, whereas the United States generates less than half this amount. The largest photovoltaic installation in the United States—the Solar Star in California—is only the 11th largest in the world. Nearly all the bigger ones are located in either China or India. But in the United States, too, there is a gathering sense that the time for solar energy has arrived—if there is a commitment to jump-start[6] the technology. "Originally it seemed like a pie-in-the-sky idea," said Michelle Price, the energy manager at the Nellis Air Force base outside Las Vegas. "It didn't seem possible." Many things seem possible now.

---

3 Something that is in the **gloom** is in partial or total darkness.

4 **Autobahn** is a word used to describe expressways in Austria, Germany, and Switzerland on which vehicles travel very fast.

5 **Condominium complexes** are apartment compounds, or living areas.

6 To **jump-start** something means to give it added energy so that it will develop faster.

GERMANY: LEADING THE WAY

In 2014, around 27% of Germany's electricity came from renewable sources, making the country a world leader among industrialized nations. Germany also has bold plans for the future. It aims to make renewable energy account for 80% of its electricity by 2050.

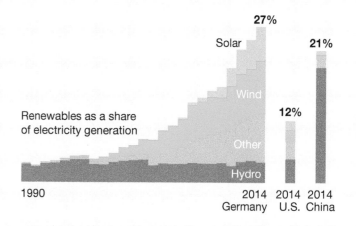

Renewables as a share of electricity generation

27%
Solar
Wind
Other
Hydro

12%

21%

1990

2014 Germany

2014 U.S.

2014 China

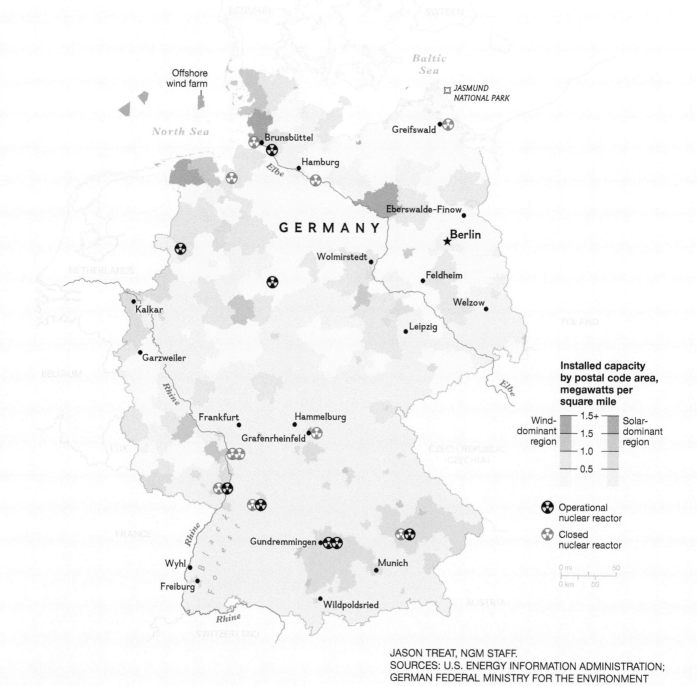

Offshore wind farm

North Sea

Baltic Sea

JASMUND NATIONAL PARK

Brunsbüttel

Greifswald

Hamburg

Elbe

Eberswalde-Finow

GERMANY

Berlin

Wolmirstedt

Feldheim

Welzow

Kalkar

Leipzig

Garzweiler

Rhine

Frankfurt

Hammelburg

Grafenrheinfeld

Gundremmingen

Wyhl

Freiburg

Munich

Wildpoldsried

Rhine

Black Forest

Installed capacity by postal code area, megawatts per square mile

Wind-dominant region

1.5+
1.5
1.0
0.5

Solar-dominant region

Operational nuclear reactor

Closed nuclear reactor

0 mi — 50
0 km — 50

JASON TREAT, NGM STAFF.
SOURCES: U.S. ENERGY INFORMATION ADMINISTRATION; GERMAN FEDERAL MINISTRY FOR THE ENVIRONMENT

A. Choose the best answer for each question.

DETAIL

1. Which of the following is NOT true about Nevada Solar One?

a. The author thinks it is a beautiful place.
b. It contains more than 150,000 mirrors.
c. It was the first solar plant to be built in the United States.
d. It is owned by a Spanish company.

DETAIL

2. What is the job of the men with the water truck in paragraph D?

a. to cool the solar plant
b. to pump water that will then be heated
c. to provide the workers with drinking water
d. to clean the surface of some of the mirrors

INFERENCE

3. In paragraph F, the phrase *barely tapped* indicates that _____.

a. the use of solar energy has been growing rapidly
b. someday, much more solar energy can be utilized
c. the supply of solar power will never meet the demand
d. no one knows how much solar energy can be generated

DETAIL

4. Which of these is NOT mentioned in paragraph H as a way to cut prices for solar energy production?

a. making mirrors from different materials
b. finding a way to store heat for use at night
c. using mirrors with a larger surface area
d. designing tubes that take in more sunlight and hold heat better

INFERENCE

5. In paragraph N, what does the author imply about the town of Freiburg, Germany?

a. It is sunny there throughout the year.
b. It does not really get that much sunshine.
c. Its solar industry helps to attract tourists.
d. It was the first town with a large-scale solar plant.

COHESION

6. The following sentence would be best placed at the end of which paragraph?
And it doesn't emit planet-warming carbon dioxide.

a. paragraph D
b. paragraph G
c. paragraph J
d. paragraph P

UNDERSTANDING INFOGRAPHICS

7. Which of the following is NOT true according to the infographic on page 110?

a. Hamburg is one of few places in the north of Germany that is solar-dominant.
b. Some of Germany's wind farms are located in the North Sea.
c. Frankfurt produces more solar energy per square mile than Munich.
d. Most nuclear power plants are located in the south of the country.

B. Scan the reading passage for quotes from the people listed below (1–5). Match each person to a paraphrase of their quote. One is extra.

1. _____ Robert Cable
2. _____ Eicke Weber
3. _____ Robert Hawsey
4. _____ Wolfgang Schnürer
5. _____ Michelle Price

a. In about a decade, as much as 20 percent of the electricity the United States produces could be from solar energy.
b. Layers of dust can affect solar mirrors.
c. People in the United States are now more optimistic about the future of solar energy.
d. The income from our personal power plant is greater than our energy costs.
e. Germany and the United States are going to remain top players in the PV market for years to come.
f. Compared with other renewable energies, solar energy is unlimited.

CRITICAL THINKING Analyzing Arguments   In paragraph Q, Eike Weber highlights two distinct types of people who might want to install a PV system in their home: those who want to save the planet (the "idealists"), and those who are financially motivated. Note answers to the questions in the chart, then discuss your ideas with a partner.

	IDEALIST	FINANCIALLY-MOTIVATED
What types of people might this group be composed of?		
What would be some incentives to get these people to install a PV system?		

∨ **A row of houses equipped with solar panels in Kanagawa, Japan**

Determining Similarities and Differences

Some texts compare two or more things in detail. To understand comparisons, you need to identify which ideas relate to each category. One way to organize this information visually is to categorize it using a Venn diagram. When information belongs to neither category, put the information outside the diagram.

CLASSIFICATION   **A.** Look back at the reading passage. Complete the Venn diagram. Match the information (a–i) to the country or countries it describes. If it doesn't describe either, write it outside the diagram.

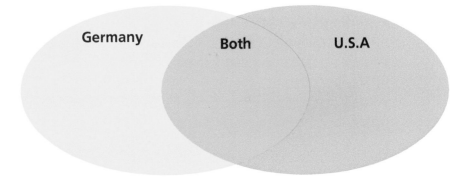

a. Despite unfavorable weather, it is a top PV power generator.

b. The mirrors for Nevada Solar One were made here.

c. Solar power produces less than 3 percent of the country's electricity.

d. The company that owns Nevada Solar One is from here.

e. A manufacturer developed very cheap, thin solar cells.

f. According to one expert, the government policies regarding solar energy appeal to people who want to make money on their investment.

g. Even the smallest solar providers are connected to the national electrical grid.

h. According to one expert, government policies regarding solar energy appeal to idealists.

i. The government gives incentives to encourage the use of solar power.

MAKING
COMPARISONS   **B.** How does the solar energy industry in Germany compare with the industry in the United States? Which do you think will be energy leaders in the future? Why?

DISCUSSION   **C.** How does your country's solar power production compare to Germany and the United States? Are there incentives for people to try solar power or other renewable sources of energy? Discuss with a partner.

COMPLETION **A. Complete the information. Circle the correct options.**

One of ¹**renewable** / **panel** energy's most problematic issues is the variable nature of wind and solar power. But a company in the small German town of Cuxhaven on the windy North Sea coast has found an ²**ingenious** / **offset** way to store wind power—in frozen fish.

The company, Erwin Gooss, operates a warehouse that stores fish caught in the North Sea. The fish need to be kept very cold. Ordinarily, air that ³**deadlines** / **circulates** inside the warehouse keeps temperatures at about –20°C. During peak wind hours, the temperature can be pushed to –30°C. The frozen fish absorb and "store" this extra energy. When winds die down, the cooling is switched off, but the warehouse remains cold.

⌃ **Globally, wind supplies seven percent of electric power.**

What's the incentive for Erwin Gooss? Storing energy in their fish helps the company ⁴**offset** / **yield** the high costs of operating in the summer when electricity is at a ⁵**subsidy** / **premium**. "It's not that we're using less power, it's just that we're using it when it's cheaper," says Gunter Krins, technical director.

DEFINITIONS **B. Match each word with its definition. One word is extra.**

deadline	panel	premium	subsidy	subtract	yield

1. _____: the date by which a project must be complete
2. _____: money paid to a person or group to support them
3. _____: to produce or provide
4. _____: a flat, rectangular device or piece of material
5. _____: to take away from a number or amount

WORD LINK **C. Some words, such as renewable, include both a prefix and a suffix (for example, re- and -able). For each bold word, create a new word by adding a prefix and a suffix from the list.**

Prefixes: *un-, dis-, re-, in-, sub-*   Suffixes: *-ly, -tion, -able, -ity, -ful*

believe: _____   **describe:** _____   **organize:** _____

respect: _____   **conscious:** _____   **equal:** _____

Sustainable eco-homes in Torup, Denmark, are partially buried to reduce heat loss.

ECO-DETECTIVES

BEFORE YOU WATCH

PREVIEWING **A.** Read the excerpts from the video. Match each word in **bold** with its definition.

> "This house is a typical three-bedroom home … But lurking beneath this innocent **façade** is an energy-eating monster."

> "He **employs** a mix of high-tech technology and good old **common sense**."

> "The house gets all the electricity it needs from the solar panels on the roof. And there's energy **to spare**."

1. employ • • a. left over
2. façade • • b. to use
3. common sense • • c. an ability to use good judgement
4. to spare • • d. the outer covering of a building

DISCUSSION **B.** In the video, "eco-detectives" discuss ways in which people can save money on home energy. What are some ways that a home can become more energy efficient? Discuss with a partner.

GIST **A.** Watch the video. Check (✓) the statements that the eco-detectives would probably agree with.

1. ☐ There are many simple things that people can do at home to save money.

2. ☐ Most people are not interested in finding ways to save money around the house.

3. ☐ We won't solve energy problems until we give up some of our conveniences.

4. ☐ The main way to save money on energy is to use energy more efficiently.

DETAILS **B.** Watch the video again. Note answers to the questions.

1. What accounts for more than half of all energy consumption in the United States?

_____

2. How does Amory Lovins know the freezer is wasting energy?

_____

3. What is a vampire load?

_____

4. What is special about Amory Lovins' house?

_____

CRITICAL THINKING Applying Ideas   How could you make your home more efficient? Note your ideas below, then discuss with a partner.

_____

_____

VOCABULARY REVIEW

Do you remember the meanings of these words? Check (✓) the ones you know. Look back at the unit and review any words you're not sure of.

Reading A

☐ appliance   ☐ audit   ☐ commonplace   ☐ commute   ☐ compact

☐ incentive*   ☐ mode*   ☐ obstacle   ☐ threshold   ☐ utility*

Reading B

☐ circulate   ☐ deadline   ☐ ingenious   ☐ offset*   ☐ panel*

☐ premium   ☐ renewable   ☐ subsidy*   ☐ subtract   ☐ yield

*Academic Word List

SURVIVAL AND PROTECTION

6

A critically endangered Sumatran rhino and her calf at Cincinnati Zoo, USA

WARM UP

Discuss these questions with a partner.

1. What animals are endangered? Why are they endangered?

2. Should some animals be protected over others? Why or why not?

117

BEFORE YOU READ

DISCUSSION

A. Look at the photo and read the caption. What do you know about bluefin tuna? Why might its future be uncertain? Discuss your ideas with a partner.

SKIMMING AND PREDICTING

B. Skim the first paragraph and each of the four sections. In your own words, write what you might learn about in each section. Then read the article to check your ideas.

The King of Fish _____

Tagging a Giant _____

Bluefin Migration _____

Uncertain Future _____

> The bluefin tuna is one of the largest and fastest fish in the sea, but it faces an uncertain future.

QUICKSILVER

Prized for sushi, the fast and powerful Atlantic bluefin tuna is being relentlessly overfished. Kenneth Brower goes in search of the story behind the king of all fish.

A One moment the undersea scenery is an empty blue cathedral, the sun an undulating[1] hot spot in the waves overhead. Its beams shine down as if from stained glass.[2] The next moment the ocean is full of giant bluefin tuna, the largest measuring over four meters and weighing three-quarters of a ton. In the sea's refracted[3] sunlight, their pale sides flash and sparkle like polished **shields**, and their long, curved fins cut the water like swords. Quick-moving tail fins drive them forward at 10 knots,[4] with bursts of speed to 25. And just as suddenly, they are gone—the ocean empty again. Here and there, a small galaxy of scales marks where a bluefin swallowed a herring. The victim's scales swirl in the **turbulence** of the departed tuna, now heading off at high speed.

The King of Fish

B Tunas are streamlined[5] to perfection and equipped with cutting-edge biological gear. The characteristics that distinguish them include great size, great range, efficient swimming, warm bodies, large gills, excellent regulation of heat, rapid oxygen uptake, and a cleverly adapted heart. All of these reach their peak in the bluefin—"the king of all fish," as Ernest Hemingway described them after seeing Atlantic bluefin off the coast of Spain.

C The three species of bluefin—the Atlantic, Pacific, and southern—are found in all the oceans except around the North and South Poles. The bluefin is a modern fish, yet its relationship with humanity is ancient. Japanese fishermen and the Haida people of the Pacific Northwest have caught Pacific bluefin for more than 5,000 years. Stone Age artists painted Atlantic bluefin tuna on the walls of Sicilian caves. Iron Age[6] fishermen watched for the arrival of bluefin schools at their Mediterranean spawning[7] grounds, and ancient coins from that region have images of giant bluefin on them.

---

1 Something that **undulates** moves up and down or back and forth in a smooth, gentle motion.
2 **Stained glass** is colored glass used to create designs and pictures in windows.
3 When a beam of light is **refracted**, it changes direction (e.g., when it enters the water).
4 A **knot** is a unit of speed measurement for boats equivalent to 1.85 kilometers per hour.
5 A **streamlined** animal has a shape that allows it to move smoothly through air or water.
6 The **Iron Age** in Europe took place from around BC 1200 to BC 1.
7 When fish **spawn**, they lay their eggs.

THE SUPER FISH

BREATHING

A bluefin swims with its mouth open, forcing water past the gills in a process called ram ventilation. Its gills have up to 30 times more surface area than those of other fish, and they extract nearly half the oxygen dissolved in the water. If the tuna ever stops swimming, it dies.

BODY HEAT

Tunas are unique among bony fish in their ability to keep key parts of their body warm. Rather than lose heat to cold water in the gills like most fish, tunas have heat-exchange systems that retain heat produced in the tissue. These systems are present in three areas (orange outline, below).

Tuna key

— Arteries carry oxygenated blood away from the heart

— Veins carry deoxygenated blood toward the heart

⋯ Heat-exchange system

↰ Retractable fins fit into grooves on the body

Two stiff fins (here and below) stabilize the fish.

White muscle
21°C (70°F)

Red muscle
31°C (88°F)

Internal organs

Cranial cavity

Heart

Blood picks up oxygen in the gills

DIVING DEEP

Tunas spend much of their lives in the sun-warmed water near the surface. Juveniles and smaller species always hover and feed there, but large adult bluefin dive to deep, cold waters, where their heat-exchange systems keep the brain and eyes alert for prey—and predators.

HEAT-EXCHANGE SYSTEM

Tunas rely on a network of tightly packed, parallel blood vessels that allow the transfer of heat between warm and cool blood moving in opposite directions. As a result, heat is retained in the tissues of the body that produced it rather than being lost through the gills.

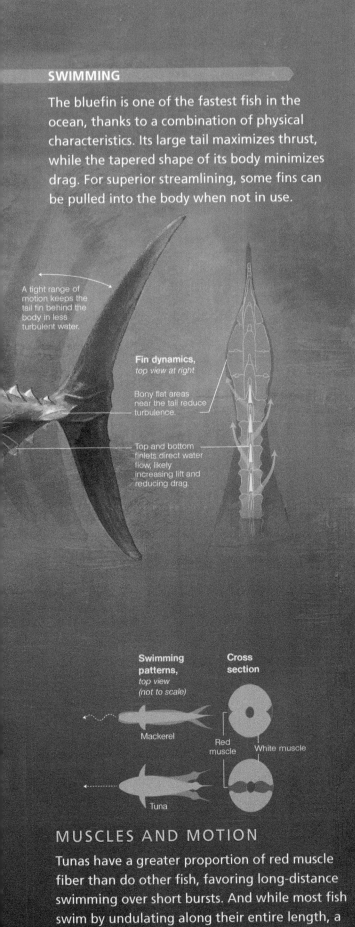

SWIMMING

The bluefin is one of the fastest fish in the ocean, thanks to a combination of physical characteristics. Its large tail maximizes thrust, while the tapered shape of its body minimizes drag. For superior streamlining, some fins can be pulled into the body when not in use.

A tight range of motion keeps the tail fin behind the body in less turbulent water.

Fin dynamics,
top view at right

Bony flat areas near the tail reduce turbulence.

Top and bottom finlets direct water flow, likely increasing lift and reducing drag.

Swimming patterns,
*top view
(not to scale)*

Cross section

Mackerel

Red muscle · White muscle

Tuna

MUSCLES AND MOTION

Tunas have a greater proportion of red muscle fiber than do other fish, favoring long-distance swimming over short bursts. And while most fish swim by undulating along their entire length, a tuna's body remains relatively rigid while only its tail whips back and forth, reducing drag.

D But this relationship with humans has lately been **detrimental** to the bluefin. They are today among the most overfished species, largely because people are prepared to pay a high price for them. One medium-sized bluefin in Japan brings in between $10,000 and $20,000, depending on quality. In 2019 a 288-kilogram bluefin sold for over $3 million at the Tokyo fish market. It is a **startling** measure of what the bluefin tuna is up against if more than a handful are to see the 22nd century.

Tagging a Giant

E The day dawned over Cape Breton, Nova Scotia, as Captain Dennis Cameron and his crew left port in his fishing boat. Along the back wall of the boat's cabin, fishing rods were racked and ready. In the open ocean ahead, fishermen catch the biggest bluefin tuna in the world.

F Cameron knows the history of the local fishing industry well. "We didn't fish tuna," he says of his father's generation. "Tuna fishing was more of a sport. Years ago they used to call it 'horse mackerel.' It was cat food back then, or fertilizer."

G To the right, we passed the big island of Cape Breton; to the left, a small island with a scattering of white houses, including the one in which Cameron grew up. The waterfront—crowded with fishing boats in the 1920s—is now **deserted**. So it goes in fishing communities worldwide. The ocean is dying, and overfishing is the primary cause.

H That day, however, we were on a different kind of fishing trip: We had come to tag and measure bluefin, not to kill them. While Cameron steered toward deep water, Steve Wilson, a Stanford University researcher who works with the Tuna Research and Conservation Center (TRCC), checked the satellite tags he hoped to attach to bluefin that day.

Nine kilometers offshore, drifting with three fishing lines in the water, we had a strike. Sheldon Gillis—Captain Cameron's assistant—fought the fish. It took twenty minutes until the fish made its first appearance, with Gillis reeling in furiously each time the tuna gave him the chance. After another 20 minutes came the loud, slapping bang of tail fin against the boat. The tuna was **hauled** aboard through a specially designed "tuna door," then laid on its side on a padded mat, perfectly still and enormous. Out of water, it looked like some kind of wonderful machine, biologically inspired and poured of living metal.

J Wilson and his tagging team worked quickly and efficiently. A wet black cloth went over the eyes, and a green hose went in the mouth, pumping seawater past the gills. The fish measured three meters long—a length that corresponds to a weight of around 550 kilograms. In nearly 20 years of work, it was the third biggest bluefin ever tagged by the team.

K Wilson then stuck a harmless dart into the fish to hold a satellite tag, and his assistant cut a thin piece of a fin for DNA analysis. Then the two men at the tail lifted their end of the mat, and the tuna plunged back into the water. Two flicks of its tail fin and it was gone. On his laptop the night before, Wilson had programmed the satellite tag to release in nine months, after which the tag will rise to the ocean's surface and send information about the tuna's movements to TRCC's home base in California.

Bluefin Migration

L Stanford University professor Barbara Block, a preeminent[8] **scholar** of the bluefin, runs TRCC out of Hopkins Marine Station in **collaboration** with the Monterey Bay Aquarium next door. The walls and cabinets of Block's lab are covered with charts, maps, and illustrations from scientific journals. One poster shows a graph of the spawning population of Gulf of Mexico bluefin above a similar graph for Mediterranean bluefin. Both populations are represented by lines that are diving toward the bottom of their graphs. They have plunged past the dotted line representing sustainable yield and are headed for zero.

M The locations of bluefin, as reported by the many satellite tags over the years, are represented by small circles in different colors. The western bluefin—represented

---

8 Someone who is **preeminent** in a group is the most important, capable, or distinguished person in that group.

Commercial fishermen unload a giant bluefin tuna on Prince Edward Island, Canada.

as reddish-orange circles—pack the Gulf of Mexico, their spawning grounds. From there they spread eastward into the western Atlantic and cross over to the eastern Atlantic, reaching all the way to Portugal and Spain. The eastern bluefin—represented as white circles—fill their Mediterranean spawning grounds, and from there spread westward, crossing over to the western Atlantic, covering the coastal waters of the United States and Canada.

N The fact of this mixing has been firmly established by Block, other taggers, and DNA researchers. The best estimates today are that around half of the bluefin caught off the eastern shores of North America were spawned in the Mediterranean. However, until recently these tuna—if caught in the west—have been mistakenly counted as fish of western origin. The discovery of the **mingling** of the two populations is making more accurate fisheries management possible.

Uncertain Future

O But an **alarming** lesson lies hidden at Hopkins Marine Station. Established by Stanford University in 1892, it was the first marine lab on the West Coast of the United States. Its old buildings, like the abandoned canneries[9] immediately to the east, were built during the age of sardines, which ended 60 years ago due to overfishing. By the 1980s sardine populations had started to come back a little, but now they are falling again.

P In a building near Hopkins are three large, waist-deep tanks, where a number of Pacific bluefin tuna are swimming. Block and her colleagues practice their tagging techniques here on fish like these. To maintain healthy populations, the bluefin tuna will need wise management assisted by good science. Here in Monterey, the consequences of the opposite are clear. Directly below the tanks of bluefin are the ruins of cannery piers that reach out into the bay for sardines that are no longer there.

---

9 A **cannery** is a factory where food is canned.

GLOBAL ANNUAL CATCH OF TUNA

Due to a dwindling population, the global annual catch of bluefin remains low compared to other species of tuna.

Skipjack

2.5 million metric tons

2.0

Yellowfin

1.5

1.0

Bigeye

0.5

Albacore

Pacific bluefin

Atlantic bluefin

0

1950   Southern bluefin   2011

A. Choose the best answer for each question.

FIGURATIVE
LANGUAGE

1. Which sentence from paragraph A does NOT contain figurative language?

a. *One moment the undersea scenery is an empty blue cathedral.*
b. *Its beams shine down as if from stained glass.*
c. *Quick-moving tail fins drive them forward at ten knots.*
d. *... their long, curved fins cut the water like swords.*

PURPOSE

2. What is the purpose of paragraph C?

a. to give reasons for the bluefin's decline
b. to explain why the bluefin is a modern fish
c. to show that ancient Sicilians worshipped the bluefin
d. to explain our long history with the bluefin

VOCABULARY

3. In paragraph D, if you are *up against* something challenging, you are _____ it.

a. denying
b. facing
c. afraid of
d. comforted by

MAIN IDEA

4. What is Captain Dennis Cameron's main point in paragraph F?

a. Tuna is popular because it can be used in many different ways.
b. In recent years, tuna fishing as a sport has increased in popularity.
c. A generation ago, tuna wasn't popular as a food for humans.
d. In the past, there were far fewer fishermen than there are today.

DETAIL

5. Why did Steve Wilson and his team want to tag the bluefin?

a. so they could later identify people who fish bluefin illegally
b. so paying tourists who enjoy fishing could help pay for their research
c. so they could determine the depths to which bluefin can dive
d. so they could track its movements

DETAIL

6. Which of the following is NOT true about western bluefin tuna?

a. Their numbers are decreasing rapidly.
b. They spawn in the Gulf of Mexico.
c. They never mix with eastern bluefin.
d. They migrate across the Atlantic Ocean.

INFERENCE

7. Why does the author discuss sardines in paragraph O?

a. to warn that bluefin could face a similar fate
b. to explain that the cause of their decline remains unknown
c. to show that research done 60 years ago is no longer relevant
d. to give hope of bringing back fish populations after overfishing

B. Look back at the Super Fish infographic. Note answers to the questions below.

1. Why would a bluefin tuna die if it stopped swimming?

_____

_____

2. In which three areas of its body does a bluefin tuna have heat-exchange systems?

_____

_____

3. What are three factors that help a bluefin tuna swim fast?

_____

_____

4. What are two ways in which a mackerel is different to a tuna?

_____

_____

5. What is the purpose of the stiff fins underneath and on top of the bluefin tuna's body?

_____

_____

CRITICAL THINKING Identifying Evidence

▶ The writer claims that the bluefin tuna is in danger. Note down evidence from the reading passage that supports this. Include any sources.

_____

_____

_____

_____

_____

_____

▶ What do you think can be done to reverse the decline in populations of bluefin tuna? Discuss your ideas with a partner. Consider the pros and cons of the following solutions.

- Ban all commercial fishing of bluefin tuna
- Protect key bluefin tuna habitat areas
- Forbid restaurants and stores from selling bluefin tuna
- Only use bluefin tuna from sustainable fish "farms"

An Atlantic bluefin tuna in the waters off the coast of Canada

Understanding Words with Multiple Meanings

Many words in English have more than one meaning. Sometimes one definition is a literal meaning and the other a figurative one. (See Unit 4A for more information about literal versus figurative meanings of words.) In other cases, a word may have different literal meanings. Use the context to help identify the most relevant meaning, as well as the correct part of speech.

IDENTIFYING
MEANING

A. Look back at Reading A and scan for the words below. Use context to check the correct meaning of each word as it is used in the passage. Circle the correct definition.

1. **beams** (paragraph A)
   a. (n) lines of light
   b. (n) heavy pieces of wood

2. **range** (paragraph B)
   a. (n) the area an animal lives in
   b. (n) a group of things that are similar

3. **yet** (paragraph C)
   a. (n) but
   b. (adv) until now

4. **measure** (paragraph D)
   a. (n) a planned action
   b. (n) a basis for comparison

5. **left** (paragraph E)
   a. (v) went away from
   b. (adj) opposite of *right*

6. **back** (paragraph F)
   a. (n) rear; opposite of *front*
   b. (adv) into the past

7. **primary** (paragraph G)
   a. (adj) coming first
   b. (adj) main

8. **perfectly** (paragraph I)
   a. (adv) completely
   b. (adv) without errors

9. **dart** (paragraph K)
   a. (v) to move quickly
   b. (n) a small object with a sharp point

10. **past** (paragraph L)
    a. (n) a time before now
    b. (prep) up to and beyond

IDENTIFYING
MEANING

B. Find the words in **bold** below in paragraphs O and P. Identify the part of speech and write a definition for each word.

1. **age** (   ): _____

2. **tanks** (   ): _____

3. **like** (   ): _____

4. **clear** (   ): _____

VOCABULARY PRACTICE

COMPLETION **A.** Complete the information by circling the correct words.

In 2006, Kiribati, a tiny island nation between Hawaii and Fiji, made a ¹**detrimental** / **startling** announcement: It would create one of the largest marine protected areas in the world. President Anote Tong called for the ²**mingle** / **collaboration** of other nations. "Let us pool our resources to protect this gift, our mother ocean," he said.

Protecting areas of ocean can actually help the fishing industry. ³**Shields** / **Scholars**, like Dr. Enric Sala, look to Spain as an example. Overfishing was ⁴**detrimental** / **turbulence** to Spain's fishing grounds decades ago, when fishermen caught and ⁵**deserted** / **hauled** away huge quantities of fish. Sala explains that once fishing was banned

⌃ **A hawkfish rests on a reef in the Phoenix Islands Protected Area.**

in a marine reserve, the number of fish increased so much that they spread outside of the reserve, reviving the fishing industry and creating jobs.

DEFINITIONS **B.** Complete the sentences. Circle the correct options.

1. A **shield** is a large piece of metal or wood carried for *protection* / *farming*.

2. If an area is **deserted**, *no one lives* / *large groups live* there.

3. When two groups **mingle**, they *mix together* / *stay separate*.

4. **Turbulence** is the *soft and gentle* / *sudden and violent* movement of air or water.

5. If something is **alarming**, it is *fascinating* / *worrying*.

WORD LINK **C.** The word **turbulence** includes the root *turb*, which means "to spin, drive, or throw into disorder." Complete these sentences with the words in the box. One word is extra.

disturb	perturb	turbulent	turbojet

1. The _____ sea made many of us on the ship sick.

2. If you see wildlife, it's best not to _____ it.

3. It did not _____ them that their son chose to quit school and pursue a career in music.

The breeding program at Sydney's Taronga Zoo has seen several successes, including the birth of a male baby gorilla, seen here with his mother Mbeli.

BEFORE YOU READ

DISCUSSION **A. Look at the photo and caption. Discuss the questions with a partner.**

1. What role can zoos play in protecting threatened species?

2. What criteria do you think zoos consider when deciding which animals to keep?

SCANNING **B. Scan the reading passage to find the following animals. Write the names of the zoos that were involved in caring for these animals.**

Sumatran rhinoceros _____

American bison _____

red wolf _____

Kihansi spray toad _____

Amur leopard _____

BUILDING THE ARK

Zoos may have to choose between keeping the animals we most want to see and saving the ones we may never see again.

A When the Cincinnati Zoo opened its gates in 1875, there were perhaps as many as a million Sumatran rhinos foraging[1] in forests from Bhutan to Borneo. Today, there may be fewer than a hundred left in the world. Three of these were born in Cincinnati—a female named Suci and her brothers, Harapan and Andalas. In 2007, the zoo sent Andalas to Sumatra, where he has since sired[2] a calf at Way Kambas National Park. If the species escapes **extinction**, it will in no small part be thanks to the work done at the zoo. And what goes for the Sumatran rhino goes for a growing list of species saved from **oblivion**. As the wild **shrinks**, zoos are increasingly being seen as modern-day arks:[3] the last **refuge** against a rising **tide** of extinction.

Who to Save?

B From the early 19th century, American zoos were involved in animal conservation. At the end of the century, the Cincinnati Zoo tried—unsuccessfully—to breed passenger pigeons, whose numbers were in rapid decline. (The bird thought to be the very last passenger pigeon, named Martha, died at the zoo in 1914; the building where she lived is now a memorial.) And in the early 20th century, when one count showed just 325 wild American bison left in North America, the Bronx Zoo started a **captive**-breeding program that helped save the species. Other animals that owe their existence to captive-breeding efforts are the Arabian oryx, the black-footed ferret, the red wolf, and the California condor.

C Because such programs tend to be expensive—the condor program costs participating institutions up to $2 million a year—they're usually led by large, big-city zoos, but smaller zoos are increasingly joining in. The Miller Park Zoo in Bloomington, Illinois, is one of the smallest zoos in the United States, at just four acres. However, it has bred red wolves and is hoping to breed the endangered Mount

---

1 When animals **forage**, they search for food.

2 The verb **sired** means to become the father of (an animal).

3 In a story from the Bible, the **Ark** was a large boat that a man named Noah built in order to save his family and two of every kind of animal from a huge flood.

Graham red squirrel. "It's a small animal that doesn't require a huge amount of space," said zoo official Jay Tetzloff.

D But zoos also have to financially support themselves, and small animals just don't attract the crowds necessary to keep business in the black.[4] Robert Lacy, a conservation biologist at the Chicago Zoological Society, says that zoos are going to have to make some difficult decisions. "Do you save a small number of large animals—the crowd favorites—or do you focus on saving a whole lot more little, unpopular creatures for the same amount of money?" he asks.

E Right now, the world's most threatened group of animals are probably amphibians. According to the International Union for Conservation of Nature (IUCN)—which maintains what's known as the Red List—about a third of the world's frog, toad, and salamander species are at risk of extinction. Unfortunately for them, amphibians are far less popular than zoo species such as pandas or lions, which are not yet facing **imminent** extinction in the wild. But there are advantages to being small. For one thing, a whole population of amphibians can be kept in less space than that required by a single rhinoceros.

F Others question whether zoos should devote resources to species, large or small, that are doing fine on their own. "I think it's a bit of a cop-out[5] to say the public wants to see x, y, or z," says Onnie Byers, chair of the Conservation Breeding Specialist Group, part of the IUCN Species Survival Commission. "Plenty of species need exactly the expertise that zoos can provide. I would love to see a trend toward zoos phasing out species that don't need that care and using the spaces for species that do."

Small Victories

G "It's an amazing responsibility to have half the remaining members of a species in your care," says Jim Breheny, the director of the Wildlife Conservation Society's Bronx Zoo. He's standing in a **state-of-the-art** breeding facility filled with tanks of Kihansi spray toads—small, yellow amphibians about 2.5 centimeters long.

H Depending on how you look at things, the Kihansi spray toad is either one of the most unfortunate or one of the luckiest species around. Until the late 1990s, the Kihansi spray toad was unknown to science. It was not actually identified until a hydroelectric[6] project was already destroying its tiny habitat—five acres of mist-soaked land in the Kihansi River Gorge in eastern Tanzania. In 2000, recognizing that the project would probably harm the newly discovered species, the Tanzanian government invited the Bronx Zoo to collect some of the toads. Exactly 499 spray toads were captured and kept in the Bronx and Toledo Zoos in the United States. Just nine years later, as a result of disease and habitat destruction, the Kihansi spray toad was declared extinct in the wild.

I In the meantime, the zoos were **struggling** to figure out how to recreate the habitat that gives the spray toad its name. In the Kihansi River Gorge, a series of waterfalls had provided the toads with constant spray, so the tanks in the Bronx Zoo were provided with spray in the same way. Among amphibians, Kihansi toads are unusual in that the young are born live: At birth, they are no bigger than a match head. For the tiny young, the zoo had to find even tinier prey; eventually, they settled on tiny insectlike animals called springtails, which the researchers also had to figure out how to raise. But then keepers noticed that the toads seemed to be suffering from a nutritional deficiency,[7] so a special vitamin **supplement** had to be designed.

J After some initial losses, the toads began to thrive and reproduce. By 2010, there were several thousand of them in New York and

---

4 If a business is **in the black**, it is making money and not losing it.

5 **Cop-out** means taking the easy way out of a difficult situation.

6 **Hydroelectric** is related to electricity made from the energy of running water.

7 If you have a **nutritional deficiency**, you are not getting the vitamins, minerals and other substances your body needs from what you eat and drink.

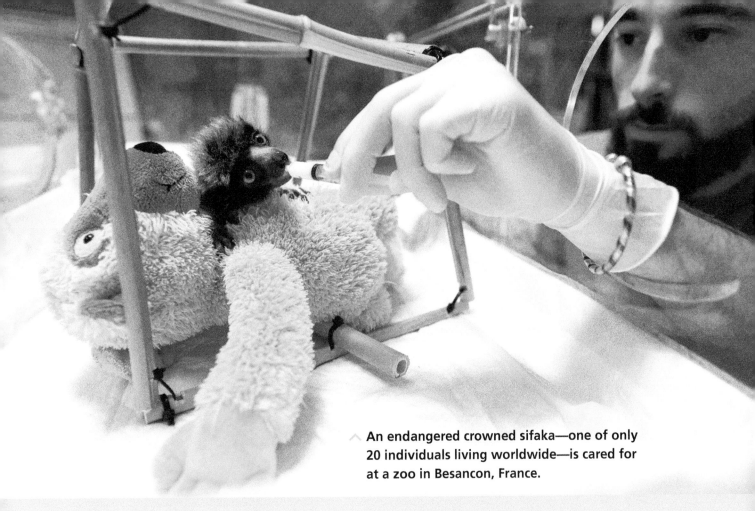

∧ An endangered crowned sifaka—one of only 20 individuals living worldwide—is cared for at a zoo in Besancon, France.

Toledo, so that year a hundred toads were sent back to the Kihansi River Gorge. But there was a problem: By diverting water from the falls, the hydroelectric project had eliminated the mist that the toads depend on. So the Tanzanians set up a system to restore the spray to the gorge. In 2012, the first toads bred in the Bronx Zoo were released back into the wild.

The Frozen Zoo

K But for every success story like the Kihansi toad, there are dozens of other species on the edge of extinction. Many of these—the Sumatran orangutan, the Amur leopard, a songbird from the island of Kauai, and a thousand other species—can be found in a single room at the San Diego Zoo Institute for Conservation Research. Vials containing cells from each of these animals are being kept in a bath of liquid nitrogen[8] where the temperature is minus 200°C. These thousands of identical-looking frozen vials represent what might be described as a beyond-the-last-ditch[9] conservation effort: the Frozen Zoo.

L For now, at least, only one of the animals in the Frozen Zoo is actually extinct: the po'ouli, a fat bird with a sweet black face and a light-colored chest that lived on the Hawaiian island of Maui until 2004. But it seems safe to predict that in the coming years, more and more will become extinct.

M "I think there are going to be more and more species where the only living material left is going to be cells in the Frozen Zoo," says Oliver Ryder, the institute's director of genetics. Native to Central Africa, the northern white rhino is down to its last two females, after the death in 2018 of the last living male. The extinction of the species is, at this point, considered inevitable. After the last two rhinos die, they will, in a way, live on— one last hope, suspended in a frozen cloud.

---

8 **Nitrogen** is a colorless element with no smell; it is usually found as a gas and is a liquid below −196°C.

9 A **last-ditch** effort is a final attempt to achieve something after all else has failed.

The Photo Ark is a 20-year-long documentary project founded by National Geographic photographer and fellow Joel Sartore. It is an extensive online archive of studio-quality photographs of animals around the world, from the largest carnivores to the smallest insects—all to showcase biodiversity. "We stand to lose half of all the planet's species by the turn of the next century," says Sartore. "The Photo Ark seeks to document as many of these as possible, using captive animals as ambassadors."

More than 9,500 species have already been photographed since the project began, and Sartore plans to continue documenting all of the roughly 12,000 species inhabiting zoos, aquariums, and breeding centers around the world. Sadly, several of the animals he photographed have already become extinct.

The goal of the project is to bring amazing images of animals to the public eye in order to inspire people everywhere to care about these species—and to do something to help save them before it's too late. "People won't work to save something if they don't know it exists," Sartore says. "That's where these photos come in."

⌄ **The Photo Ark features a diverse range of animal species**

READING COMPREHENSION

A. Choose the best answer for each question.

MAIN IDEA

1. According to the article, what is the main ethical question that zoos are facing?
   a. Do we return zoo animals back to the wild?
   b. Should we try and bring back extinct animals?
   c. Which of the many threatened animals do we save?
   d. Is it right to put animals like pandas and lions in zoos?

DETAIL

2. According to the passage, which of the following was NOT a conservation success story?
   a. red wolves at Miller Park Zoo
   b. American bison at the Bronx Zoo
   c. passenger pigeons at Cincinnati Zoo
   d. Sumatran rhinos at Way Kambas National Park

VOCABULARY

3. In paragraph F, *phasing out* can be replaced with _____.
   a. slowing increasing
   b. gradually removing
   c. humanely sending back
   d. partially using

CAUSE AND EFFECT

4. Why did the Tanzanian government decide to invite the Bronx Zoo to collect Kihansi spray toads?
   a. They realized a hydroelectric dam was destroying their habitat.
   b. Scientists said the toads could no longer reproduce in the gorge.
   c. Disease had begun to spread through the toad population.
   d. The toads started to suffer from a nutritional deficiency.

COHESION

5. This sentence would best be placed at the end of which paragraph?
   It is estimated that a third of all reef-forming corals, a quarter of all mammals, a fifth of all reptiles, and a sixth of all birds are headed toward oblivion.
   a. paragraph C
   b. paragraph F
   c. paragraph G
   d. paragraph L

DETAIL

6. What is the Frozen Zoo?
   a. a place to see frozen but now extinct animals
   b. another name for the Bronx Zoo
   c. a place to keep frozen cells of threatened animal species
   d. a part of the San Diego Zoo where people see endangered animals

INFERENCE

7. Which animal is probably the most in danger of becoming extinct?
   a. the panda
   b. the northern white rhino
   c. the po'ouli
   d. the Kihansi spray toad

B. Complete the summaries of each section of the passage. Use one word from the passage for each answer.

As animal habitats shrink and more species are threatened with extinction, zoos are taking on a bigger role in helping to ensure species survival.

Who to save?

Zoos have long been involved in [1]_____ efforts. Captive-breeding programs have been especially effective. However, they can be very [2]_____—which is challenging for zoos that have to financially support themselves. This means that the focus has been on [3]_____ animals because they're popular with the public. This, according to Robert Lacy, raises an ethical question: which animals do you [4]_____?

Small Victories

There have been some breeding success stories, such as that of the Kihansi spraying toad. While the toad was [5]_____ extinct in the wild, zookeepers recreated the toad's [6]_____ at the Bronx Zoo. After a careful breeding program, the toads were successfully released back into the wild.

The Frozen Zoo

However, a large number of species still face the possibility of extinction. Researchers, scientists, and concerned citizens are exploring ways to help. The Frozen Zoo, for example, stores [7]_____ from animals under threat in thousands of ice-cold [8]_____.

CRITICAL THINKING Analyzing Arguments   In paragraph D, Robert Lacy asks, "Do you save a small number of large animals—the crowd favorites—or do you focus on saving a whole lot more little, unpopular creatures for the same amount of money?" Note down some arguments for each viewpoint. Then discuss your ideas with a partner.

Arguments for saving ...	
a few large, popular species	many smaller, unpopular species

Determining the Meaning of Root Words

Many words in English are composed of a root word and one or more affixes (prefixes or suffixes). By understanding root words—especially those of Greek and Latin origin—you can build and greatly increase your vocabulary. If you come across an unknown word, having knowledge of its root can help you make an educated guess at its meaning.

DETERMINING
MEANING

A. Work with a partner. Look at these words from the reading. What does each underlined root relate to? Choose the option that is closest in meaning.

1. <u>nutri</u>tional (para I)   a. food   b. water   c. age
2. <u>bio</u>logist (para D)   a. two   b. life   c. death
3. centi<u>meter</u> (para G)   a. small   b. measure   c. weight
4. <u>zoo</u>logical (para D)   a. animal   b. inside   c. true
5. <u>hydro</u>electric (para H)   a. slow   b. planet   c. water

DETERMINING
MEANING

B. Work with a partner. Complete the charts using the words in the box.

carry	distant	earth	earth	feel	hear
see	self	sound	speak	study of	write

	Root meaning	Examples
Greek root		
1. *auto*		autograph, autobiography, automobile
2. *geo*		geography, geology, geopolitics
3. *graph*		calligraphy, autograph, graphic
4. *ology*		biology, zoology, archeology
5. *phon*		phonetics, telephone, microphone
6. *tele*		television, teleport, televise
Latin root		
7. *audi*		audience, auditory, auditorium
8. *dict*		dictate, predict, contradict
9. *port*		import, export, transport
10. *sens / t*		sensitive, sensation, resent
11. *terr*		terrain, territory, terrestrial
12. *vis*		visible, vision, supervise

COMPLETION **A. Complete the information. Circle the correct words.**

The IUCN has added two new species to its Red List—and has reassessed the status of another.

- Populations of the Brazilian three-banded armadillo have declined by an estimated 30 percent in the past 20 years, primarily because its habitat is [1]**oblivion / shrinking**. The armadillo faces a [2]**struggle / refuge** to survive and remains vulnerable.

- The Chinese crocodile lizard has declined by 84 percent in the past 35 years. According to the IUCN, the species might not survive in the wild much longer. Its [3]**imminent / state-of-the art** decline may mean that zoos are the lizard's last [4]**supplement / refuge**.

△ **The Brazilian three-banded armadillo rolls into a ball when threatened.**

- Once on the edge of [5]**shrinking / extinction**, the Yarkon bream stands out as a success story. The fish disappeared from the wild in 1999. After a successful breeding program, 9,000 fish were released into their native habitat.

DEFINITIONS **B. Complete the definitions using the words in the box. One word is extra.**

captive	oblivion	state-of-the-art	struggle	supplement	tide

1. If you _____ something, you add something extra in order to improve it.
2. A(n) _____ animal is one that lives in a zoo or park, not in the wild.
3. Something that is considered _____ has the most advanced ideas or technological features.
4. The _____ of something (e.g., history) refers to the way it is changing.
5. _____ is a state of nothingness.

WORD WEB **C. Complete the diagram with synonyms for imminent. Three words are extra.**

about to happen	approaching	dangerous	forthcoming
impending	looming	identical	unusual

_____

_____ — imminent — _____

_____   _____

VIDEO

In addition to its animal exhibits, the Smithsonian Institution's Museum of Natural History also contains frozen specimens from hundreds of thousands of plant and animal species

LIFE ON ICE

BEFORE YOU WATCH

DEFINITIONS **A.** The words in **bold** appear in the video. Match each one with its definition. Use a dictionary to help.

1. archive •	• a. happening very quickly
2. genome •	• b. a process or system used to produce a result
3. ecology •	• c. detailed and complicated in design
4. plunge •	• d. a complete set of genetic material in an organism
5. instantaneous •	• e. a place where historical records are kept
6. elaborate •	• f. to thrust or throw forcefully into a substance
7. mechanism •	• g. a test of excellence used to judge other things by
8. the gold standard •	• h. the study of the relationships between organisms and their environment

PREVIEWING **B.** Look at the photo and read the caption. Then discuss the questions with a partner.

1. Why do you think researchers might be interested in storing frozen specimens?

2. How do you think they store the specimens?

GIST **A.** Watch the video. Check your predictions in Before You Watch B.

SUMMARIZING **B.** Watch the video again. Complete the summary using no more than three words for each answer.

According to scientist Jonathon Coddington, much of biology over the next few decades will involve [1]_____ of the many kinds of life on Earth. Frozen specimens, such as those at the Smithsonian, are extremely useful for this.

Coddington collects and creates the frozen specimens using [2]_____. The method is fast and [3]_____ for the animals. It also allows the specimens to be preserved for an extremely long time. Spiders are just one example of a species Coddington and his team have collected. Scientists who study the spider specimens will be able to learn more about the [4]_____ they produce.

Amy Driskell sees the collection of frozen specimens as just an extension of more traditional methods, such as keeping specimens in ethanol, or [5]_____ them. The frozen tissue collection now has around [6]_____ samples, and this will provide great support for future scientific research.

CRITICAL THINKING Synthesizing Information   Consider the animal conservation methods described in this unit. Which might be the most successful? Discuss with a partner.

- Tagging and monitoring animals in the wild
- Keeping animals in zoos
- Taking photos of animals for the Photo Ark
- Keeping frozen samples in an archive

VOCABULARY REVIEW

Do you remember the meanings of these words? Check (✓) the ones you know. Look back at the unit and review any words you're not sure of.

Reading A

☐ alarming ☐ collaborate ☐ deserted ☐ detrimental ☐ haul

☐ mingle ☐ scholar ☐ shield ☐ startling ☐ turbulence

Reading B

☐ captive ☐ extinction ☐ imminent ☐ oblivion ☐ refuge

☐ shrink ☐ state-of-the-art ☐ struggle ☐ supplement* ☐ tide

* Academic Word List

HUMAN BODY

7

A climber with a prosthetic leg scales a rock face.

WARM UP

Discuss these questions with a partner.

1. In what ways can people use technology to alter or improve their body?

2. What further changes or improvements do you think will be made over the next 50 years?

139

BEFORE YOU READ

DISCUSSION **A.** Discuss the questions below with a partner.

1. What kinds of things might brain researchers hope to learn about the brain?

2. In what ways could a greater knowledge of the brain help individuals or society?

SKIMMING **B.** Look at title of the reading and the three subheadings. What do you think the passage will be about? Discuss with a partner, then read the passage to check your ideas.

> An engineer wears a helmet of sensors—part of an
advanced scanner that creates maps of the brain.

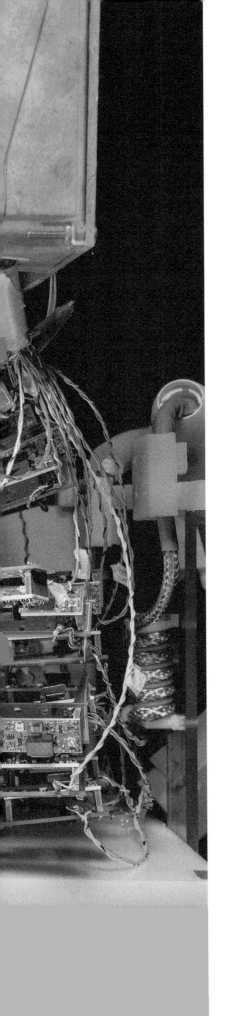

SECRETS
OF THE BRAIN

New technologies are helping researchers solve a great biological mystery: how the brain really works. Carl Zimmer takes a journey into his own head to see what it's all about.

My Contribution to Science

A In a scanning room at the Martinos Center for Biomedical Imaging in Boston, Massachusetts, I lay on my back on a slab,[1] my head resting in an open plastic box. I had offered myself as a guinea pig[2] to neuroscientist Van Wedeen and his colleagues who were now going to scan my brain. A white plastic helmet was lowered over my face, and the slab slowly glided into the scanner tube.

B The magnets that surrounded me began to rumble[3] and beep. For an hour I lay still, eyes closed, and tried to remain calm in the narrow scanner—it wasn't easy. To suppress feelings of panic, I breathed smoothly and transported myself to places in my memory. At one point I recalled walking my nine-year-old daughter to school through the snow. And as I lay there, I reflected on the fact that all my thoughts and emotions were the creation of the 1.3-kilo loaf of flesh that was being **scrutinized**: my brain.

C Submitting to this uncomfortable scanning procedure was part of reporting on the stunning advances in understanding the human brain. Wedeen, who is at the **forefront** of brain imaging, creates in **unprecedented** detail representations of the brain's wiring. My brain scan was the first step in creating an image of my own brain, but I would have to make a second appointment to see the final product.

D On my return trip to his lab, Wedeen opened up the image on a computer screen. His technique—called diffusion spectrum imaging—translates radio signals given off by the brain. What I saw was a map of the nerve fibers that form hundreds of thousands of pathways, carrying information from one part of my brain to another. Wedeen had painted each path a rainbow of colors so that my brain appeared as an explosion of colorful fur, like a psychedelic[4] Persian cat.

---

1 A **slab** is a thick, flat piece of a hard material.
2 If someone is used as a **guinea pig**, they are used in an experiment or a test.
3 Something that **rumbles** makes a deep, vibrating sound.
4 **Psychedelic** art has bright colors and strange patterns.

Mapping the Brain

E   Cutting-edge techniques for mapping the brain are giving researchers greater access to that **organ** than ever before. Some neuroscientists focus in on the structure of individual nerve cells, or neurons. Others chart genes that interact with those neurons. Still others—Wedeen among them—work on revealing as much of the brain's vast **neural** network as they can.

F   Jeff Lichtman and his colleagues at Harvard University are creating extremely detailed three-dimensional images of neurons, revealing every bump and stalk branching from them. They begin by slicing preserved mouse brains into thin layers of tissue, each less than a thousandth the thickness of a human hair. An electron microscope[5] is then used to take a picture of each layer, and the images are put in order using a computer. Slowly a three-dimensional image is built—one that the scientists can explore as if they were in a tiny submarine. "Everything is revealed," says Lichtman.

G   The problem is that even a mouse brain is unbelievably complex. Lichtman and his colleagues have managed to recreate a piece about the size of a grain of salt. Its data alone is equal to the amount of data in about 25,000 high-definition movies. "It's a wake-up call to how much more complicated brains are than the way we think about them," says Lichtman. When asked if his method could be used to scan an entire human brain, which contains a thousand times more neurons than a mouse brain, Lichtman says with a laugh, "I don't dwell on that—it's too painful."

H   When and if Lichtman completes his 3-D portrait of the brain, it will reveal much—but it will still be only an **exquisitely** detailed sculpture. Living neurons, on the other hand, are full of active genes that are integral to brain function. Researchers at the Allen Institute in Seattle, Washington, have developed a method for mapping these genes—the Allen Brain Atlas. First, the donated brains of recently deceased people are scanned using a powerful

> A colored 3-D scan of nerve fibers in the brain. The fibers transmit nerve signals between brain regions, and between the brain and spinal cord.

MRI[6] scanner. This scan is used for reference as a kind of 3-D road map. The brain is then sliced into sections so thin that they are nearly invisible, and the slices are mounted on glass. Finally, chemicals are applied to reveal the active genes in the neurons.

I   So far, the researchers have mapped the brains of six people. It's a huge amount of data, and they've only just begun to understand the genetic landscape of the brain. The scientists estimate that 84 percent of all the genes in our DNA become active in the adult brain. Certain combinations of genes are activated by neurons to carry out important tasks in different locations. The secret to certain **disorders** may be hiding in these complex networks, as certain genes shut down or switch on abnormally.

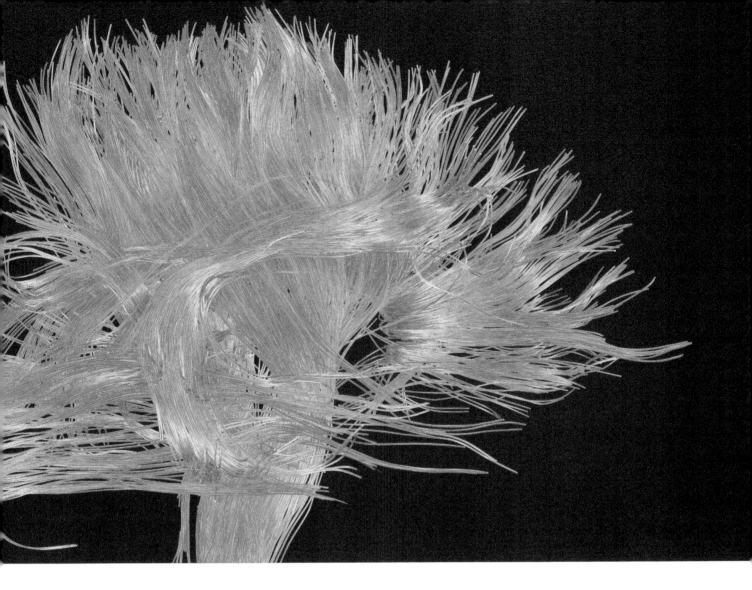

J Of all the new ways of visualizing the brain, perhaps the most remarkable is one invented by neuroscientist Karl Deisseroth and colleagues at Stanford University. They have found a way to make a mouse brain as transparent as glass, allowing researchers to see inside the brain while it is still intact. The technique involves replacing the naturally occurring substances in the brain with transparent ones. They can then color the brain with chemicals that show different pathways of connecting neurons. "You don't have to take it apart to show the wiring," says Deisseroth.

K It's not easy to **dazzle** neuroscientists, but Deisseroth's method, called CLARITY, has left his colleagues awestruck.[7] Wedeen has called the research "spectacular ... unlike anything else in the field." Deisseroth's ultimate goal is to make a human brain transparent—a far more difficult task, not least because a human brain is 3,000 times larger than that of a mouse. He anticipates that CLARITY may someday help patients with autism[8] or depression, but for now he's keeping those hopes in check. "We have so far to go before we can affect treatments that I tell people, 'Don't even think about that yet.' It's just a voyage of discovery for now."

5 An **electron microscope** is a tool that allows the viewer to see objects as small as an atom.

6 Magnetic Resonance Imaging (**MRI**) is a technique for creating detailed images of organs in the body.

7 If a person is **awestruck**, he or she is very impressed and amazed by something.

8 **Autism** is a mental disorder that affects a person's ability to communicate and interact with others.

Connecting Brain with Machine

L For the most part, brain research has yet to change how doctors treat patients. But there is one line of research—brain-machine interfaces[9]—where the mapping of the brain has started to change people's lives.

M At 43 years old, Cathy Hutchinson suffered a massive stroke, leaving her unable to move or speak. Lying in her bed in Massachusetts General Hospital, she gradually figured out that her doctors didn't know if she was brain-dead or still aware. Her sister asked Hutchinson if she could understand her, and she managed to answer by moving her eyes up as a signal. "It gave me such a relief," Hutchinson tells me 17 years later, "because everybody talked about me as if I was dying."

N Still almost completely unable to move or speak, she communicates by looking at letters on a computer screen. A camera tracks the movement of a tiny metal disk attached to the center of her eyeglasses, thanks to a system developed by Brown University neuroscientist John Donoghue.

O Donoghue wanted to find a way to help people with paralysis by using signals from the brain's motor cortex—the area where signals to move muscles **originate**. He spent years developing such a device, testing it on monkeys. Once he and his colleagues knew it was safe, they were ready to start working with human patients.

A volunteer takes part in a brain scan at the Neuroimaging Research Centre in Paris, France.

P Surgeons inserted the device into Hutchinson's motor cortex. After she had healed from her surgery, the researchers plugged in wires to send signals from her brain to nearby computers. The computers recognize the signals and use them to move a computer cursor around a screen. Two years later, they attached a robot arm with a hand to the computers, and Hutchinson quickly learned to use it.

Q "It felt natural," she says. So natural that one day she reached out for a cup of coffee, grabbed it, and brought it to her lips to drink. "Cathy's smile when she put down that drink—that's everything," Donoghue says.

R Today Donoghue and other scientists are building on that success, hoping to create human-machine interfaces that will be powerful, safe, and easy. At Duke University, Miguel Nicolelis has gotten monkeys to control full-body exoskeletons using methods similar to those that helped Hutchinson. "Eventually brain implants[10] will become as common as heart implants," says Nicolelis. Predicting the future is a **tricky** game, however, and advances in the past have inspired expectations that have not been met. But it is clear that current research is moving neuroscience to a remarkable new stage.

---

9 An **interface** is a device or program that enables a person to interact with a computer.

10 An **implant** is something inserted into a person's body, especially by surgery.

A. Choose the best answer for each question.

MAIN IDEA

1. Why did Carl Zimmer get his brain scanned?
   a. to help him recollect childhood memories
   b. because the neuroscientist Van Wedeen asked him to
   c. to aid him in reporting on how the brain works
   d. because he wants to learn to suppress feelings of panic

PARAPHRASE

2. When asked if his method could be used to scan an entire human brain, Jeff Lichtman said with a laugh, *"I don't dwell on that—it's too painful."*
What did he mean by his response?
   a. He can't answer that because it's not ethical to do that to a human.
   b. He doubts he would do it since it would cause so much pain.
   c. He finds it funny that people would suggest that since the mice died in the process.
   d. He doesn't think about it much because it would be such a huge challenge.

SEQUENCE

3. When mapping genes, what do researchers at the Allen Institute do last?
   a. cut the brain into thin sections
   b. apply chemicals to reveal active genes
   c. scan the brain of a dead person
   d. mount brain slices on glass

AUTHOR ATTITUDE

4. How does Carl Zimmer feel about the work of Karl Deisseroth?
   a. He feels it's amazing, as even other scientists are impressed.
   b. He finds it impressive, even though most scientists are skeptical.
   c. He finds it interesting, but worries it may not be practical.
   d. He thinks his work has not been fully appreciated by other scientists.

VOCABULARY

5. In paragraph K, the phrase *in check* is closest in meaning to _____.
   a. in focus   c. under control
   b. at a glance   d. without fear

DETAIL

6. How was Cathy Hutchinson able to raise a coffee cup?
   a. She controlled a machine using verbal commands.
   b. Wires carried signals directly from her brain to the cup.
   c. She used a special bionic hand that was attached to her arm.
   d. A computer used signals from her brain to move a robot arm.

INFERENCE

7. According to the writer, which researcher is the farthest along in finding practical ways to use recent brain research?
   a. Van Wedeen   c. Karl Deisseroth
   b. Jeff Lichtman   d. John Donoghue

B. **Complete each sentence using no more than three words from the passage.**

1. Van Wedeen uses a technique called diffusion spectrum imaging, which detects _____ produced by the brain.

2. Jeff Lichtman and his colleagues use a(n) _____ to take pictures of mouse brains.

3. Lichtman and his colleagues have recreated a piece of a mouse brain about the size of a(n) _____.

4. A human brain contains around a thousand times more _____ than a mouse brain.

5. Scientists working on the Allen Brain Atlas use a(n) _____ to scan human brains.

6. Karl Deisseroth and his colleagues have found a way to make mouse brains _____, so they can be studied while still whole.

7. Cathy Hutchinson had a device inserted into a part of her brain called the _____. This allows her to move a robot arm.

8. Using similar methods to those that helped Hutchinson, Miguel Nicolelis has enabled monkeys to control _____.

CRITICAL THINKING Reflecting   Carl Zimmer describes himself as a "guinea pig" for undergoing a brain scan. Discuss the following questions with a partner.

▶ Would you have your brain scanned like Zimmer did? Explain your answer.

▶ Would you ever be a guinea pig for other medical tests or procedures you didn't need? Under what circumstances?

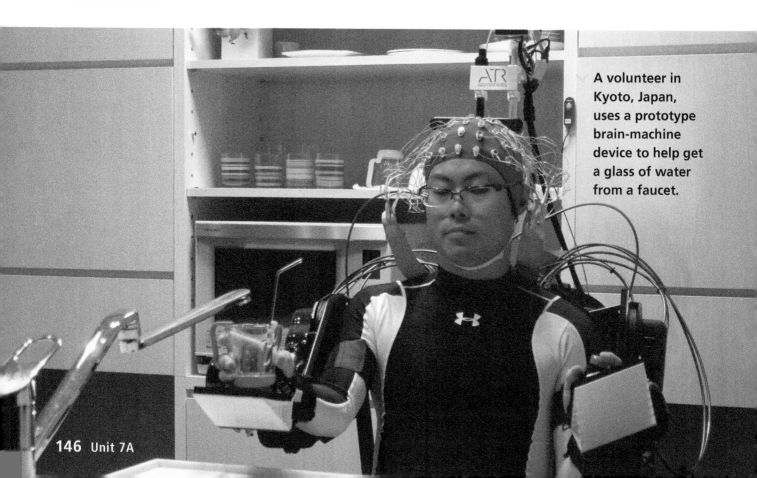

A volunteer in Kyoto, Japan, uses a prototype brain-machine device to help get a glass of water from a faucet.

Understanding the Use of the Passive Voice

Most sentences in English are in the active voice. However, there are times, especially in scientific and technical texts, when the passive is the structure of choice and the writer chooses to omit the agent (the "doer" of the action). These include:

1. when the person who performed the action is either unimportant or obvious

The brain is then sliced into sections.

2. when the writer does not know who performed the action

A box of chocolates was left on my bedside table.

3. when the writer wishes to be vague

Advances in the past have inspired expectations that have not been met.

IDENTIFYING PASSIVE SENTENCES

A. Read the excerpt from the reading. Underline the verbs in the passive voice. Can you identify the doer of the actions? Discuss with a partner.

They begin by slicing preserved mouse brains into thin layers of tissue, each less than a thousandth the thickness of a human hair. An electron microscope is then used to take a picture of each layer, and the images are put in order using a computer. Slowly a three-dimensional image is built—one that the scientists can explore as if they were in a tiny submarine. "Everything is revealed," says Lichtman.

UNDERSTANDING AUTHOR'S PURPOSE

B. Look at the sentences below (1–5). Why did the writer use the passive voice in each one? Circle the most likely reason.

1. The patient was told that he would need brain surgery.

a. The person who told the patient is obvious.
b. The person who told the patient is not known.

2. His mail was delivered to his house while he was in the hospital.

a. The person who delivered the mail is not important.
b. The writer wishes to be vague.

3. Some expensive medicines were stolen from the lab.

a. The person who stole the medicines is obvious.
b. The person who stole the medicines is not known.

4. Somewhat low brain activity was seen during the brain scan.

a. The person who saw the low brain activity is obvious.
b. The writer wishes to be vague.

5. Various instruments were handed to the doctor during the surgery.

a. The person who handed the doctor the instruments is obvious.
b. The writer wishes to be vague.

COMPLETION **A.** Complete the information using the words in the box.
Three words are extra.

dazzle	disorder	forefront	neural
organ	originate	scrutinize	unprecedented

Depending on where you're from, you might see a man, a rabbit, or a pair of hands in the full moon.

Joel Voss is a researcher working at the

¹_____ of research focusing on our most

complex ²_____: the brain. He studies

how our brains find meaning in random shapes.

In his studies, he shows people shapes and

measures ³_____ activity by tracking

changes in blood flow. When a person looks at

the shapes, certain regions of the brain become

active—the same areas that are involved in processing

meaningful images.

Where does seeing images like this ⁴_____? Voss says the brain must

quickly ⁵_____ unfamiliar information and figure out what to pay

attention to. Seeing faces or figures in the moon, for example, is a consequence of the

brain matching stored information with new information.

DEFINITIONS **B.** Complete the sentences. Circle the correct options.

1. Something **unprecedented** has *never / frequently* been done before.
2. If someone has a brain **disorder**, the brain is acting *normally / abnormally*.
3. A **tricky** problem is probably *easy / difficult* to solve.
4. Something that is drawn **exquisitely** is drawn *carelessly / beautifully*.
5. If someone **dazzles** you, you are *impressed / disappointed* by their skill or beauty.

COLLOCATIONS **C.** The words in the box are frequently used with the adjective **unprecedented**.
Complete the sentences with the correct words. One word is extra.

detail	opportunity	scale	step

1. Brain scans can show neurons in unprecedented _____.
2. Recent breakthroughs offer an unprecedented _____ to find a cure for cancer.
3. Warming oceans may lead to environmental change on an unprecedented _____.

BEFORE YOU READ

PREVIEWING
A. Look at the photo and read the caption. Then discuss the questions with a partner.

    1. What is a bionic arm? How do you think it works?

    2. What do you think might be the challenges of using a bionic arm?

SKIMMING AND PREDICTING
B. Skim the reading passage to answer these questions about Amanda Kitts. Then read the passage to check your ideas.

    1. Why does she need a bionic arm? _____

    2. What are things she can now do with her bionic arm? _____

    3. What are things she can't do yet? _____

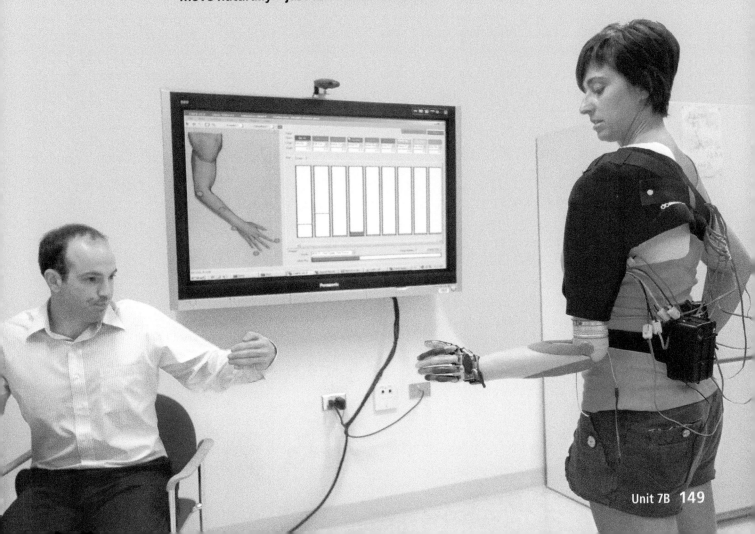

In Chicago, Amanda Kitts trains her bionic arm's computer system to obey her thoughts and move naturally—just as a real arm would.

HUMAN BIONICS

A Amanda Kitts is mobbed by four- and five-year-olds as she enters the classroom. "Hey, kids, how're my babies today?" she says, patting shoulders and ruffling[1] hair. Slender and energetic, she has operated this Knoxville, Tennessee, daycare center and two others for almost 20 years. She crouches down to talk to a small girl, putting her hands on her knees.

B "The robot arm!" several kids cry. "You remember this, huh?" says Kitts, holding out her left arm. As she turns her hand palm up, there is a soft whirring sound. If you weren't paying close attention, you'd miss it. She bends her elbow, accompanied by more whirring.

C "Make it do something silly!" one girl says. "Silly? Remember how I can shake your hand?" Kitts says, extending her arm and rotating her wrist. A boy reaches out, hesitantly, to touch her fingers. What he brushes against is flesh-colored plastic, fingers curved slightly inward. Underneath are three motors, a metal framework, and a network of sophisticated electronics. The assembly is topped by a white plastic cup midway up Kitts's biceps, encircling a stump[2] that is almost all that remains from the arm she lost in a car accident in 2006.

D Almost all, but not quite. Within her brain, below the level of consciousness, lives an intact image of that arm—a phantom. When Kitts thinks about flexing[3] her elbow, the phantom moves. Impulses racing down from her brain are picked up by electrode sensors in the white cup and converted into signals that turn motors, and the artificial elbow bends.

E "I don't really think about it. I just move it," says Kitts, who uses both this standard model and a more experimental arm with even more control. "After my accident, I felt lost. These days I'm just excited all the time, because they keep on improving the arm. One day

I'll be able to feel things with it and clap my hands together in time to the songs my kids are singing."

F Kitts is one of "tomorrow's people," a group whose missing or ruined body parts are being replaced by devices **embedded** in their nervous systems that respond to commands from their brains. The machines they use are called neural prostheses or—using a term made popular by science fiction writers—bionics.

G The kind of prosthesis that Amanda Kitts uses is controlled by her brain. A technique called targeted muscle reinnervation uses nerves remaining after an amputation[4] to control an artificial limb. It was first tried in a patient in 2002. Four years later, Tommy Kitts, Amanda's husband, read about the research, which took place at the Rehabilitation Institute of Chicago (RIC). His wife lay in the hospital at the time; the truck that had crushed her car had also crushed her arm, from just above the elbow down.

H "I was angry, sad, depressed; I just couldn't accept it," she says. But the news Tommy brought her about the Chicago arm gave her some reassurance, and some hope. "It seemed like the best option out there, a lot better than motors and switches," Tommy says. "Amanda actually got excited about it." Soon they were on a plane to Illinois.

I Todd Kuiken, a **licensed** medical practitioner and biomedical engineer at RIC, was the person responsible for what the institute had begun calling the "bionic arm." He knew that nerves in an amputee's stump could still carry signals from the brain, and he knew that a computer in

---

1 If you **ruffle** someone's hair, you lightly rub it.
2 A **stump** is the base portion of a body part that remains after the rest has been amputated.
3 When you **flex** something, usually a muscle, you bend it.
4 An **amputation** occurs when a body part is removed, usually for medical reasons.

a prosthesis could direct electric motors to move the limb. However, making the connection was far from straightforward. Nerves conduct electricity, but they can't be spliced together with a computer cable. (Nerve fibers and metal wires are not mutually **compatible**, and an open wound where a wire enters the body would be a dangerous avenue for infections.)

J Kuiken needed an amplifier to boost the signals from the nerves, avoiding the need for a direct contact between nerve and wire. He found one in muscles. When muscles tense, they give off an electrical burst strong enough to be detected by an electrode placed on the skin. He developed a technique to reroute severed nerves from their old, damaged spots to other muscles that could give their signals the proper boost.

K In October 2006, Kitts consented to have Kuiken try out his new technique on her. The first step was to **salvage** major nerves that once went all the way down her arm. "These are the same nerves that work the arm and hand, but we had to create four different muscle areas to lead them to," Kuiken says. The nerves started in Kitts's brain—in the motor cortex, which holds a rough map of the body—but they terminated at the end of her stump. In an **intricate** operation, a surgeon rerouted those nerves to different regions of Kitts's upper-arm muscles. For months the nerves grew, millimeter by millimeter, moving deeper into their newly **assigned** homes.

L "At three months, I started feeling little tingles and twitches," says Kitts, "and by four months, I could actually feel different parts of my hand when I touched my upper arm. I could touch it in different places and feel different fingers." What she was feeling were parts of the phantom arm that were mapped into her brain, now reconnected to flesh. When Kitts thought about moving those phantom fingers, her real upper-arm muscles contracted.

BIONIC MAN

As scientists work to link machine and mind, artificial bones, organs, joints, and limbs (parts shaded green and blue) are gaining many of the capabilities of human ones.

1 Images captured by a video camera in glasses are converted to signals and sent wirelessly to an implant in the eye. Electrodes in the eye send the signals to the optic nerve, which sends them to the brain, and a person is able to "see" the images.

2 Implants stimulate nerves inside the ear, allowing people who are partially or completely deaf to hear.

3 Signals are sent from the brain to the bionic arm via electrodes attached to nerves in the injured arm. The result: a person is able to grasp and manipulate objects.

4 A bionic ankle copies the action of a real one by pushing the wearer forward, helping the person to walk again.

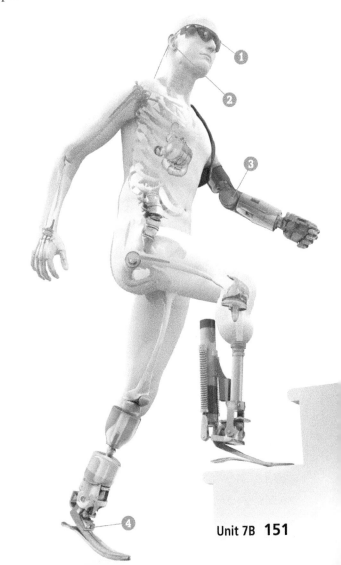

M A month later, she was fitted with her first bionic arm, which had electrodes in the cup around the stump to pick up the signals from the muscles. Now the challenge was to convert those signals into commands to adjust the elbow and hand. A storm of electrical noise was coming from the small region on Kitts's arm. Somewhere in there was the signal that meant "straighten the elbow" or "turn the wrist." A microprocessor inserted in the prosthesis had to be programmed to differentiate the right signal and send it to the right motor.

N Kitts practiced using her arm one floor below Kuiken's office in an apartment set up by occupational therapists. The apartment had a kitchen with a stove, silverware in a drawer, a bed, a closet with hangers, a bathroom, and stairs—things people use every day without a second thought but that pose huge obstacles to someone missing a limb.

O Watching Kitts make a peanut butter sandwich in the kitchen is a startling experience. With her sleeve rolled back to reveal the plastic cup, her motion is fluid. Her live arm holds a slice of bread, her artificial fingers close on a knife, the elbow flexes, and she swipes peanut butter back and forth. "It wasn't easy at first," she says. "I would try to move it, and it wouldn't always go where I wanted." But she worked at it, and the more she used the arm, the more lifelike the motions felt.

P What Kitts would really like now is **sensation**. That would be a big help in many actions, including one of her favorites—gulping coffee. "The problem with a paper coffee cup is that my hand will close until it gets a solid grip. But with a paper cup, you never get a solid grip," she says. "That happened at Starbucks once. It kept squeezing until the cup went 'pop.'"

Q There are **valid** reasons for supposing that one day she'll get that sensation, says Kuiken. In partnership with bioengineers at the Johns Hopkins University Applied Physics Laboratory, RIC has been developing a new prototype[5] for

Kitts and other patients that not only has more flexibility—more motors and joints—but also has pressure-sensing pads on the fingertips. The pads are connected to small rods that poke into Kitts's stump. The harder the pressure, the stronger the sensation in her phantom fingers.

R "I can feel how hard I'm grabbing," she says. She can also differentiate between rubbing something rough, like sandpaper, and smooth, like glass, by how fast the rods **vibrate**. "I go up to Chicago to experiment with it, and I love it," she says. "I want them to give it to me already so I can take it home. But it's a lot more complicated than my take-home arm, so they don't have it completely reliable yet."

S Today, Kitts has a new, more elastic cup atop her arm that better aligns electrodes with nerves that control the arm. "It means I can do a lot more with the arm," she says. "A new one up in Chicago lets me do lots of different hand grasps—I want that. I want to pick up pennies and hammers and toys with my kids." These are reasonable hopes for a substitute body part, Kuiken says. "We are giving people tools, and they are better than what previously existed. But they are still **crude**, like a hammer, compared with the complexity of the human body."

T The work of neural prostheses is extremely delicate, a series of trials filled with many errors. As scientists have learned that it's possible to link machine and mind, they have also learned how difficult it is to maintain that bond. Still, bionics represents a major leap forward, enabling researchers to give people back much more of what they've lost than was ever possible before.

U "That's really what this work is about: restoration," says Joseph Pancrazio, program director for neural engineering at the National Institute of Neurological Disorders and Stroke. "When a person with a spinal cord injury can be in a restaurant, feeding himself, and no one else notices, that is my definition of success."

---

5 A **prototype** is an early model of a product that is tested so that the design can be changed if necessary.

A. Choose the best answer for each question.

GIST

1. The best alternative title for this reading would be _____.

   a. Bionics, the Next Generation of Prosthetics
   b. The Latest Varieties of Robots
   c. Amanda Kitts: A Brief Biography
   d. A Short History of Prosthetic Limbs

VOCABULARY

2. In paragraph C, the phrase *brushes against* is closest in meaning to _____.

   a. looks at carefully
   b. touches briefly
   c. grasps tightly
   d. pushes away quickly

DETAIL

3. In paragraph F, who does *tomorrow's people* refer to?

   a. doctors who treat people who have lost limbs
   b. all people who have a missing or damaged body part
   c. scientists who are developing advanced bionic limbs
   d. people who have prosthetics controlled by their brains

DETAIL

4. According to the author, the term *bionics* _____.

   a. is older than the term *neural prosthesis*
   b. was popularized by science fiction authors
   c. is no longer in regular use today
   d. refers to the people who wear prostheses

DETAIL

5. In paragraph J, the *amplifier* proposed by Kuiken _____.

   a. is an electric motor that is placed directly on the skin
   b. sends signals from damaged nerves to the brain
   c. is a muscle that helps link nerve signals to electrodes
   d. receives a signal directly from a computer cable

REFERENCE

6. In the last sentence of paragraph M, the word *it* refers to _____.

   a. the correct signal
   b. the prosthesis
   c. the right motor
   d. a microprocessor

INFERENCE

7. In paragraph P, the author implies that the paper coffee cup *went 'pop'* because Kitts _____.

   a. did not know how hard she was squeezing the cup
   b. could not feel how hot the coffee was
   c. did not realize how full the cup was
   d. could not tell that the cup was already empty

∧ **Motorized springs in a powered ankle push off like a real leg.**

B. Complete each sentence using no more than three words from the passage.

1. In her subconscious, Amanda Kitts has an image of an arm called a(n) _____.

2. The Rehabilitation Institute of Chicago first described a prosthetic limb as a(n) _____.

3. One problem with trying to control a prosthetic limb with your brain is the fact that _____ and wires are not compatible.

4. Kitts said she could feel _____ in her arm three months after surgery.

5. It took time and a lot of hard work before Kitts felt she could make the motions in her bionic arm _____.

6. Todd Kuiken says that he is giving people _____, though these devices are still quite limited.

7. The work being done in prosthetics is, in many ways, a series of _____ with lots of mistakes.

< **Amanda Kitts with a Proto1 bionic arm**

CRITICAL THINKING Justifying Opinions

▶ Read each opinion and decide if you agree or disagree with it. Circle **1** (strongly disagree) to **5** (strongly agree).

1. People with bionic parts may have an unfair advantage over others.   **1 2 3 4 5**
2. Bionic research will likely only benefit wealthy people.   **1 2 3 4 5**
3. In 100 years, everyone will be partly bionic.   **1 2 3 4 5**
4. I would consider replacing a healthy limb to get a better, bionic one.   **1 2 3 4 5**
5. There is a danger of creating a new race of bionic "superbeings."   **1 2 3 4 5**

▶ Discuss the reasons for your choices with a partner.

Distinguishing Fact from Opinion

Most explanatory articles contain both facts and opinions. An opinion (the author's own or one given by an expert) can be supported with evidence, but unlike a fact, it cannot be verified. Distinguishing a fact from an opinion can help you better assess the information in a passage. Opinions are often (but not always) indicated by the following:

1. Hedging verbs: *think, believe, seems, suggests*
2. Subjective adjectives: *terrific, beautiful, smart*
3. Comparative adjectives: *better, greater*
4. Modals: *might, could*

FACT OR
OPINION

A. The following sentences are based on information from the article. Write **F** (fact) or **O** (opinion).

1. _____ Signals run from Amanda Kitts's brain to electrode sensors in the white cup, where they are transmitted into signals that power motors, and she can then bend her elbow. (paragraph D)

2. _____ The bionic arm seems like the best option, much better than the older prosthetics that use motors and switches. (paragraph H)

3. _____ An amputee's nerves can still carry signals from the brain. (paragraph I)

4. _____ The point where a metal wire enters the body may also allow germs to come in, causing an infection. (paragraph I)

5. _____ It's amazing to watch Amanda make a sandwich. (paragraph O)

6. _____ One day Kitts will be able to feel sensations through her prosthetic fingers. (paragraph Q)

7. _____ One prosthetic arm that Kitts has experimented with allows her to tell the difference between rough surfaces and smooth surfaces. (paragraph R)

8. _____ If people who have spinal cord injuries can feed themselves, and no one notices they have been injured, that is the definition of success. (paragraph U)

SCANNING

B. Look at the opinions you identified in Activity A. Which person from the reading passage expresses each opinion? Scan the passage and note the name of the person next to each one.

VOCABULARY PRACTICE

COMPLETION **A.** Complete the information by circling the correct words.

The effectiveness of bionic technology is continuing to improve, helping thousands of people to regain abilities and [1]**sensations / salvages** they had previously lost. For example, a(n) [2]**valid / intricate** piece of equipment [3]**embedded / assigned** in a patient's chest can help restore hand movement lost due to paralysis. Scientists also hope to develop new materials that will help make machine parts more [4]**compatible / licensed** with the human body.

∧ **An advanced bionic hand allows for a range of movement.**

DEFINITIONS **B.** Complete the sentences. Circle the correct options.

1. Something that is **crude** is *simple and basic / complex and refined*.

2. A **valid** argument or idea is based on *incorrect / sensible* reasoning.

3. If you manage to **salvage** a difficult situation, you make it *better / worse*.

4. Something that **vibrates** shakes with *small, quick / large, uneven* movements.

5. If something is **assigned** to someone, it is officially *given to / taken from* them.

6. A **licensed** individual has an official *qualification / request* to do something.

COLLOCATIONS **C.** The nouns in the box below are often used with the adjective **valid**. Complete the sentences using the correct words.

concern	data	point	reason

1. Many people were unhappy with the tax increase. They could see no valid _____ for it.

2. The rising crime rate is a valid _____ for people in many parts of this country.

3. Before proposing their new theory, the scientists ensured they had obtained valid _____.

4. I thought the President made a valid _____ when she suggested that more needed to be done to help the country's poorest people.

> Thanks to new advances in bionics, many paralyzed patients are being given the chance to walk again.

A GIANT STEP

BEFORE YOU WATCH

PREVIEWING **A.** Read the information below. The words in **bold** appear in the video. Match each word with its definition.

Cutting-edge bionic devices are giving **paralyzed** people the chance to walk again. The technology is still at an early stage, but trials on a number of patients have been hugely promising, with many participants noting the **overwhelming** sensation of standing upright for the first time in years. Today's devices are not yet able to provide a full-time replacement for wheelchairs—they are very slow, heavy, and difficult to turn. However, in addition to helping with injury **rehabilitation**, they also provide relief to **paraplegic** patients from the medical side-effects of being confined to a wheelchair for long periods.

1. paraplegic   •

  • a. the treatment of physical disabilities

2. paralyzed   •

  • b. someone who cannot move the lower half of their body

3. rehabilitation   •

  • c. affecting someone very strongly

4. overwhelming   •

  • d. being unable to move and having no feeling in a part of the body

WHILE YOU WATCH

GIST **A.** Watch the video. Note answers to the questions.

1. How did Frank get injured?

_____

2. What is Frank able to do for the first time since his accident?

_____

3. What does Frank need to make sure he can do first?

_____

4. What does Frank's mother say about the experience?

_____

DEFINITIONS **B.** Watch the video again and read the quotes below. Write what you think each phrase in **bold** means.

1. "Today is **an absolute milestone** for Frank." _____

2. "Frank is **facing tough odds**."_____

3. "I'm **in the rhythm**."_____

4. "We're **reaching the stars** right now." _____

CRITICAL THINKING Applying Ideas   Discuss these questions with a partner.

▶ What are some possible applications of bionic technology in each of the following fields?

exploration   military   medical   sports   transportation

▶ What might be some concerns or drawbacks in the use of bionic technology in these fields?

VOCABULARY REVIEW

Do you remember the meanings of these words? Check (✓) the ones you know. Look back at the unit and review any words you're not sure of.

Reading A

☐ dazzle   ☐ disorder   ☐ exquisitely   ☐ forefront   ☐ neural

☐ organ   ☐ originate   ☐ scrutinize   ☐ tricky   ☐ unprecedented*

Reading B

☐ assign*   ☐ compatible*   ☐ crude   ☐ embed   ☐ intricate

☐ licensed*   ☐ salvage   ☐ sensation   ☐ valid*   ☐ vibrate

* Academic Word List

SOCIAL
BEHAVIOR

8

A pack of gray wolves
howl in the Rocky Mountains,
Montana, USA.

WARM UP

Discuss these questions
with a partner.

1. What aspects of social
   behavior are unique to
   humans?

2. Which animals do you
   think are closest to us in
   terms of social behavior?

159

8A

DISCUSSION **A.** Look at the photo and read the caption. What do you think are the advantages and disadvantages of animals of living in large groups? Discuss your ideas with a partner.

SKIMMING **B.** Quickly skim the reading passage. Why do you think researchers are interested in how insects such as ants and bees behave in groups? Note your answers below. Then read through the passage again to check your ideas.

_____

_____

> Insect swarms—like this swarm of mosquitoes—live in tight groups, often acting as a single entity.

THE GENIUS OF SWARMS

A single ant or bee isn't smart, but ant and bee colonies are. The reason, as writer Peter Miller discovers, is something called swarm intelligence.

A I used to think ants knew what they were doing. The ones marching across my kitchen counter looked so confident. I figured they had a **coherent** plan, knew where they were going, and what needed to be done. How else could ants create highways, build elaborate nests, organize epic[1] raids, and do all the other things ants do?

B It turns out I was wrong. Ants aren't clever little engineers, architects, or warriors after all—at least not as individuals. When it comes to deciding what to do next, most ants don't have a clue. "If you watch an ant try to accomplish something, you'll be impressed by how inept[2] it is," says Deborah M. Gordon, a biologist at Stanford University.

C How do we explain, then, the success of Earth's 12,000 or so known ant species? They must have learned something in 140 million years. "Ants aren't smart," Gordon says. "Ant colonies are." A colony can solve problems unthinkable for individual ants, such as finding the shortest path to the best food source, allocating workers to different tasks, or defending a **territory** from neighbors. They do it with something called swarm intelligence.

D Where this intelligence comes from raises a fundamental question in nature: How do the simple actions of individuals add up to the complex behavior of a group?

E One key to an ant colony is that no one's in charge. No generals command ant warriors, no managers boss around ant workers, and the queen plays no role except to lay eggs. Even with half a million ants, a colony operates as a single entity without any management at all—at least none that we would recognize. Such a system—described by scientists as *self-organizing*—relies upon countless interactions between individual ants, each of which is following simple rules.

F That's how swarm intelligence works: simple creatures following simple **protocols**, each one acting on local information. No ant sees the big picture, or tells any other ant what to do. Some ant species may go about this with more sophistication than others. (*Temnothorax albipennis*, for example, can

---

1 If something is **epic,** it is very large or grand.
2 People or animals that are **inept** are awkward, clumsy, or unable to do things.

rate the quality of a potential nest site using multiple **criteria**.) But in each case, says Iain Couzin, a biologist at Oxford and Princeton Universities, no leadership is required. "Even complex behavior may be coordinated by relatively simple interactions," he says.

G Inspired by this idea, computer scientists have been using swarm behavior to create mathematical **procedures** for resolving complex human problems, such as routing trucks and scheduling airlines.

H In Houston, for example, a company named American Air Liquide has been using ant-based guidelines to manage a complex business problem. The company produces industrial and medical gases at about a hundred locations in the United States and delivers them to 6,000 sites, using pipelines, railcars, and 400 trucks. Air Liquide developed a computer model inspired by the foraging behavior of Argentine ants (*Linepithema humile*). The species, like other ant species, deposits chemical substances called pheromones.

I "When these ants bring food back to the nest, they lay a pheromone trail that tells other ants

to go get more food," says Charles N. Harper, who oversees the supply system at Air Liquide. "The pheromone trail gets reinforced every time an ant goes out and comes back, kind of like when you wear a trail in the forest to collect wood. So, we developed a program that sends out billions of software ants to find out where the pheromone trails are strongest for our truck routes."

J Air Liquide used the ant approach to consider every permutation[3] of plant scheduling, weather, and truck routing—millions of possible decisions and outcomes a day. Every night, forecasts of customer demand and manufacturing costs are fed into the model. "It takes four hours to run, even with the biggest computers we have," Harper says, "but at six o'clock every morning, we get a solution that says how we're going to manage our day."

K Other companies have also profited by **imitating** ants. In Italy and Switzerland, fleets of trucks now use ant-foraging rules to find the best routes for bulk deliveries. In England and

---

3 A **permutation** is one of the ways in which a number of things can be ordered or arranged.

∨ **Researchers on Appledore Island observe swarming bee behavior.**

France, telephone companies improved their network speed by having messages deposit virtual pheromones at switching stations, just as ants leave signals for other ants to show them the best trails.

L But ants are not the only insects with something useful to teach us. On a small island off the southern coast of Maine, biologist Thomas D. Seeley of Cornell University has been studying how colonies of honeybees (*Apis mellifera*) choose a new home. In late spring, when a hive gets too crowded, a colony normally splits. The queen, some drones,[4] and about half the workers migrate a short distance to cluster on a tree branch, while a small number of scouts go searching for a new site for the colony.

M To find out how, Seeley's team put out five nest boxes—four that weren't quite big enough and one that was just about perfect—and released a colony of bees. Scout bees soon appeared at all five boxes. When they returned to the main group, each scout performed a waggle dance urging other scouts to go have a look. These dances include a **code** giving directions to a box's location; the strength of each dance reflected the scout's enthusiasm for the site.

N The decisive moment didn't take place in the main cluster of bees, but out at the boxes, where scouts were building up. As soon as the number of scouts visible near the entrance to a box reached about 15—a threshold confirmed by other experiments—the bees at that box sensed that a quorum[5] had been reached, and they returned to the swarm with the news. "It was a race," Seeley says. "Which site was going to build up 15 bees first?"

O Scouts from the chosen box then spread through the swarm, signaling that it was time to move. Once all the bees had warmed up, they lifted off to secure their new home. To no one's surprise, it turned out to be the best of the five boxes. The bees' rules for decision-making—seek a diversity of options, encourage a free competition among ideas, and use an effective mechanism to narrow choices—so

impressed Seeley that he now uses them at Cornell as chairman of his department.

P "I've applied what I've learned from the bees to run **faculty** meetings," he says. He wants to avoid going into a meeting with his mind made up, hearing only what he wants to hear, and pressuring people to conform. Therefore, Seeley asks his group to identify all the possibilities, discuss their ideas for a while, and then vote by secret ballot.[6] "It's exactly what the swarm bees do, which gives a group time to let the best ideas emerge and win."

Q In fact, almost any group that follows the bees' rules will make itself smarter, says James Surowiecki, author of *The Wisdom of Crowds*. "The analogy is really quite powerful: The bees are predicting which nest site will be best, and humans can do the same thing, even in the face of exceptionally complex decisions." Investors in the stock market, scientists on a research project, even kids at a county fair guessing the number of beans in a jar can be smart groups, he says. That is, if their members are diverse, independent-minded, and use a mechanism such as voting, auctioning, or averaging to reach a collective, **aggregate** decision.

R That's the wonderful appeal of swarm intelligence. Whether we're talking about ants, bees, or humans, the ingredients of smart group behavior—decentralized control, response to local cues, simple rules of thumb—add up to an effective strategy to cope with complexity.

S Consider the way an Internet search engine like Google uses group smarts to find what you're looking for. When you type in a search query, the engine surveys billions of Web pages on its **index** servers to identify the most relevant ones. It then ranks them by the number of

4 A **drone** is a male bee that does not work but can fertilize the queen. The term can also be used to describe one who performs menial or tedious work.

5 A **quorum** is the minimum number of members required to be present in a meeting before any business can be transacted.

6 A **ballot** occurs when people select a representative or course of action by voting.

pages that link to them, counting links as votes. The most popular sites get weighted votes[7] since they're more likely to be reliable, and the pages that receive the most votes are listed first in the search results.

T With free collaborative encyclopedias available to anyone online, "it's now possible for huge numbers of people to think together in ways we never imagined a few decades ago," says Thomas Malone of the Massachusetts Institute of Technology (MIT) Center for Collective Intelligence. "No single person knows everything that's needed to deal with problems we face as a society, such as health care or climate change, but collectively we know far more than we've been able to tap[8] so far."

U Such thoughts underline an important truth about collective intelligence: Crowds are wise only if individual members act responsibly and make their own decisions. A group won't be smart if its members imitate one another, unthinkingly follow fads, or wait for someone to tell them what to do. When a group is being intelligent, whether it's made up of ants or attorneys,[9] it relies on its members to do their own part. For those of us who sometimes wonder if it's really worth recycling that extra bottle to lighten our impact on the planet, the fact is that our actions matter, even if we don't see how.

V "A honeybee never sees the big picture any more than you or I do," says Thomas D. Seeley, the bee expert. "None of us knows what society as a whole needs, but we look around and say, oh, they need someone to volunteer at school, or mow the church lawn, or help in a political campaign." If you're looking for a role model in a world of complexity, you could do worse than to imitate an ant or a bee.

---

7 **Weighted voting** systems are voting systems based on the idea that not all voters are equal.

8 When we **tap** something, like a resource, we access and use it.

9 **Attorneys** is another term used for lawyers.

ARTICULATE ANTS

Weaver ants communicate with each other by combining physical movements with chemical signals from their glands.

Rectal gland

Sternal gland

Mandibular gland

We have food

- CHEMICAL SIGNAL
Ant lays odor trail to food site using rectal gland.

- MOVEMENT
When meeting another worker, ant waves head and mimes offering food.

There's an intruder nearby

- Ant emits alarm pheromones from mandibular gland.

- Ant drags abdomen and leaves a short, looping trail from sternal gland.

Join a new nest

- Ant uses rectal gland to lay odor trail to new nest site.

- Ant jerks its body, tugs on nest mate's mandibles.

READING COMPREHENSION

A. Choose the best answer for each question.

MAIN IDEA

1. What is the main idea of the passage?

    a. Although colonies of ants display intelligence, they are not as smart as colonies of bees.

    b. Insects such as ants and bees can teach humans lessons about collective decision-making.

    c. Individual ants and bees are far more intelligent than other types of insects.

    d. A group of humans that uses the bees' methods of decision-making will be smarter than one that doesn't.

INFERENCE

2. In paragraph A, what does the author imply?

    a. He has changed his mind about the behavior of ants.

    b. He has performed research on ants himself.

    c. He was not really interested in ants until he wrote this article.

    d. He now believes that ants can make coherent plans.

RHETORICAL PURPOSE

3. Why does the author quote Deborah M. Gordon in paragraph C?

    a. to present an idea that supports his own point of view

    b. to show how much ants have learned in 140 million years

    c. to support the idea that individual ants are not intelligent

    d. to explain why ants travel in a large group

REFERENCE

4. The word *it* in the last sentence of paragraph C refers to _____.

    a. the shortest path

    b. an ant colony

    c. solving difficult problems

    d. the best food source

DETAIL

5. According to the information in paragraph E, what is the primary role of queen ants?

    a. They manage the worker ants.

    b. They create more members of the colony.

    c. They command warrior ants on raids.

    d. They allow the colony to operate as a single entity.

RHETORICAL PURPOSE

6. How does Charles N. Harper explain the concept of a pheromone trail in paragraph I?

    a. by contrasting it with a computer program

    b. by explaining the chemical composition of pheromones

    c. by comparing it with a similar human activity

    d. by giving examples of several types of pheromone trails

UNDERSTANDING INFOGRAPHICS

7. According to the infographic *Articulate Ants*, what does a weaver ant NOT do when an intruder is nearby?

    a. release pheromones

    b. drag its abdomen

    c. wave its head

    d. leave a trail

B. Choose the best heading for each section of the passage.

1. Paragraphs A–B

   a. The Ant's Plan   b. Are Ants Clever?   c. How Ants March

2. Paragraphs C–F

   a. A Lack of Leadership   b. Swarm Intelligence   c. Role of the Queen

3. Paragraphs G–K

   a. Ants as Computers   b. Finding the Smartest Ants   c. Real World Applications

4. Paragraphs L–Q

   a. Decision-Making Bees   b. Flaws of Centralization   c. Artificial Pheromones

5. Paragraphs R–T

   a. The Google Problem   b. How Insects "Vote"   c. Dealing with Complexity

6. Paragraphs U–V

   a. The Crowd is Right   b. Individuals Matter   c. A Honeybee Expert

CRITICAL THINKING Identifying Pros and Cons   Look back at paragraphs R–T. Note answers to the questions below. Discuss your ideas with a partner.

▶ What are some other examples of collective intelligence in human society?

_____

▶ Do you think collective decision-making usually results in a positive outcome? Can you think of any exceptions?

_____

▶ What are some pros and cons of applying swarm intelligence to human activities on the Internet?

_____

A flock of starlings fly in formation over Suffolk, England.

Making Inferences (2)

Not all details are stated directly in a text. Often a reader will need to make inferences—to look at other details and references to work out what is being stated. Look at the example from Reading A.

I used to think ants knew what they were doing.

Though it is not stated directly, we can infer from the author's use of "used to" that he has changed his opinion about ants.

Making inferences is also an important skill for taking exams. Questions of this type will often contain words like "imply," "suggest," or "infer." For example:

In paragraph A, what does the author imply/suggest?
According to the passage, we can reasonably infer that …
Based on the passage, it could be suggested that …

MAKING
INFERENCES

A. Choose the best answer for each question.

1. According to the information in paragraph E, we can reasonably infer that an ant colony would not work if _____.

   a. there was more than one queen
   b. it grew to over half a million ants
   c. the queen made decisions

2. Based on the information in the passage about swarm intelligence theory, it could be suggested that a successful business should _____.

   a. hire workers who are likely to follow orders
   b. ensure workers spend enough time with their families
   c. encourage a democratic approach to decision-making

3. What first step would Thomas Seeley likely agree is the best way to start a business meeting?

   a. see what other companies do
   b. brainstorm ideas openly
   c. have a secret vote to elect a leader

4. In paragraphs M–O, what does the author imply?

   a. Only some scouts communicate information by dancing.
   b. The researchers could guess which home the bees would choose.
   c. The scouts moved as a group and visited each box in turn.

5. Based on the reading passage, we can infer that _____ is an example of swarm intelligence.

   a. a political party that follows the teaching of a charismatic leader
   b. a collaborative travel website where users share tips and resources
   c. a crowd at a rock concert that refuses to follow any rules or regulations

JUSTIFYING

B. Work with a partner. Compare your answers to the questions in Activity A and explain your reasoning.

COMPLETION **A.** Complete the information by circling the correct words.

For animals in the wild—such as caribou—traveling in very large groups offers several advantages. Biologist Karsten Heuer has spent years studying caribou. During one expedition, he spotted a wolf creeping into the ¹**code** / **territory** of a caribou herd, causing one animal to turn and run. This movement was a message to the rest of the herd. The caribou near it ran in all directions, confusing it, but the rest ran in a(n) ²**imitated** / **coherent** and orderly mass. In the end, the entire herd escaped—and the wolf was left exhausted.

△ **Migrating caribou in Alaska, USA**

Each individual caribou was engaged in its own life or death struggle, and yet the ³**aggregate** / **procedure** behavior of the herd was characterized by precision, not fright. Every caribou knew the ⁴**criteria** / **territory** that determined when and where to run, even if it didn't know exactly why. Swarm intelligence ensured that each animal followed simple ⁵**faculties** / **protocols** evolved over thousands of years.

DEFINITIONS **B.** Match each word in the box with its definition.

code	faculty	imitate	index	procedure

1. _____: to copy behavior

2. _____: an alphabetical list of items used for reference

3. _____: an established or official way of doing something

4. _____: the teaching staff at a university or college

5. _____: a system of signs, symbols, or movements that has a meaning

COLLOCATIONS **C.** The nouns in the box are commonly used with the adjective **coherent**. Complete the sentences using the correct words.

message	strategy	whole

1. While comprised of thousands of individuals, an ant colony functions as a coherent _____.

2. The dances performed by honeybees convey a coherent _____ to the rest of their colony.

3. The company's leaders met to develop a coherent _____ for the next financial year.

> According to Dr. E. O. Wilson, ants are one of the world's most successful **organisms**. They are also the planet's principle **scavengers**, helping keep the forest **habitats** clear and healthy.

8B

BEFORE YOU READ

DEFINITIONS **A.** Look at the photo and read the caption. Match each word in **bold** with its definition.

1. an animal that feeds on dead or decaying matter •   • a. habitat
2. an animal or a plant •   • b. scavenger
3. an animal's natural home or environment •   • c. organism

PREDICTING **B.** Reading B is an interview with the American biologist and author Edward O. Wilson. Skim the passage and note three topics you think the interview will cover. Then read the whole passage to check your ideas.

_____

_____

_____

OF ANTS AND HUMANS

E. O. Wilson, one of the world's foremost authorities on biodiversity, discusses his lifelong love of the natural world, including its smallest members.

∧ **Leafcutter ants can carry leaf pieces that weigh 20 times their own weight.**

A **National Geographic:** How did you develop a passion for nature?

Edward O. Wilson: When I was nine years old and living in Washington, D.C., I somehow got excited about the idea of expeditions to far-off jungles to collect the sorts of things you saw in *National Geographic.* So I decided I would do some expeditions to Rock Creek Park,[1] and I got bottles and everything, and I started collecting there. I would go on my own and wander for hours. Then I went to the National Zoo, which was paradise on Earth for me. How could you avoid becoming a naturalist in that kind of environment?

B **NG:** Is that kind of exploration a rarer experience for kids today?

Wilson: I worry about that. I have no data, but it appears to me that many of our young people are staying at home or being influenced by an increasingly stimulating "artifactual" world. **Fake** nature, sci-fi movies, videos, being drawn into lives that are pursued in front of a computer. That's a trend that would take young people away from a naturalist's experience. But there are counter-influences. More people go to zoos in the United States than attend professional sports; did you know that? There's a strong pull remaining that I think is primal.

C **NG:** Darwin loved beetles. What was it about ants for you?

Wilson: Originally, I was going to work on flies because I felt that was a wide-open area to do exploration, but I couldn't get the special insect pins to collect them. It was 1946, just after the Second World War, and those pins were not available. So, I turned to ants because I could collect them in bottles of alcohol.

D **NG:** Do some say that this isn't serious science, it's just collecting?

Wilson: Well, when people say that sort of thing, you can respond quickly that you're not going to get anywhere until you do this science, and furthermore, you're going to make all sorts of new discoveries while you're doing it. You never know when someone is going to be looking for some kind of lead in this growing body of information from mapping life on Earth.

---

1 **Rock Creek Park** is an urban park in Washington, D.C.

For instance, someone might say, "What I need for my work is an ant that hunts underwater and walks around submarine fashion and then comes out and goes back to a dry nest. Does any such thing exist?" It turns out, yes!

E **NG:** A submarine ant?
Wilson: Yes, in Malaysia, on the pitcher plant *Nepenthes*. This plant collects water in which insects fall and drown, and there are substances in the water that help digest the insects. *Nepenthes* gets **organic** material from the insects it captures. There is this ant that lives on *Nepenthes*, and the workers walk in, right down into the mouth of hell. They just walk right in submarine-like and pick up insects that have fallen to the bottom.

F **NG:** Are you doing any field trips these days?
Wilson: I get together with younger ant specialists—they all seem younger to me, these days—and we go into the field. On a recent trip to the Dominican Republic, we went up to 2.4 kilometers above sea level. Most people don't know the Dominican Republic has mountains. We were all the way up in cold pine forests, discovering new species at every mountain site.

G **NG:** There's no feeling that the world has been conquered now?
Wilson: Oh, no. That's the point—we're just beginning exploration. For animals, we probably know as few as 10 percent of the species. Even in a fairly familiar group like ants, we're discovering them right and left. I estimate that maybe half the ants in the world remain undiscovered.

H **NG:** How well did Darwin know his ants?
Wilson: Darwin knew his ants very well. He spent a lot of time watching ants, and part of the reason was that ants **exemplified** a peculiarity that he said might have proved **fatal** to his theory of evolution. And that potential flaw was that worker ants are so completely different from queen ants, yet they are **sterile**. So how would you explain that by natural selection? If worker ants couldn't have offspring, how are their traits developed and passed on?

I **NG:** The problem was how this kind of self-sacrifice—tending the queen while giving up reproduction—evolved?
Wilson: Yes, and Darwin solved the problem: What counts is the group, and that worker ants are just part of the colony, just an extension of the queen. Her heredity is what matters. If she is producing separate organisms that serve her purpose, then all together, these colonies can prevail over **solitary** individuals. That was the solution, and actually, that isn't too far from the way we see it today. The most recent theories [are] spelled out in a book that Bert Hölldobler and I wrote called *The Superorganism*.

J **NG:** Why that title?
Wilson: The colony is the next level of biological organization. The colony, by group selection, has developed traits that could not be possible otherwise—communication, the "caste" system,[2] cooperative behavior. It's a unit of activity and of evolution. One colony against another is what's being selected. This happens to be close to Darwin's idea but in modern genetic terms.

K **NG:** How does this kind of social behavior get started?
Wilson: It has to do with defense against enemies. Naturalists have discovered more and more groups that have **altruistic** workers and soldiers—ants, termites, certain beetles, shrimp, and even a mammal, the naked mole rat. What's **consistently** the case is that these animals have a resource, usually a place to live with food, that's very valuable. If you're a solitary individual and you build a chamber like that, somebody could chuck you out.[3] The idea is that these lines are going to find it advantageous to develop sterile castes for maintaining and protecting the colony.

L **NG:** So, this is a story about community and home.
Wilson: I've learned my lesson about jumping from ants or sponges to humans! But it does, in my opinion, call for another look at human

---

2 A **caste system** is a rigid hereditary system of social ranking.
3 When you **chuck** something **out**, you throw it out.

origins. Anthropologists now pretty much agree that a major factor in human origins was having a habitation, a campsite, which allowed for certain specialization, where some stayed and looked after the site and the young and so on, while others ventured out to bring food back. And the pressures from predators must have been pretty intense.

M **NG:** But we don't have sterile castes.
Wilson: No, we have a division of labor. That is very true, and that's a fundamental difference between us and insects and these other creatures, and that's why we have to be very careful about drawing analogies. Because human beings are so flexible and intelligent, we can divide labor without physical castes.

N **NG:** That system has worked pretty well for ants.
Wilson: They dominate ecosystems. In tropical forests, from one study, ants alone make up four times the weight of all the land vertebrates put together—amphibians, reptiles, birds, mammals. The weight of all the ants in the world is roughly the weight of all the humans ... They are the principal predators of small animals, the principal scavengers in much of the world, and the principal turners of the soil.

O **NG:** It's interesting that ants and humans are both social and that both dominate their environment.
Wilson: Sure enough, we're the one highly social vertebrate with altruism and high levels of division of labor, though not sterility. We're the one species that has reached this level, and we dominate.

P **NG:** We also have a tremendous effect on other species.
Wilson: More than any kind of ant. But I'm always at risk of having it said, "That nut[4] wants to compare ants and humans." Well, obviously not. Beyond the fact that we both reached high levels of social behavior based on altruism and division of labor, the resemblance between humans and ants pretty much comes to an end. For example, they communicate almost entirely by taste and smell. They live in a sensory world that's totally different from humans. It's like ants are from another planet. And ants are constantly at war. Well, so are we! But they are the most warlike of animals.

Q **NG:** It makes you wonder whether war and complex societies go together.
Wilson: It may turn out that highly evolved societies with this level of altruism tend strongly to divide into groups that then fight against each other. We humans are constantly at war and have been since prehistory. I know a lot of people would like to believe that this is just a nasty habit we developed, just a cultural **anomaly**, and all we have to do is get enlightened[5] and drop it. I hope that's true.

R **NG:** Do the ants offer any lessons?
Wilson: At least not any we would care to put in practice. Ant colonies are all female; males are tolerated only part of the year. Slavery and cannibalism[6] are commonplace. There is one lesson we have already learned, however: Ants keep themselves **fanatically** clean, so epidemics[7] are rare.

S **NG:** But now ants and many other creatures are threatened with extinction. Are you hopeful that we can save enough in time?
Wilson: Actually, I am. The best funded global conservation organizations are now scoring successes in persuading developing countries to set up sustainable reserves—sustainable meaning they provide an actual increase in the quality of life for people living in and around them. That doesn't take as much money as some have thought. It can be achieved in many of these countries where the greatest destruction is occurring because incomes may be just a few hundred dollars a year. There are reasons to believe that where most of the biodiversity occurs—the tropical forest, grasslands, and shallow marine areas—a lot can be saved.

---

4 The term **nut** is sometimes used to describe someone who is eccentric.
5 An **enlightened** person is someone who has great understanding and is therefore tolerant and unprejudiced.
6 **Cannibalism** is the eating of an animal by an animal of its own kind.
7 **Epidemics** are widespread occurrences of a disease.

A. Choose the best answer for each question.

DETAIL **1.** Why did E. O. Wilson study ants and not flies?

    a. He found ants much more interesting than flies.
    b. He couldn't find the equipment he needed to study flies.
    c. He was inspired by the works of Charles Darwin to study ants.
    d. He liked the idea that the study of ants was wide open.

DETAIL **2.** What is *Nepenthes*?

    a. a plant that grows underwater
    b. an insect that is digested by certain plants
    c. a submarine ant from Malaysia
    d. a plant that captures insects

DETAIL **3.** According to Wilson, what would many people find surprising about the Dominican Republic?

    a. It has mountainous areas.
    b. It has cold pine forests.
    c. It has many species of ants.
    d. It is located in the Caribbean.

DETAIL **4.** What is the book *The Superorganism* about?

    a. newly discovered species of insects and their importance
    b. the idea that worker insects were once fertile
    c. theories about the role of colonies in the evolution of species
    d. species of animals that were researched by Darwin

REFERENCE **5.** In paragraph L, the word *some* refers to _____.

    a. anthropologists
    b. ancient humans
    c. predators
    d. ants or sponges

RHETORICAL PURPOSE **6.** Wilson mentions the statistics in paragraph N to _____.

    a. present the results of some research that he recently completed
    b. show that there are more types of ants than of any other animals
    c. indicate that ants are one of the world's most dominant species
    d. compare the number of ants in the tropics with the number of ants elsewhere

MAIN IDEA **7.** According to Wilson's responses, how are humans unique?

    a. We are the most warlike of all the creatures on the Earth.
    b. We have division of labor but no biological castes.
    c. We have a strong effect on other species with which we share territory.
    d. We are the only social creatures that do not form colonies.

B. Are the following statements true or false according to the reading passage, or is the information not given? Circle **T** (true), **F** (false), or **NG** (not given).

1. According to Wilson, more people visit zoos in the United States than attend professional sporting events. **T F NG**

2. The insects that fall to the bottom of the water inside the Malaysian pitcher plant are mostly ants. **T F NG**

3. Darwin spent more time studying ants than he did studying beetles. **T F NG**

4. Solitary animals find it more difficult to maintain and defend a nest than colonial animals. **T F NG**

5. The average human weighs about the same as a million ants. **T F NG**

6. Ants communicate by taste and smell because they evolved in dark conditions. **T F NG**

7. Female ants are usually not found in ant colonies. **T F NG**

8. Ants keep themselves so clean that epidemics seldom occur in ant colonies. **T F NG**

CRITICAL THINKING Analyzing Arguments

▶ In what ways does E. O. Wilson think ants are similar to humans? Check (✓) the areas which have similarities.

☐ Social behavior ☐ Conflict resolution ☐ Reproduction

☐ Division of labor ☐ Habitation

▶ Discuss your answers with a partner. How are ants similar to humans?

Workers dismantle scaffolding from the façade of a museum in Moscow, Russia. Like ants, humans are able to complete complex tasks via a division of labor.

Identifying Multiple Answers to Questions

On some standardized exams, certain multiple-choice questions may have more than one correct answer. These types of questions usually have five options. While all the options may be true, you must identify the ones *mentioned in the text*.

Always read the instructions carefully and note how many answers you need to identify. Determine what is being asked and find the section of the passage that contains the answers. As with any scanning task, look for key words, synonyms, and paraphrases.

SCANNING **A. Read each question carefully and follow the instructions. Circle the best answers.**

1. Which TWO activities did E. O. Wilson say he did as a child?

   a. He moved to Washington, D.C.
   b. He went to a park in Washington, D.C.
   c. He went to sports events.
   d. He visited the zoo.
   e. He took a trip to the Dominican Republic.

2. What TWO examples does E.O. Wilson give to support his claim that "we're just beginning exploration"?

   a. The plant *Nepenthes* was only discovered a few years ago.
   b. Scientists have only discovered about 10 percent of all animal species.
   c. An estimated 50% of ant species remain undiscovered.
   d. There are areas of the Dominican Republic that no one has visited before.
   e. Scientists still can't explain why worker ants are sterile.

3. What TWO examples does E.O. Wilson give to support his claim that ants "dominate ecosystems"?

   a. In tropical forests, there are four times as many ants as there are mammals.
   b. The weight of all the world's ants is about the same as the weight of all humans.
   c. Ants are the world's primary predators of small animals.
   d. Ants have a greater effect on other species than humans do.
   e. Ants are one of the only animal species not threatened with extinction.

4. Which TWO features does E. O. Wilson say are common in an ant colony?

   a. There can be more than one queen.
   b. They are populated by females for most of the year.
   c. They can be built in trees.
   d. They can connect to other ant colonies.
   e. They are clean.

COMPLETION **A.** Complete the information by circling the correct words.

When it comes to war, army ant colonies ¹**fake** / **exemplify** an extreme fighting spirit. Army ants are able to kill prey vastly larger than themselves. Although a ²**consistently** / **solitary** ant can do no real damage, a large swarm can inflict ³**fatal** / **sterile** attacks on thousands of insects and small animals within hours.

Although violent, attacks by army ants also benefit the forest by helping maintain biodiversity. The ants turn the soil, move nutrients and ⁴**altruistic** / **organic** matter, and help disperse seeds. The devastation left by an ant raid also creates opportunities for new species to enter the habitat.

△ **A team of ants forms a ladder to reach a leaf.**

DEFINITIONS **B.** Complete the sentences. Circle the correct options.

1. An **anomaly** is something *better than* / *different from* what is usual.
2. Something **consistent** is done in *the same* / *a different* way over time.
3. If something is **fake**, it's not *real* / *cheap*.
4. Something done **fanatically** is done in *a funny* / *an extreme* way.
5. An animal that is **sterile** is unable to *live a long life* / *produce young*.
6. Someone who is **altruistic** is *unselfish* / *unreliable*.

COLLOCATIONS **C.** The nouns in the box are frequently used with the adjective **fatal**. Complete the sentences using the correct words. One word is extra.

accident	blow	illness	shootings

1. Police are investigating a fatal _____ involving three cars.
2. Cancer is not always a fatal _____. There are many cancer survivors.
3. Unless we get guns off the streets, I fear there will be more fatal _____.

CRANE MIGRATION

> Around 600,000 sandhill cranes flock to Nebraska's Central Platte River Valley each spring in one of the world's largest bird migrations.

BEFORE YOU WATCH

DEFINITIONS **A.** The words in **bold** appear in the video. Match each one with its definition. Use a dictionary to help.

1. **abundant** •
2. **adapt** •
3. **coexist** •
4. **migration** •
5. **resilience** •

- a. (v) to live together with success
- b. (n) the ability to survive challenging or damaging events
- c. (v) to change in order to cope with a new situation
- d. (n) the act of moving from one place to another
- e. (adj) large in number or quantity

PREVIEWING **B.** Read the excerpts from the video. Complete the sentences using the correct form of the words in Activity A.

1. "This is [...] without doubt, one of the most spectacular _____ that you can witness in North America."

2. "[The cranes] are gone before we put seed in the ground, so we really _____ pretty well."

3. "It's another measure of their _____ and their opportunism; they're taking advantage of a new food source."

4. "These birds are _____ to water, [...] and water obviously is affected by climate."

5. "So just because the cranes are _____, it doesn't mean they're not fragile."

GIST **A.** Watch the video. Check your answers in Before You Watch B.

DETAILS **B.** Watch the video again. Note answers to the questions.

1. How long have the cranes been doing this migration?

_____

2. What is "staging"?

_____

3. What do the cranes mainly eat?

_____

4. What is the main threat to sandhill cranes?

_____

5. How has climate change affected the sandhill cranes' migration?

_____

6. What happened to sandhill cranes in the 1930s?

_____

^ **A sandhill crane**

CRITICAL THINKING Applying Ideas   Consider what you learned in Reading A. In what ways do you think sandhill cranes might make use of swarm intelligence? Note some ideas below, then discuss with a partner.

_____

_____

_____

VOCABULARY REVIEW

Do you remember the meanings of these words? Check (✓) the ones you know. Look back at the unit and review any words you're not sure of.

Reading A

☐ aggregate* ☐ code* ☐ coherent* ☐ criteria* ☐ faculty

☐ imitate ☐ index* ☐ procedure* ☐ protocol* ☐ territory

Reading B

☐ altruistic ☐ anomaly ☐ consistently* ☐ exemplify ☐ fake

☐ fanatically ☐ fatal ☐ organic ☐ solitary ☐ sterile

* Academic Word List

CREATIVITY

9

Researchers in Italy use ultraviolet light to search behind a 16th-century mural for a lost Leonardo da Vinci painting.

Discuss these questions with a partner.

1. Who do you think were the most creative people in the past?

2. To what extent is creativity something that people are born with?

BEFORE YOU READ

A. Look at the photo and read the caption. What do you know about Leonardo da Vinci? Discuss your ideas with a partner.

B. Quickly scan the reading passage. Which of Leonardo da Vinci's works of art does the author discuss? Note them below.

_____

_____

Visitors take photos of the Mona Lisa at the Louvre Museum, Paris.

DECODING LEONARDO

A According to legend, in the year 1505 near the Tuscan town of Fiesole, a great bird rose from Monte Ceceri (Swan Mountain) and took to the air. No witness testimony remains of the event, but if anyone was present on that hillside, the most likely candidate is Leonardo da Vinci, a man whose ambition for many years had been to fly like a bird. Some 50 years later, an acquaintance, Gerolamo Cardano, wrote, "Leonardo da Vinci ... attempted to fly, but failed. He was an excellent painter."

B To call Leonardo an excellent painter is like labeling Shakespeare a clever wordsmith.[1] He was a true genius, recognized in his own time and idolized in ours. His paintings are as secret and seductive as himself, done with the hand of an angel, the intellect of a scientist, and the soul of a romantic. His drawings are among the most beautiful ever made; his most treasured painting, the *Mona Lisa*, is undoubtedly the most famous in the world.

C His love of painting notwithstanding, it was knowledge itself that was Leonardo's great love—knowledge, and the experience from which it may be drawn. To acquire it, Leonardo turned to a diverse array of fields: mathematics, geometry, optics, astronomy, geology, botany, zoology, hydraulics, mechanics, and anatomy, as well as painting and drawing. As an engineer, he could think in four dimensions, visualizing not only the shapes of mechanical parts but also their interrelated motions.

D Among his designs for flight, Leonardo imagined parachutes, landing equipment, even an aerial screw that acted like the blades of a helicopter. But, like so much else in his life, Leonardo's attempts to actually create a workable flying machine are a mystery. There remains only one enigmatic[2] reference, in a notebook characteristically filled with phrases and sketches, in which he proclaims that his great bird "will bring eternal glory to the nest where it was born ..."

Birth of a Genius

E Leonardo da Vinci was born in 1452, the illegitimate child of a peasant girl named Caterina and respected notary[3] Piero da Vinci. Leonardo lived at first with his mother in a three-room stone house on a hill just outside the village of Vinci, some 20 kilometers west of Florence. In that idyllic Tuscan countryside began the youngster's lifelong love of nature—a love that would remain **implicit** in all his later works.

---

1 A **wordsmith** is someone who is good with words and language.
2 A person, thing, or situation that is **enigmatic** is mysterious or puzzling.
3 A **notary** is a clerk licensed to prepare legal documents.

F Around 1469, Leonardo's father took him to Florence, where the statesman Lorenzo de Medici had established a society that actively encouraged all forms of artistic expression. For years, art had been an instrument of religious expression, and the **parameters** of what was **ideologically** acceptable had been decided by the Church. But in the more tolerant atmosphere of Florence, painters represented things as they saw them, rather than as the Church said they must be. It was a society well suited to the ever-questioning country boy.

G Leonardo commenced an apprenticeship at the **academy** of Andrea del Verrocchio, with whom he studied for at least six years. The boy mastered every medium and continued his studies of nature, discovering so much so fast that it seemed to him that everything must eventually be revealed to his searching. In painting, he not only outshone his more mature colleagues but also his teacher. Assigned to paint the figure of an angel, he gave it a whole new dimension that drew the viewer directly into the painting, in a way that Verrocchio's inhibited style could never do. Some say that Verrocchio never painted again.

Early Masterworks

H Leonardo left Florence in 1482 at the age of 30, and he stayed away for 18 years. The young Florentine hoped to find the glory he sought in the court of Ludovico Sforza, ruler of Milan. A practical city, Milan cared more for knowledge than for the arts. Leonardo came as a musician but presented himself as an engineer, describing in a long boastful letter his inventiveness in the field of weapons. He assured Sforza that, "... also I can do in painting whatever may be done, as well as any other, whoever he may be."

I It was as an artist that Leonardo was accepted. He established an art factory much like Verrocchio's shop in Florence and at once accepted assignments. These included a portrait of Sforza's beautiful and learned mistress Cecilia Gallerani, a portrait of a musician that some scholars believe is really a self-portrait, and a brilliant early version of *Virgin of the Rocks*, begun in 1483 and now in the Louvre.

J Around 1485 he began his notebooks. These are detailed, cryptic[4] compilations of material on a seemingly **arbitrary** range of topics, from geology and geometry to anatomy and astronomy, all interwoven as one burning interest gave way to the next. His notes are written left-handed from right to left, and there are sketches everywhere that complement his text. His discussions were addressed to himself, leaving an extraordinary record of the movements of his mind.

Bronze Horse and Last Supper

K Two great works mark Leonardo's years with Sforza: One was to be a bronze statue of the duke's late father as a conquering hero riding a horse. The other, ordered by Sforza for his favorite church, was a "Last Supper." The themes were not unlike other **commissions** of the time, but if the subjects lacked originality, their treatment did not.

L The horse was to be colossal, in a pose full of motion and life, and the concept was so bold, so ambitious, that it finally brought the artist the praise he sought. His contemporaries thought it could not be created, but Leonardo devised workable

---

4 Something that is **cryptic** is mysterious in meaning, puzzling, or ambiguous.

plans. Sadly, he was **denied** the chance to complete his project; war broke out, and the bronze was used for cannons instead.

M *The Last Supper*, too, was presented as never before. Leonardo arranged the 13 figures in a brilliant composition reflecting the terrible moment following Christ's words, "One of you shall betray me." He gave the figures deep emotions, varying according to their natures, perfectly illustrating the intention of each subject's soul.

N Unfortunately, Leonardo's brilliance was not matched by his planning. He hated deadlines and fixed schedules; painting fresco (that is, on freshly prepared plaster) imposed both. So he worked with oil mixtures, which could be applied whenever the mood struck him. The technique suited the artist, but not the wall; the paint soon blistered and began to peel away from the damp surface. With his doomed masterworks behind him, Leonardo left Milan, and in the spring of 1500, he was back in Florence.

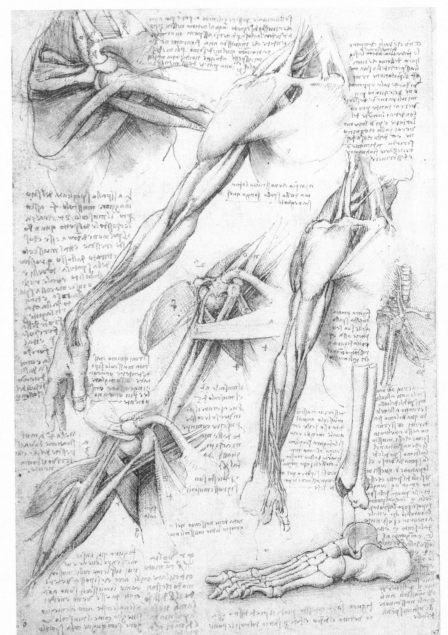

∧ **A page from a Leonardo da Vinci notebook, filled with anatomical sketches and notes**

Battle of the Giants

O Leonardo came home a famous man. No one knew or cared much about his science and his inventions, but everyone had heard of his horse and his *Last Supper*.

P Many of his competitors had either died or gone to Rome. His most serious rival was Michelangelo Buonarroti, 23 years his junior, surly,[5] ambitious, and a great painter. The two Florentines hated each other wholeheartedly.

Q Once again, two great works drew Leonardo's artistic effort: One was a huge mural for the Council Chamber depicting the Battle of Anghiari, an important political victory for Florence. The other was a life-size portrait of a middle-class woman. He

---

5 Someone who is **surly** is usually bad-tempered and rude.

worked on the paintings **concurrently**, the portrait offering him pleasant relief from the subject of the battle.

R Some say the subject of the portrait is Lisa, wife of Florentine merchant Francesco del Giocondo, while others suggest different identities. Known today as *Mona Lisa*, it hangs in the Louvre, glass shrouded and guarded. Its colors have suffered a strange change, as if bathed in undersea light, but the lady still glows with an inner radiance, both troubling and serene.

S The battle scene thrust Leonardo into an artistic rivalry with Michelangelo, who was to paint another wall of the same chamber. The rivals did their **preliminary** sketches in separate quarters. Both sketches were magnificent in their own way: The younger man's picture of male bathers interrupted by a call to arms was as dynamic as Leonardo's cavalry[6] confrontation. Benvenuto Cellini, who saw them both while they were still intact, wrote that "they were the school of the world."

T Michelangelo never transferred his **draft** to the Council Chamber wall. Leonardo did, or at least, he began to. Forgetting the fate of *The Last Supper* (or perhaps not yet aware of it), he again used an oil paint for greater freedom and brighter colors. The paint, however, soon began to flake and run. The work was doomed, another masterpiece lost—at least until its traces were rediscovered in the 1970s.

A Life Unfinished

U Leonardo now turned from art to his old love: flight. By this time, his knowledge went far beyond the limits of his age and was approaching the understanding that much later gave men wings. But his efforts, including his legendary attempt on Monte Ceceri, brought him no satisfaction, only the certainty that he himself would never fly or witness manned flight.

V In 1513, Leonardo journeyed south to Rome to work for the new pope, Leo X; three years later, he set out once again, this time for France, on the last journey of his life. France's young new king, Francis I, regarded Leonardo as the wisest of men and wanted him nearby, whether he painted or not. Thus, he lived the three remaining years of his life in a small chateau in the peaceful landscape near Amboise.

W In his heart, Leonardo felt defeat. His greatest works crumbling, his great knowledge undisclosed, Leonardo grieved for what might have been, for all the wondrous, unfinished projects that forever filled his extraordinary mind. He had no way to know that the few magnificent works he did complete would alone make his name immortal. And so the universal man—symbol of his time and anticipator[7] of ours— passed into eternal fame.

---

6 The **cavalry** is the part of an army that is mounted on horseback.

7 An **anticipator** is someone who foresees future events.

The Art of War

Leonardo's innovations were often conceptual experiments developed for patrons or his own amusement. Even though he called war a "beastly madness," Leonardo was attracted to the creative challenge of imagining tools that amplified human strength. Most of his weapons were never built.

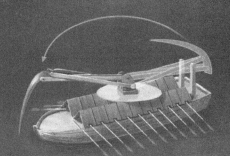

Manuscript B, f 98r

Armored carriage, ca 1487–1490
A fresh take on a concept from the Middle Ages, Leonardo's tank had new movement systems, and a ring of cannons for a 360-degree attack. It would require eight men to turn the cranks to move the wheels.

British Museum

Sail shredder, ca 1484–86
A blade on a wooden pole rotates 360 degrees and—when activated by rowers—can tear through ships and masts of enemy ships.

Wheels

Cranks

Eight men would turn the cranks to move the wheels. A turret helped them aim.

Giant crossbow, ca 1485–1490
More than 30 drawings illustrate Leonardo's ambitions for a crossbow that would shoot cannonballs. It was built, but not during his lifetime.

Screw   Trigger   Stone

Width: 25 meters

Codex Atlanticus, f 149 Br

He specified that the armature should be composed of strips of wooden beams, joined for better flexibility.

① The bow is aimed left and right by lifting the back and pivoting the front wheels.

② A gear connected to a screw is rotated, pulling back the ropes and trigger.

③ Men load the bow with a 100-pound stone, and activate the trigger by a lever or a hammer blow.

A. Choose the best answer for each question.

GIST

1. What does the author say about Leonardo in paragraph B?

 a. Today he is considered much more talented than Shakespeare.
 b. He was known in his own era and is greatly respected today.
 c. His drawings are thought to be more beautiful than his paintings.
 d. His painting *Mona Lisa* was not well-known when he first painted it.

REFERENCE

2. The word *it* in the second sentence of paragraph C refers to _____.

 a. love   b. experience   c. knowledge   d. painting

INFERENCE

3. In paragraph G, the author implies that Verrocchio _____.

 a. was not able to teach Leonardo much because he was not a very good painter
 b. was a great inspiration for his apprentice Leonardo
 c. taught Leonardo more about nature than about the art of painting
 d. stopped painting because he was not as skillful as Leonardo

DETAIL

4. The metal for the bronze horse sculpture was eventually _____.

 a. used to create other works of art
 b. stolen by enemies of Milan
 c. used to make weapons
 d. used for plumbing in a palace

INFERENCE

5. The section title "Battle of the Giants" refers to _____.

 a. Cellini's criticism of Michelangelo and Leonardo
 b. Florence's victory at the battle of Anghiari
 c. the dispute about the identity of the subject of *Mona Lisa*
 d. the competition between Leonardo and Michelangelo

INFERENCE

6. What is the likely reason for Leonardo and Michelangelo's rivalry?

 a. They felt threatened by each other's talents.
 b. Michelangelo was jealous of Leonardo.
 c. Leonardo wanted art commissions that Michelangelo got.
 d. Michelangelo felt that Leonardo did not respect his work.

PARAPHRASE

7. In paragraph W, what does the author mean when he says, *He had no way to know that the few magnificent works he did complete would alone make his name immortal?*

 a. Leonardo could not predict that the few great works he finished would be enough to make him famous for years to come.
 b. Leonardo could not decide which of the works he produced were best and would make him famous after his death.
 c. At the end of his career, Leonardo had no way to be certain how many of his great works were still in existence.
 d. Although he produced many great works, Leonardo would be surprised to know that only a few are still famous.

B. Complete the information about key moments in Leonardo's life. Use dates and words from the reading passage. Then label the map (1–6) to show his movements over the course of his life.

1. _____–1469
   Leonardo da Vinci spends his childhood in the beautiful Tuscan _____.

2. 1469–1482
   Leonardo moves to Florence and studies art for at least _____ years with Andrea del Verrocchio.

3. _____–1500
   Leonardo sets up a studio in the court of Ludovico Sforza. There he paints a portrait of a musician (which some historians think is a _____ of the artist) and *The Last Supper*. He also begins writing in his famous _____.

4. 1500–_____
   Leonardo is commissioned to paint a giant _____ at the Council Chamber—in competition with Michelangelo.

5. _____–1516
   Leonardo goes to work for the Pope.

6. 1516–_____
   Leonardo works for the King of France.

CRITICAL THINKING Justifying Opinions

▶ Leonardo da Vinci was interested in many different fields. What accomplishments, if any, are mentioned in the reading passage for each of the fields below?

painting   engineering   anatomy   zoology
sculpture   cartography   architecture   science

▶ In your opinion, which accomplishment stands out above the others? Discuss with a partner.

▶ Can you think of anyone alive today who, like Leonardo, excels in multiple fields? Share your ideas with a partner.

Understanding Complex Infographics (2)

Many infographics make use of technical drawings to allow the reader to better visualize how complex objects such as machines work. The following are common techniques used in technical drawings:

- The same object is often drawn from **multiple perspectives** (e.g., front, side, top) to allow the reader a complete understanding of its shape.

- The **scale** of a drawing is indicated by giving measurements or by including drawings of people or everyday items such as houses or cars.

- A **cutaway drawing** is one in which selected parts of an object's surface are removed to show internal features.

- **Arrows** are used to show how parts of an object move.

- **Numbering** is used to show how the different parts of a machine connect to each other.

- **Labels** highlight key components.

ANALYZING **A.** Look back at the infographic The Art of War. Note answers to the questions below.

    1. How many different perspectives are given of the giant crossbow? _____

    2. Which object is presented as a cutaway drawing? _____

    3. How does the illustrator show the scale of the armored carriage? _____

UNDERSTANDING INFOGRAPHICS **B.** Choose the best answer for each question.

    1. Which of the drawings did Leonardo complete first?

        a. sail shredder   b. armored carriage   c. giant crossbow

    2. When the giant crossbow is preparing to fire, which of these happens last?

        a. the stone is loaded   b. the bow is aimed   c. the ropes are pulled back

    3. Around how high is the armored carriage?

        a. 3 meters   b. 6 meters   c. 9 meters

    4. How is the sail shredder powered?

        a. by water   b. by people   c. by wind

DISCUSSION **C.** According to the infographic, most of Leonardo's weapons were never built. What do you think are some possible reasons? Note your ideas below, then discuss with a partner.

_____

_____

_____

VOCABULARY PRACTICE

COMPLETION **A.** Complete the information using the correct form of the words in the box. One word is extra.

arbitrary	commission	concurrently	deny	draft	preliminary

Leonardo da Vinci primarily worked as a painter and received several large ¹_____ from some of the wealthiest people in Italy. But Leonardo was a restless multitasker—while painting, he worked ²_____ as a scientist and inventor. His notebooks are filled with notes and drawings on a vast variety of subjects. Very few of his paintings have survived, ³_____ many people the chance to see Leonardo's amazing work.

In 2019, 500 years after Leonardo's death, museums around the world celebrated his life and work. In Denver, museum-goers were able to see early ⁴_____ of his paintings, as well as models based on ⁵_____ designs for a helicopter, an airplane, and a submarine.

∧ **A museum visitor views a working model of a machine sketched by Leonardo da Vinci.**

DEFINITIONS **B.** Match each word in the box with its definition.

academy	arbitrary	ideology	implicit	parameter

1. _____: an institution for teaching and learning
2. _____: a limit or guideline
3. _____: expressed in an indirect way
4. _____: not based on any system or plan
5. _____: a set of beliefs on which actions are based

COLLOCATIONS **C.** The nouns in the box are often used with the word **deny**. Complete each sentence with the correct word.

access	opportunity	payment

1. Visitors without proper tickets are denied _____ to special exhibits in a museum.
2. If you pay for something with an expired credit card, your _____ will be denied.
3. Injury denied her the _____ to compete in the Olympics.

BEFORE YOU READ

DISCUSSION **A.** In what ways is your language similar to, and different from, English? Discuss with a partner.

SKIMMING AND PREDICTING **B.** Quickly look at the title, captions, and first two paragraphs of the reading passage. What topics do you think the author will cover? Note them below. Then read the rest of the article to check your predictions.

_____

_____

> Hieroglyphs cover the interior walls of the Ancient Egyptian temple Medinet Habu. This early system of writing required scribes to learn hundreds of distinct characters.

THE POWER OF WRITING

Joel L. Swerdlow investigates the history and future of one of humanity's most potent forms of artistic and cultural expression.

A   No other invention—perhaps only the wheel comes close—has had a longer and greater impact on humanity's development than writing. Written words have overthrown governments and changed the course of history. So powerful is writing that the beginnings of civilization and history are most often defined as the moment cultures develop it. The transformation of language into written words has immortalized passion, genius, art, and science.

B   Much of writing's power comes from its flexibility. Ever since the Sumerians[1] began keeping records by carving signs on clay tablets 5,000 years ago, humans have searched for the ideal tool to portray words. They have carved symbols in stone and bone and written on leaves, bark, silk, papyrus, parchment, paper, and electronic screens. This skill, once known only to a few professional scribes, grew into mass **literacy**: More than five billion people—over 86 percent of the world's population—can now read and write.

C   To understand how writing evolved, I visited Serabit el-Khadim, a flat-topped, wind-eroded mountain of reddish sandstone in the southwestern Sinai Peninsula of Egypt. Here, in a turquoise mine dug by Egyptians almost 3,500 years ago, is one of the earliest examples of a phonetic alphabet.

D   "What do you think?" asked Avner Goren as we stooped to enter a dark hole. Goren, an archeologist who supervised excavations in the Sinai for 15 years, was pointing to a wall just ahead of us. Carved into the stone were crude sketches of a fish, an ox head, and a square. The simplicity of the marks belied[2] their significance. The people who made them were among the first to use characters that denote sounds—an alphabet. The alphabetic symbols each represented the initial sound of an object. The picture of the square—a house—thus stood for the *b* sound because the word for house was *beit*.

---

1 The **Sumerians** were an ancient people in southern Mesopotamia, modern Iraq.
2 If one thing **belies** another, it hides it and gives a false impression of it.

E The signs were remarkably different from the Egyptian hieroglyphs found elsewhere at the site. If these ancient writers were not Egyptians, who were they? Most researchers now believe that this alphabet was invented in Canaan, a region between the Jordan River and the Mediterranean Sea. Most likely, Canaanites, who were brought in to work the mines, left these messages.

F Egyptian scribes had to master hundreds of symbols. I asked Goren if alphabetic writing must have seemed attractive to those scribes. "Probably not," he says. "About 30 of the symbols in Egyptian hieroglyphs represent single sounds, just like the alphabet. They knew about using symbols to represent sounds, so to the Egyptians, the Semitic writing may have looked too primitive to be significant."

G Goren warned me against seeing an alphabet as "**superior**" to pictographic writing. "If you came from outer space and wrote a report, you'd give the alphabet high marks," he says. "It's flexible and easy to learn. But what actual effect did that have? There was no mass literacy until after the development of the printing press in the mid-15th century."

H Nevertheless, although it took hundreds of years, alphabets would eventually change the way people thought. From a small patch in the Middle East, the notion of one symbol per sound gradually became widespread around the world, taking root first among the Greeks, who adapted some characters into written vowels. The Latin alphabet of the Romans evolved from the Greek around the sixth century B.C. By the ninth century A.D., Japan had **integrated** phonetic components into its written language; Korea did so by the 15th century.

I Indeed, of the several hundred written languages in the world today, only Chinese still relies on a traditional writing system whereby individual characters represent individual words. These characters often mean one thing when used alone, but something else when combined. The Chinese character for *trust*, for example, shows

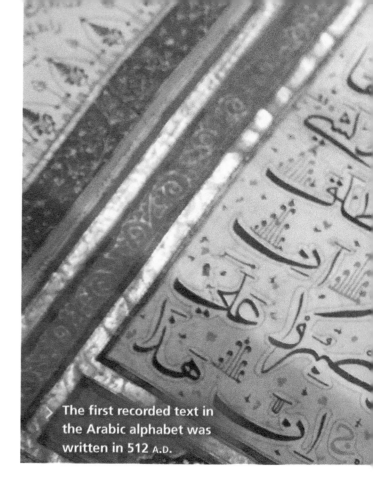

> **The first recorded text in the Arabic alphabet was written in 512 A.D.**

the character for *man* alongside the one for *word*, literally a man standing by his word.

J Since its beginning as a means for keeping records, writing has evolved into one of humanity's most powerful forms of self-expression. People have used writing to counter loneliness and to establish a sense of self. In the fourth century B.C., Aristotle[3] saw writing as a way to express "affections of the soul." Recent studies have shown that writing about feelings can **alleviate** depression, boost the immune system, and lower blood pressure.

K And yet, of the more than 10,000 languages ever spoken, most had no written form. How, then, do people in societies without writing express themselves? "We talk to each other, listen, visit, and trust the spoken word," says Guujaaw, a leader of the Haida Nation. "Writing is not essential to living; expressing yourself without writing is natural."

---

3 **Aristotle** (384–322 B.C.) was a Greek philosopher and scientist.

L The Haida have lived on the Queen Charlotte Islands off the coast of British Columbia for more than 10,000 years. I suggest to Guujaaw that things get distorted when people repeat them to one another, especially over a long **duration** of time. "Things get distorted in writing as well," he says. "People with writing are a brief chapter in our history, but oral histories from our people go back thousands of years. They are a living history and provide a link between storyteller and listeners that written stories cannot. In fact, human intimacy and community can best come through oral communication."

M Plato, Aristotle's teacher, would probably agree. Living at a time when writing began to challenge Greece's oral-based culture, he warned that writing would make people "trust to the external written characters and not remember of themselves ... They will be hearers of many things and will have learned nothing."

N But Plato lived in the fifth century B.C., when reading was physically difficult. Books were papyrus scrolls often more than 15 meters long; the idea of pages only emerged in Europe in the second century A.D. Spaces between words did not become standard in Western society until the seventh century. Long after Plato's time, writing served mostly as an aid to memory, something to stimulate the spoken word.

O The transition from the spoken to the written word occurred because writing meets certain needs so much more effectively. Writing permits analysis, precision, and communication with both current and future generations in a way that is much more powerful than the spoken word.

P Thousands of years ago, China's rulers learned the value of a uniform written language, recognizing that it has the power to unite people. In the third century B.C., Chinese people spoke at least eight languages and countless dialects, but with the establishment of a unified empire and a standard writing system around 200 B.C., everyone could read the same characters.

Q Today, the extra work needed to **manually** enter Chinese into a computer—up to five keystrokes for one Chinese character—raises an important issue. China could become the wealthiest country in the world; it already is a major factor in the international economy. As this economy relies more on computers, does the Chinese writing system act as a **constraint** on its development?

R Perhaps not. Usama Fayyad, a former researcher at Microsoft Corporation, whose job was to think about the long-term future of computers and data storage, says technology will eventually offer efficient and economical ways to bypass[4]

∧ **An exhibitor demonstrates the benefits of electronic paper at the Educational IT Solutions Expo in Tokyo, Japan.**

keyboards. Technology that **incorporates** voice and handwriting recognition, he claims, could make it irrelevant which writing system is used.

S Fayyad also says that the distinction between an alphabet and Chinese characters does not matter in terms of how a computer operates. He explains that when you hit a letter on the keyboard, the computer enters that action into its memory as a number. Each letter is a different number, and a sentence inside the computer is a string of numbers. It's up to the computer program to interpret how the string of numbers **corresponds** to an instruction.

T Overall, computers are terrifically useful machines, but perhaps paper is still superior. You can hold it, fold it, put it in your pocket, look at it again later when it's convenient. This thought leads me to Joseph Jacobson, a professor of physics at the Massachusetts Institute of Technology. He helped found a company, E Ink, whose technology has transformed ink from a permanent medium to a **format** that can change electronically.

U "Paper is fantastic," Jacobson tells me. "If books or newspapers on paper had not already been invented, if we lived in a world only with computer screens, then paper would be a breathtaking breakthrough. But the way we use paper is incredibly wasteful." E Ink is a major developer of electronic-paper—the kind you see on tablets such as Amazon's Kindle. E-paper works by printing electronic letters on squares of plastic that look and feel like paper but can be erased and reused. Jacobson believes that using e-paper will significantly reduce the cost and pollution associated with paper manufacturing.

V "Paper needs to be taken into the digital age. We need writing that changes on paper," says Jacobson. With that in mind, E Ink has just released a new kind of e-paper called JustWrite that promises to offer an experience just like writing on real paper. Users can write on the paper, roll it up, and even cut holes in it—all with very low power usage and no backlight.

W As I observe E Ink's latest technology, I feel as if I'm back in the cave at Serabit el-Khadim—looking at a piece of the future.

---

4 If you **bypass** something, you go or get around it, trying to avoid it.

A. Choose the best answer for each question.

DETAIL
1. According to the passage, what percentage of people in the world today cannot read or write?

    a. 4 percent   c. 50 percent
    b. 14 percent   d. 86 percent

VOCABULARY
2. The phrase *crude sketches* in paragraph D is closest in meaning to _____.

    a. rough drawings   c. old statues
    b. faded pictures   d. mysterious signs

DETAIL
3. What was the probable occupation of the Canaanites who wrote the inscriptions in stone in the Sinai?

    a. supervisors   c. farmers
    b. scholars   d. miners

DETAIL
4. According to Avner Goren, how did Egyptian scribes probably feel about the Canaanite alphabet?

    a. It was too complicated because it had so many letters.
    b. It was confusing because it used symbols to represent sounds.
    c. It was not as sophisticated as their own writing system.
    d. It was not easy to understand as it was based on pictures.

REFERENCE
5. The word *it* in the first sentence of paragraph H refers to _____.

    a. the creation of the Roman alphabet
    b. the development of the printing press
    c. alphabets changing the way people thought
    d. a small section of the Middle East

INFERENCE
6. What can we infer about Plato?

    a. He was probably older than Aristotle.
    b. He invented the first forms of writing.
    c. He lived in the tenth century B.C.
    d. He was a great supporter of the development of writing in Greece.

INFERENCE
7. Which of these opinions would Usama Fayyad most likely agree with?

    a. A new type of keyboard now under development will soon make it easier to enter information on computers.
    b. The Chinese should develop a special writing system that can be used more easily with computers.
    c. In China, computers may one day be replaced with a new generation of technology.
    d. New technology will allow us to enter data on computers in various languages, without using a keyboard.

B. Scan the reading for the names in the box. Complete each sentence (1–10) with the correct name. Each name should be used twice.

a. Avner Goren	b. Guujaaw	c. Plato	d. Usama Fayyad	e. Joseph Jacobson

1. _____ is working on ways to reduce paper use.
2. _____ felt writing would stop people remembering spoken words.
3. _____ feels oral histories bring people together in ways writing cannot.
4. _____ is doing research on an alphabet that was invented in Canaan.
5. _____ points out that computers don't see the difference between an alphabet and pictographs.
6. _____ warned that reading does not always mean you have learned anything.
7. _____ does not think pictograph writing is necessarily inferior to alphabets.
8. _____ thinks communication without writing is more natural.
9. _____ developed a product that looks and feels like paper.
10. _____ is confident that technology related to voice recognition and handwriting recognition will overcome any limitations with current computers.

CRITICAL THINKING Identifying Pros and Cons

▶ List some pros and cons of the kinds of e-paper E Ink is developing. Share your list with a partner. Overall, do you think e-paper will have a positive or negative impact on writing?

_____

_____

_____

▶ How do you think writing will continue to develop in the next 100 years? Discuss with a partner.

A child in Boston, United States, uses an electronic pen to write on a smart board.

Using Graphic Organizers to Organize Key Ideas

A graphic organizer is a good way to record and organize facts and other specific information. Some tests ask you to complete a graphic organizer using words or numbers from a reading passage. To fill out a graphic organizer, follow these steps:

1. Check which type of graphic organizer is being used so that you know the kind of information you need. For example, a Venn diagram usually compares and contrasts information, while a flow chart shows a sequence or a process.

2. Look for clues in the chart that will tell you what to look for—a number, a name, a specific term.

3. The notes may use different language from the reading passage and are sometimes not presented in the same order.

4. Most of the answers will be nouns.

COMPLETING A CHART **A. The reading passage describes the evolution of writing. Complete the timeline using no more than three words for each answer.**

About 5,000 years ago	The ¹_____ used clay tablets to record information.
Around ²_____ years ago	Canaanite people carved alphabetic symbols into stone in a mine in Sinai.
6th century B.C.	The ³_____ alphabet starts to form
⁴_____ B.C.	In Plato's time, writing began to challenge the Greek oral-based tradition.
4th century B.C.	⁵_____ recognized the emotional benefits of writing.
3rd century B.C.	Chinese people spoke eight languages and countless dialects.
200 B.C.	China develops a ⁶_____ which the whole country could understand
2nd century A.D.	The concept of ⁷_____ first appeared in Europe.
7th century A.D.	⁸_____ started to become common.
9th century A.D.	Japan began using ⁹_____ elements in its writing.
¹⁰_____ A.D.	The Korean language included phonetic elements in its written language.
Mid 15th century A.D.	Development of the ¹¹_____.

INTERPRETING **B. Which events in Activity A do you think were the most significant? Share your ideas with a partner.**

COMPLETION   **A.** Complete the information by circling the correct words.

On the back of a letter pulled from the ruins of a Peruvian church in 2008, archeologists have discovered words written 400 years ago in a previously unknown language. The author ¹**incorporated / alleviated** a series of numbers in the letter, in the ²**format / literacy** of a list. The left column contained Spanish numbers along with numerals; in the right column, these were translated into a language never seen before by modern scholars. The numbers ³**correspond / superior** to a decimal system, suggesting the language may have ⁴**alleviated / integrated** elements of other decimal-based Incan languages.

The fragment was just one of hundreds of historic papers trapped inside the ruined church for almost four centuries. Despite the long ⁵**duration / literacy**, the extremely dry climate allowed the papers to remain in good condition.

Ancient written pages were salvaged from the ruins of a Spanish colonial church in 2008.

WORDS IN CONTEXT   **B.** Complete the sentences using the words in the box.

alleviate	constraint	literacy	manually	superior

1. _____ is defined as the ability to read and write.

2. Some people say that writing on paper is _____ to using computers.

3. Before the printing press was invented, books had to be written and copied out _____.

4. Some scholars argue that the complex system of Chinese writing may be a _____ on the nation's future development.

5. Writing about your emotions can help _____ negative feelings like anxiety.

WORD LINK   **C.** The word root *man* in **manual** means "hand." Match each word below with its definition.

1. **manuscript**   •   • a. a cosmetic treatment of the hands

2. **manipulate**   •   • b. a book, document, or piece of music written by hand

3. **manufacture**   •   • c. to handle or control (a tool) in a skillful way

4. **manicure**   •   • d. to make in a factory

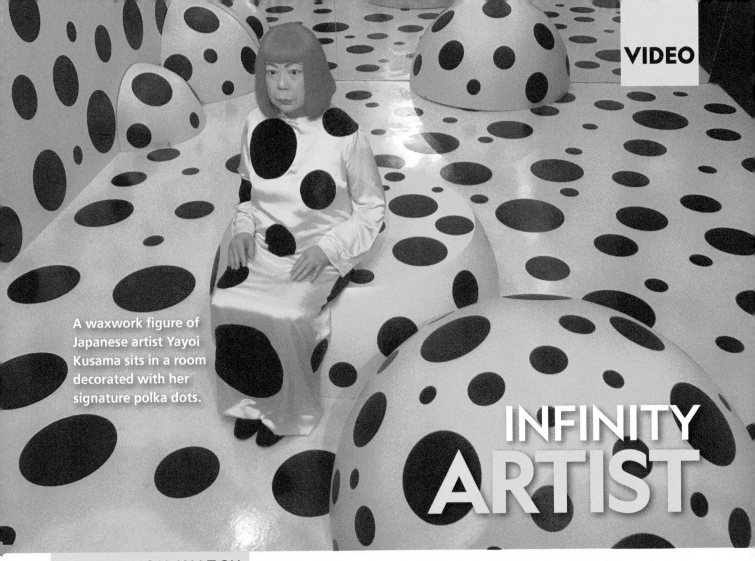

A waxwork figure of Japanese artist Yayoi Kusama sits in a room decorated with her signature polka dots.

INFINITY ARTIST

BEFORE YOU WATCH

DEFINITIONS **A.** The words in **bold** appear in the video. Match each one with its definition. Use a dictionary to help.

1. **hallucination** • • a. (n) a piece of art constructed within a gallery
2. **installation** • • b. (n) the experience of seeing something that is not really there
3. **reputation** • • c. (n) the general opinion people have about someone
4. **renowned** • • d. (adj) unable to fully express yourself
5. **stifled** • • e. (adj) well-known, usually in a positive way

PREVIEWING **B.** Read the excerpts from the video. Complete the sentences using the words in Activity A.

1. "Yayoi Kusama is one of the most _____ artists in the world."
2. "Kusama's iconic polka dots are inspired by a recurring _____ from her childhood."
3. "[Kusama left Japan] at the age of 27, feeling _____ by the expectations from her family."
4. "[She] quickly gained a(n) _____ in the avant garde movement."
5. "One of her most popular _____ is her infinity mirror room."

GIST **A.** Watch the video. Check your answers in Before You Watch B.

DETAILS **B.** Watch the video again. Why are each of the things below mentioned? Note your answers, then discuss with a partner.

1. the Praemium Imperiale

_____

2. a vast field of flowers

_____

3. Seattle

_____

4. Donald Judd and Eva Hesse

_____

5. 50 hours

_____

6. Seiwa Hospital for the Mentally Ill

_____

⌃ **Yayoi Kusama in front of a newly finished painting**

CRITICAL THINKING Synthesizing Information

How does Kusama's artistic style differ from that of Leonardo da Vinci? Which style do you prefer? Discuss with a partner.

VOCABULARY REVIEW

Do you remember the meanings of these words? Check (✓) the ones you know. Look back at the unit and review any words you're not sure of.

Reading A

☐ academy* ☐ arbitrary* ☐ commission* ☐ concurrently* ☐ deny*

☐ draft* ☐ ideology* ☐ implicit* ☐ parameter* ☐ preliminary*

Reading B

☐ alleviate ☐ constraint* ☐ correspond* ☐ duration* ☐ format*

☐ incorporate* ☐ integrate* ☐ literacy ☐ manually* ☐ superior

* Academic Word List

10

NEW DISCOVERIES

In preparation for a future mission to Mars, a NASA scientist studies five samples of potential spacesuit materials.

10A

PREVIEWING **A.** Look at the photo and read the caption. What makes the ALMA telescope different from traditional telescopes? Discuss your ideas with a partner.

PREDICTING **B.** Quickly skim the section headings. What do you think each section will be about? Note your predictions. Then read the passage to check your ideas.

An Eye on the Heavens _____

The Perfect Location _____

Assembling the Array _____

Early Discoveries _____

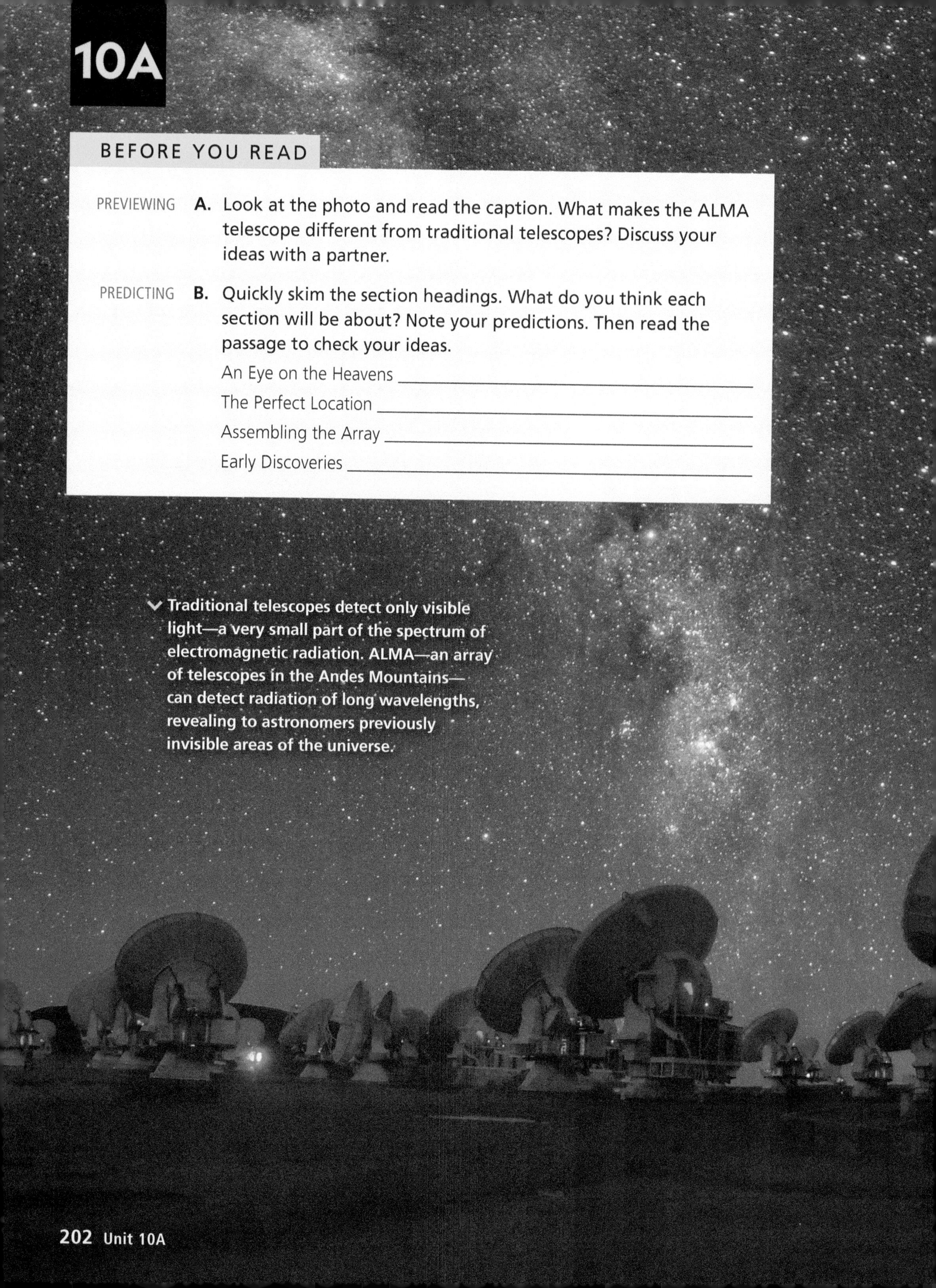

⌄ Traditional telescopes detect only visible light—a very small part of the spectrum of electromagnetic radiation. ALMA—an array of telescopes in the Andes Mountains— can detect radiation of long wavelengths, revealing to astronomers previously invisible areas of the universe.

COSMIC
DAWN

High in the Andes Mountains, an array[1] of telescopes larger than many cities reveals the secrets of the universe.

An Eye on the Heavens

A Telescopes have come a long way since the first ones were invented early in the 17th century. Traditional telescopes allow astronomers to view objects in space thanks to the visible light those objects **emit** or reflect. However, for modern telescopes, any electromagnetic radiation will suffice for the purpose of viewing objects in space. Extremely hot objects, such as stars, emit not only visible light but also high-energy gamma radiation. Specialized telescopes—such as NASA's space-based Chandra X-ray Observatory[2] —are built to detect such radiation. Cold objects—like comets and asteroids—emit low-energy radiation, which is invisible to the naked eye. Much of the universe is even colder than this. The clouds of dust and gas of which stars are made are only slightly warmer than absolute zero— the temperature at which atoms stop moving. To capture images of cold objects, astronomers use radio telescopes.

B A radio telescope is a device that typically uses a large dish antenna to collect the low-energy radiation emitted by objects in space. In the 1960s, astronomers started using them to view asteroids, planets, comets, and other objects. However, it was challenging to get a clear image of those objects using ground-based antennas because low-energy radiation is absorbed and **distorted** by water vapor in the Earth's atmosphere. The signal that a dish antenna on the ground finally receives is therefore weak.

C The signal can be strengthened by **positioning** the antenna on a site with very dry air, and it can be made even stronger by arranging several antennas in an array, combining their signals so that they function together as a single, more powerful

---

1 An **array** of instruments, such as antennas, is a number of them that are connected together to form a single unit.

2 An **observatory** is a building with a large telescope from which scientists study objects in space.

 Workers prepare to deliver a new antenna to the ALMA site.

telescope. By the 1980s, several small arrays were operating in Japan, Europe, and the United States. Technological advances soon made much larger arrays possible, provided that a high, flat site could be found where the antennas could be set up. And if the antennas were portable, the distance between them could be adjusted to change the sensitivity of the telescope. Placed far apart, they could zoom in to focus on a small target, such as a planet. Grouping the antennas closer together would have the effect of zooming out, which would be useful for capturing images of an object as large as a galaxy. In the 1990s, astronomers began searching the world for the ideal place to set up a large array of antennas.

The Perfect Location

D One May morning, two small trucks passed through the quiet town of San Pedro in Chile's Atacama Desert and headed up a mountainside. It was 1994, and the men inside the trucks were trying to find the highest, driest, flattest place on Earth. They had already spent a week and a half checking other locations in this desert. Now, guided by a map and a Chilean astronomer named Hernán Quintana, they were searching for the Chajnantor plateau. At 5,000 meters, it is almost as high as the two base camps used by climbers on Mount Everest (Qomolangma).

E The Atacama Desert is one of the driest places on Earth, with less than 1.2 centimeters of rain a year on average. The desert's remoteness and thin, dry air make the area ideal for observing the night sky. Astronomers from several countries were very interested in setting up observatories there. For the most part, these were observatories to view the fraction of the universe visible using the portion of the light spectrum that the human eye can see. Quintana and his **companions** were looking for a location to set up an array of dish antennas for a large radio telescope. Quintana felt that the Atacama Desert was likely the best possible place—but it wasn't easy to get to.

F "The trip was slow and painful, because the tires kept getting stuck in the sand," remembers Riccardo Giovanelli of Cornell University, one of the researchers who accompanied Quintana. When they finally arrived, the group was not disappointed. "The sky was beautiful—it was the deepest blue one can expect to see," remembered Giovanelli. "There was no doubt that somewhere nearby was the place." One of the astronomers brought along an instrument to measure water vapor. It was lower than any other place they had been.

G News of the discovery inspired a cooperative effort among astronomers in the United States, Europe, and Japan. Scientists in these countries began to realize that by working together, they could build a larger and more powerful array than any one of them could alone. In 1999, an agreement was signed to cooperate on a telescope project.

Assembling the Array

H It would take more than 10 years to transform one of the world's loneliest spots into a busy modern observatory. Land mines[3] planted decades before by the Chilean military had to be located and removed, and an oil company needed to be convinced to choose a different route for a planned pipeline that would have crossed the site. **Prototype** antennas were redesigned after testing in New Mexico, and new ones needed to be manufactured. The infrastructure for the installation had to be built from scratch, including many kilometers of service roads.

I The first of the dish antennas—12 meters in diameter and weighing more than a hundred tons—arrived from the United States at the Chilean port of Antofagasta in April 2007. Escorted by police cars, a truck carried the massive dish up the mountain, its progress occasionally interrupted by herds of llamas crossing the road.

J Over the next five years the dishes continued to arrive. Two specially made 28-wheel transporters—nicknamed Otto and Lore—stood ready to move the antennas to new locations on the plateau as needed. Setting the dishes up to work together required astonishing **precision**: They would need to turn together on command and point at the same target in the sky within a second and a half of one another. A massive supercomputer had to be installed on-site to **coordinate** their movements and **interpret** the signals received.

Early Discoveries

K The installation was officially opened in March 2013 and named the Atacama Large Millimeter/submillimeter[4] Array, or ALMA for short. Even before it was completely set up, it had already produced results. The year before, with only 16 antennas **in operation**, researchers led by Caltech's[5] Joaquin Vieira had used ALMA to view 26 distant galaxies. From the images they gathered, they were able to **deduce** that many stars in those galaxies were a billion years younger than astronomers had previously thought.

L Since the official opening of ALMA, there has been a steady stream of other discoveries of great interest to astronomers. In July 2013, the telescope's high-resolution[6] images provided clues that may help answer a question that has long puzzled astronomers: Why are massive galaxies so rare in the universe? ALMA is also helping researchers understand how planets are born, by providing the first-ever images of the planet-forming process.

M One of the ALMA's most notable achievements is the role it played in creating the first image of a black hole. ALMA collaborated with six other observatories to form an array that functions as one Earth-sized telescope. This network collected and processed more than a petabyte of data while staring at a black hole in the distant Messier 87 galaxy. The image—a circular void surrounded by a ring of orange light—made headline news in April 2019.

N These achievements are just the beginning. In the future, ALMA will show us even finer details of galaxies and star systems. On a dry plateau a few kilometers from where shepherds[7] once slept, our eyes will open upon an unseen universe.

---

3 A **land mine** is an explosive device that is placed on or under the ground and explodes when a person or vehicle touches it.

4 1 **millimeter** = 0.001 m; 1 **submillimeter** = 0.0001 m; the array's name refers to the range of radiation wavelengths that it can detect.

5 **Caltech** is the abbreviation for the California Institute of Technology, located in California, USA.

6 **High-resolution** images or photographs are extremely clear, down to the smallest details.

7 A **shepherd** is a person whose job is to look after herds of sheep.

ALMA'S TEN-MILE-WIDE ZOOM

Elevation: 5,000 meters

Rearranging antennas on the wide plateau is like adjusting a camera's zoom. When the antennas are far apart, the telescope focuses on tight sections of the sky and fine details. Grouping the antennas closer together is like using a wide-angle lens and takes in wider areas of the sky.

ALMA consists of two telescope arrays working together. Two massive transporters relocate antennas in the main array with submillimeter precision. The Morita Array, a separate group of 16 antennas built by Japan, targets large-scale structures in the universe.

THE ELECTROMAGNETIC SPECTRUM
(in meters)

Visible spectrum

Radio waves   Microwaves   Infrared   Ultraviolet   X-rays   Gamma rays

10^3 10^2 10^1 1 10^{-1} 10^{-2} 10^{-3} 10^{-4} 10^{-5} 10^{-6} 10^{-7} 10^{-8} 10^{-9} 10^{-10} 10^{-11} 10^{-12}

ALMA range

THE MORE THE BETTER

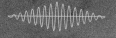

A single-dish telescope can detect faint signals, but its images are blurry. By combining signals from two dishes spaced a distance apart, much clearer images can be produced. The longer the distance, or baseline, the finer the details that can be seen.

Expanding from two to three antennas creates three baselines, further improving sensitivity.

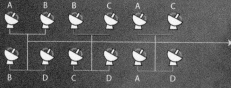

Adding one more antenna provides six baselines. Adding even more antennas further sharpens the signal and reduces noise.

ALMA's 66 antennas can create 1,291 separate baselines, giving the telescope superb sensitivity and the ability to capture fine details.

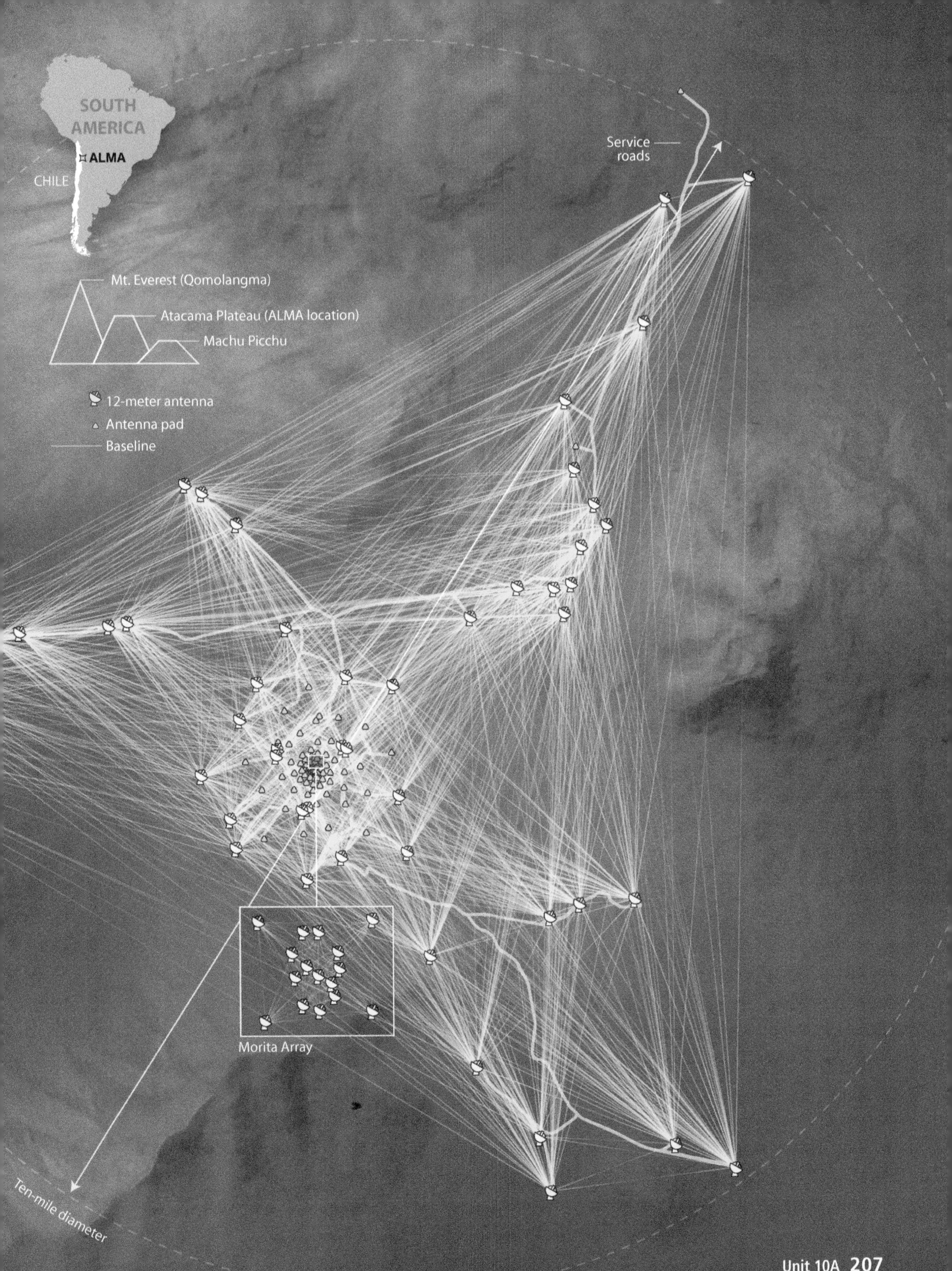

SOUTH
AMERICA

☐ ALMA

CHILE

Mt. Everest (Qomolangma)

Atacama Plateau (ALMA location)

Machu Picchu

12-meter antenna

Antenna pad

Baseline

Service
roads

Morita Array

Ten-mile diameter

A. Choose the best answer for each question.

DETAIL

1. What images can radio telescopes capture that other telescopes cannot?

  a. images of distant hot objects
  b. images of distant cold objects
  c. images of objects that emit light
  d. images of objects that emit high-energy radiation

PURPOSE

2. What is the purpose of paragraph B?

  a. to describe how radio telescopes have changed since the 1960s
  b. to point out a limitation of ground-based dish antennas
  c. to argue that radio telescopes can best view asteroids, planets, and comets
  d. to give reasons that low-energy radiation is absorbed and distorted by water vapor in the atmosphere

DETAIL

3. What did the group that included Chilean astronomer Hernán Quintana find challenging about the Chajnantor plateau?

  a. It was very hard to get to.
  b. No one was used to the thin air.
  c. The high elevation made everyone cold.
  d. The best spots were already taken by other astronomers.

DETAIL

4. Which of the following is NOT mentioned as a reason for choosing Chajnantor plateau for the observatories?

  a. It is in a remote location.   c. It receives little rain.
  b. It is near the equator.   d. The elevation is very high.

VOCABULARY

5. In paragraph H, the phrase *from scratch* is closest in meaning to _____.

  a. without receiving permission to start
  b. from local materials that anyone can find
  c. from old materials that are difficult to find
  d. from the beginning and without using any work done before

COHESION

6. Where would be the best place to insert this sentence?
*"We had to assemble a little city on the mountainside in the middle of nowhere,"
said Al Wootten, the lead North American scientist on the project.*

  a. the end of paragraph G   c. at the end of paragraph H
  b. at the beginning of paragraph H   d. at the end of paragraph I

SEQUENCE

7. Which of these things happened most recently?

  a. The installation site was officially opened.
  b. Two transporters were brought to the installation site.
  c. A massive supercomputer was installed at the installation site.
  d. ALMA was used to view 26 distant galaxies.

B. Look back at the infographic ALMA's Ten-Mile-Wide Zoom. Complete the sentences by choosing the correct options.

1. The wavelengths of electromagnetic radiation that ALMA detects are _____ those of visible light.

    a. shorter than   b. longer than   c. the same length as

2. ALMA is located in the _____ of Chile.

    a. north   b. south   c. west

3. Moving the antennas nearer together helps ALMA look at a _____ area of space.

    a. narrower   b. wider   c. specific

4. Increasing the baseline between two antennas will result in _____ images.

    a. blurrier   b. more colorful   c. clearer

5. In order to have six baselines, at least _____ antennas are required.

    a. three   b. four   c. six

6. The Morita Array _____ ALMA.

    a. is part of   b. is larger than   c. is located to the South of

7. From the information in the infographic, we can infer that five antennas would provide _____ baselines.

    a. 8   b. 10   c. 12

CRITICAL THINKING Justifying Opinions   Where else in the world could a project like ALMA be viable? Consider the following factors. Discuss your ideas with a partner.

typical climate   environmental conditions
quality of infrastructure   ease of transporting material

⌄ **The ALMA antennas stand at an altitude of 5,000 m on the Chajnantor plateau, Chile.**

Increasing Your Reading Speed

When you read, you will want to speed up for some parts or some text types. Increase your reading speed when there are general ideas, simple sentences, and familiar vocabulary. However, decrease your reading speed when there are abstract concepts, detailed technical material, complex structures, unfamiliar terms, and when you need to retain information.

Your brain does not process words individually. Instead, it processes them in groups of three to five, or "chunks." One way to increase your reading speed is to learn to read in chunks. As you read, look for logical chunks based on grammar, vocabulary, and meaning. At first you may want to mark the chunks in a text to practice this technique.

INCREASING READING SPEED

A. Read the text. Try to read it in chunks.

More than 50 million light-years away, / in the heart of a galaxy / called Messier 87, / a gargantuan beast is devouring anything / that strays too near. / Stars, planets, gas, and dust /—not even light—/ escapes the monster's grasp / once it crosses a threshold / called the event horizon. Today, / scientists unveiled an image / of that object, / a supermassive black hole. / This landmark image / is the world's first glimpse / of a black hole's silhouette.

INCREASING READING SPEED

B. Mark the chunks in the text. Then read it as fast as you can.

The new image is the stunning achievement of the Event Horizon Telescope project, a global collaboration of more than 200 scientists using an array of observatories scattered around the world, from Hawaii to the South Pole. Combined, this array acts like a telescope the size of Earth. It was able to collect more than a petabyte of data while staring at M87's black hole in April 2017. It then took two years for scientists to assemble the shot.

ANALYZING

C. Look back at Reading A. Which parts of the passage are possible to read quickly? Which require a slower reading speed? Discuss with a partner.

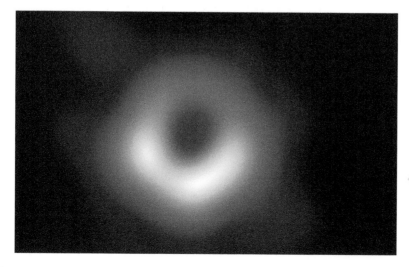

< The image of the supermassive black hole was created using observatories all around the world.

VOCABULARY PRACTICE

COMPLETION **A.** Complete the information by circling the correct words.

Expectations are high for NASA's new $10 billion telescope. Completed in 2016—and currently undergoing tests on Earth—the James Webb Space Telescope (Webb for short) will launch sometime in 2021. When put into ¹**operation** / **companion**, Webb will allow astronomers to look back in time to when stars began to form.

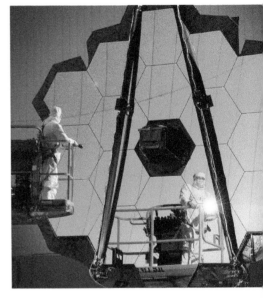

Once Webb's 18 hexagon-shaped mirror sections are ²**positioned** / **interpreted** in space, they will create the largest ever orbiting mirror. Targeting infrared light (a wavelength that warm objects ³**coordinate** / **emit**) the telescope will be able to peer with ⁴**precision** / **prototype** into the star-creating centers of galaxies. And because the telescope is in space, light does not need to pass through the Earth's atmosphere, which can ⁵**interpret** / **distort** an image.

∧ **Technicians inspect the hexagonal mirrors of the James Webb Space Telescope.**

"We're going to find all sorts of new things—and when we do that, we're going to change the astronomical landscape again," says Jason Kalirai, project scientist for Webb.

DEFINITIONS **B.** Match each word in the box with its definition.

companion	coordinate	deduce	interpret	prototype

1. _____ (n) someone you spend a lot of time with

2. _____ (v) to work out the meaning of something

3. _____ (v) to make many things work together effectively

4. _____ (v) to come to a conclusion based on evidence

5. _____ (n) the first working model of a product or machine

WORD LINK **C.** The word root *mit* in **emit** means "send" or "throw." Complete the sentences with the correct form of the words in the box.

omit	submit	transmit

1. A good essay should not _____ the sources an author has used.

2. Radio waves are used to _____ radio and television signals around the world.

3. Many companies now allow people to _____ their job applications online.

BEFORE YOU READ

DISCUSSION **A.** Look at the photo and read the caption. Discuss these questions with a partner.

1. Which of the elements in the periodic table are you familiar with? What uses do they have?

2. Why do you think scientists are interested in creating new elements?

SCANNING **B.** Scan the reading passage for information about the three scientists below. Then match the names to their accomplishments.

1. Georgy Flerov • • a. led a team that created the first atom of element 114

2. Glenn Seaborg • • b. helped launch Soviet nuclear weapons research

3. Yuri Oganessian • • c. helped create an atomic bomb for the U.S. military

ELEMENT HUNTERS

All the elements found in nature—the different kinds of atoms—were found long ago. To find a new one these days, you need to create it.

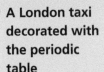

A London taxi decorated with the periodic table

A Everything you know and love on Earth, and everything you don't, is built of elements—the different types of atoms. Most of them are billions of years old, scattered into space by the Big Bang[1] or by exploding stars. They were then incorporated into the newly born Earth, endlessly recycled as they moved from rock to bacteria, president, or mouse.

B In the late 1800s, the Russian chemist and inventor Dmitry Mendeleyev tried to make sense of Earth's elements, grouping them by mass—the scientific term for weight—and other **attributes** in his periodic table of the elements. Later, scientists connected the order of elements in the periodic table to the structure of atoms. Each element got a number: its atomic number—the number of protons in its atomic nucleus.

C By 1940, researchers had discovered every element on Earth, right up to uranium (element 92). They had filled in every gap Mendeleyev had left in his table, but they weren't finished. Beyond uranium lay a world of possibilities— elements too radioactive and unstable to have survived billions of years. To explore that world, you have to create it first.

D The first steps of creation not only extended the periodic table, but played a fateful[2] role in world history. It was 1940, the year after World War II began, and U.S. scientists led the race to create new elements. Element 93, neptunium, was created in a laboratory at the University of California, Berkeley. The next year, Glenn Seaborg and his colleagues at the same university produced element 94, plutonium. Seaborg was promptly recruited to the Manhattan Project[3] to create an atomic bomb for the U.S. military.

E The intensified level of nuclear research in the United States did not go unnoticed by the world's other superpower at the time—the Soviet Union. Georgy Flerov was a prominent physicist who had helped launch that country's nuclear weapons research. Early in World War II, Flerov had noticed that the flow of articles about radioactive elements from U.S. and German scientists had suddenly stopped. This heightened secrecy led him to suspect that they were building atomic bombs, and in April 1942, he wrote to

---

1 The **Big Bang** refers to the cosmic explosion that marked the beginning of the universe.

2 If an action is **fateful**, it is considered to have an important and often disastrous effect on future events.

3 The **Manhattan Project** was the name of the U.S. government project that developed the first atomic bombs during World War II.

TWENTY-SIX NEW ELEMENTS

Since the 1940s, scientists have probed the frontiers of the atomic nucleus, synthesizing heavier elements one by one. The first step beyond uranium (the heaviest natural element) was neptunium, number 93 in the periodic table. The synthetic atoms are all radioactive: They decay into lighter elements, sometimes within milliseconds. In general, the heavier the element, the shorter its half-life. For decades researchers have been searching for the "island of stability," where "magic numbers" of protons and neutrons might combine to make superheavy atoms that last long enough to be studied.

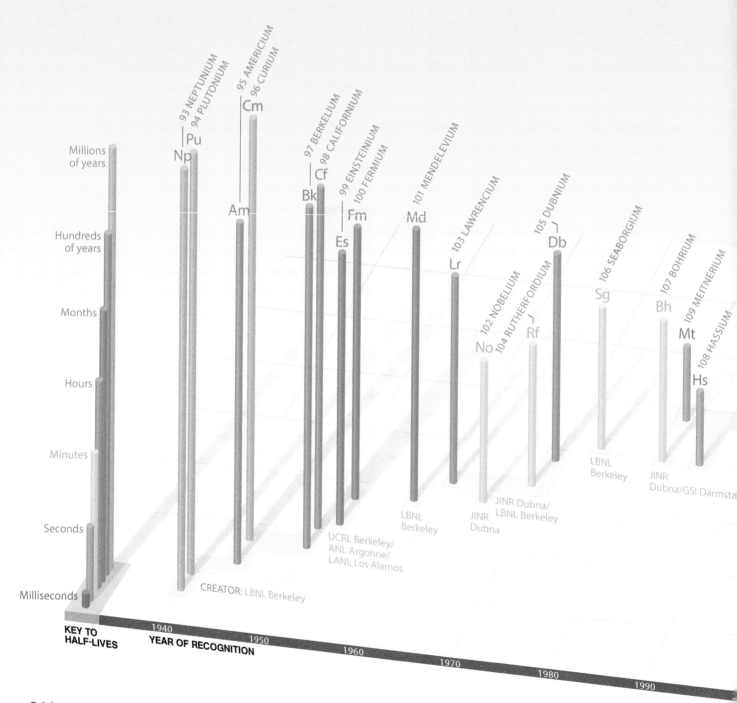

Soviet leader Joseph Stalin explaining his fears. Flerov's suspicions were confirmed, and Stalin asked Russian physicists to build a bomb, too.

F For his part in the war effort, Flerov was rewarded with a car, a house, and, most significantly, a laboratory in the town of Dubna, north of Moscow. There, Flerov focused his attention on the hunt for new elements. His American **counterpart**, Glenn Seaborg, returned to Berkeley after helping to engineer the bomb that the U.S. military dropped on Nagasaki at the end of the war. He continued to make new elements, with less fateful applications—smoke detectors, for instance—or no applications at all. By 1955, his team had gotten as far as element 101—he named it mendelevium.

G For a time it seemed Mendeleyev's table might end there, with his namesake.[4] The protons in an atomic nucleus are always trying to tear it apart; their positive electric **charges** repel[5] one another. Neutrons—electrically neutral particles that outnumber the protons—help **bind** the nucleus together. But that binding force works only at extremely close range, and it weakens sharply as the size of the nucleus increases. So there has to be a final box on the periodic table, a maximum size beyond which an atom won't be stable even for an instant. With mendelevium, which has a half-life[6] of 51.5 days, researchers seemed to be getting close to the final box.

Beyond Mendelevium

H The Berkeley team continued its research regardless, rivaled by Flerov's team in Dubna. From 1965 to 1974, Berkeley claimed to have produced elements 102–106—but so did the Dubna lab. Although those short-lived elements died within hours, the tense **disputes** over who made them first were fueled by the competitive atmosphere of the Cold War.[7] In the end, a spirit of compromise **prevailed**: Element 105 was named dubnium and element 106 seaborgium.

I Meanwhile, theorists had given a new purpose to the **quest** for elements. They calculated that a very large nucleus might be surprisingly stable if it had "magic numbers" of protons and neutrons. That insight, if correct, would change everything. It would mean that there could be an "island of stability" where extremely heavy elements might last minutes, weeks, or even thousands of years.

ISLAND OF STABILITY
Home of superheavy elements lasting years

4 Someone's or something's **namesake** has the same name as that person or thing.

5 When two charged particles **repel** each other, they push each other away.

6 **Half-life** is the time needed for half the atoms in a radioactive substance to disintegrate.

7 The **Cold War** was a period of hostility between the United States and the Soviet Union from 1945 until 1991.

J Around the time that this new theory appeared, a brilliant physicist named Yuri Oganessian joined Flerov's lab in Dubna. The island of stability had captured his imagination. However, reaching it seemed to him an impossible task at that point. The Berkeley and Dubna labs had gotten only as far as element 106 by shooting light atoms against heavy ones with such force that they joined to create a single superheavy nucleus. But beyond 106, the **collisions** were so energetic that they were ripping the new nucleus apart before it even formed. To overcome this problem, Oganessian proposed that shooting slightly heavier atoms at lighter targets might create gentler collisions that were more likely to create new elements. Unfortunately, before he could put his proposal into action, a lab in Darmstadt, Germany, used the idea to make elements 107 through 112. Oganessian's historic moment would have to wait another quarter century.

K In the coming years, the Dubna lab went through hard times. Flerov died in 1990; the Soviet Union collapsed in 1991. The lab went months without being able to pay its researchers. Scientists gathered mushrooms in the forests and fished in the Volga River. Oganessian, now in charge of the lab, could have directed it toward more practical goals and made some money for himself and his staff, but he decided instead to continue toward element 114 and the promised island of stability.

Achieving the Dream

L To make element 114, Oganessian would shoot calcium at plutonium. He persuaded U.S. physicists at the Lawrence Livermore National Laboratory in California—who just a few years earlier had been his rivals—to give him a small amount of plutonium. The plan was to use a cyclotron[8] to shoot a beam of calcium atoms at high speed into a thin sheet of metal covered with the precious plutonium atoms. Among the trillions of atoms spraying out the other side—the metal sheet was thinner than hair—Oganessian expected at most one atom of element 114. His team—along with Livermore's—invented a new device to detect it.

M They turned the cyclotron on in November 1998. It wasn't a very **trustworthy** piece of machinery, and it required constant attention. Nevertheless, in late November, the cyclotron managed to produce a single atom of element 114. It lasted only a few seconds—but that was thousands of times longer than would be expected if there were no island of stability. It also proved that the calcium method worked. Dubna and other labs have since made elements 115–118, and isotopes[9] with different numbers of neutrons. They are still nowhere near the island's peak, where an element might last years, but the creation of element 114 was the great breakthrough that Oganessian had been dreaming about for decades.

N It wasn't until 2011, however, that element 114 was officially admitted to the periodic table. This is because no newly discovered element is officially recognized until another laboratory can **duplicate** the experiment, which sometimes takes years. Element 114 was given the name *flerovium*. This belated[10] but welcome recognition came when Oganessian was 78 years old. After such a triumph, other scientists might have decided it was time to retire to a quiet and grateful life—but not Yuri Oganessian.

O The island of stability still captures his imagination, inspiring him on to further discoveries. As Oganessian put it, "We have discovered the island. Now it is time to explore it, to walk along its western beach." Techniques must be developed to shoot the magic number of neutrons into flerovium to reach its peak of stability. Scientists need to discover if there are peaks at other elements. Although at the moment those goals seem almost impossible, Oganessian has no intention of giving up the hunt for new elements.

---

8 A **cyclotron** is a device that can accelerate charged atoms, protons, or other particles, direct them into a beam, and "shoot" them at a target.

9 **Isotopes** are elements that have the same number of protons and electrons, but a different number of neutrons.

10 A **belated** action happens later than it should have.

A. Choose the best answer for each question.

DETAIL

1. What contribution to science is Dmitry Mendeleyev noted for?

    a. the discovery of the element uranium
    b. the understanding that elements have different weights
    c. the creation of the periodic table of elements
    d. the connection of elements in the periodic table to atoms

CAUSE AND EFFECT

2. What led Georgy Flerov to suspect that the Americans and Germans were building atomic bombs?

    a. The Russians had already started to build atomic weapons.
    b. Glenn Seaborg and his colleagues had recently discovered plutonium.
    c. Glenn Seaborg and his colleagues were about to work on a military project.
    d. U.S. and German scientists stopped writing about radioactive elements.

SEQUENCE

3. Which of these elements was the last to be created?

    a. flerovium
    b. dubnium
    c. mendelevium
    d. neptunium

DETAIL

4. What evidence is there that the Berkeley and Dubna teams were able to compromise?

    a. Element 105 was named dubnium and element 106 seaborgium.
    b. The teams worked together to produce 102–106.
    c. They reached agreement on who discovered each element first.
    d. Flerov worked with Seaborg to jointly discover mendelevium.

DETAIL

5. Why were physicists excited about the theory of the "island of stability"?

    a. They could increase the number of protons in a nucleus.
    b. They could create an unlimited number of new elements.
    c. Heavy elements could exist for a significant amount of time.
    d. It allowed them to study the nucleus in great detail.

COHESION

6. Where would be the best place in paragraph O to insert this sentence?
*In other words, there is more work to do before we understand
how the new elements behave alone and in reaction with others.*

    a. after the first sentence
    b. after the second sentence
    c. after the third sentence
    d. after the fourth sentence

UNDERSTANDING INFOGRAPHICS

7. Since 2000, how many newly created elements have lasted longer than a few milliseconds?

    a. none
    b. two
    c. four
    d. five

> **Yuri Oganessian is considered
> the world's leading researcher in
> superheavy chemical elements**

B. Scan the reading for the names in the box. Complete each sentence (1–8) with the correct name. Each name should be used twice.

> a. Dmitry Mendeleyev   b. Georgy Flerov   c. Glenn Seaborg   d. Yuri Oganessian

1. _____ created element 114.

2. _____ invented the periodic table.

3. _____ named element 101 mendelevium.

4. _____ thought American and German scientists were building a nuclear bomb.

5. _____ was a 19th-century chemist and inventor.

6. _____ was part of the Manhattan Project.

7. _____ helped create the Soviet Union's nuclear weapons research.

8. _____ did experiments to shoot calcium at plutonium.

CRITICAL THINKING Identifying Pros and Cons

▶ Work with a partner. Look at these discoveries from human history. Discuss with a partner what you know about each one.

Gunpowder, 10th century

Oil, 1859

Electricity, late 19th century

Penicillin, 1928

> British bacteriologist Sir Alexander Fleming discovered the antibiotic powers of penicillin in 1928.

▶ What are the pros and cons (if any) of each discovery? Note your ideas in the chart below.

Discovery	Pros	Cons
Gunpowder		
Oil		
Electricity		
Penicillin		

▶ Which of the discoveries has had the greatest positive effect on the world? Which has had the most negative effect? Share your ideas with a partner.

Understanding Long Sentences

Answering comprehension questions can be challenging when a reading passage contains long, complex sentences. As you learned in 10A, long sentences may be easier to understand if you break them down. Follow these steps:

1. Use a "/" to divide the sentence into clauses.

2. Identify the subject, verb, and object of each key clause.

3. Ask yourself questions like *Who / What does what?* and *How / Why / Where / When did they do it?*

4. Circle the verb, underline the subject, and double-underline the object. Finally, draw parentheses around any modifiers, phrases, or adverbs.

Look at the example:

(For his part in the war effort), Flerov was rewarded with a car, a house, and, (most significantly), a laboratory (in the town of Dubna), (north of Moscow).

ANALYZING   **A. Break down the sentences (1–3). Then answer the questions.**

1. His [Flerov's] American counterpart, Glenn Seaborg, returned to Berkeley after helping to engineer the plutonium bomb that the U.S. military dropped on Nagasaki, Japan, at the end of the war.

    a. Who returned to Berkeley? _____

    b. What did he help engineer? _____

    c. When was it used? _____

2. He [Oganessian] persuaded U.S. physicists at the Lawrence Livermore National Laboratory in California—who just a few years earlier had been his rivals—to give him a small amount of plutonium.

    a. Who did he persuade? _____

    b. What was their relationship? _____

    c. What did he persuade them to do? _____

3. The Berkeley and Dubna labs had gotten only as far as element 106 by shooting light atoms against heavy ones with such force that they joined to create a single superheavy nucleus.

    a. What were the names of the two labs? _____

    b. How far did they get with their experiments? _____

    c. How did they get this far? _____

    d. What happened when the atoms joined? _____

COMPLETION **A.** Complete the information by circling the correct words.

The [1]**bind** / **quest** for new elements begins with expensive ingredients: rare isotopes of calcium and an existing element like plutonium. If there is a high-speed [2]**collision** / **duplicate** between the two kinds of atoms, they sometimes [3]**bind** / **charge** together and form a new superheavy one. Here are the key steps.

A. Bake a solid calcium compound in an oven at 700 degrees Celsius. The calcium vaporizes, forming a gas that can be shaped into a high-energy beam.

B. Ionize the calcium atoms by stripping off some of their electrons. The positively [4]**charged** / **disputed** ions can now be accelerated by electric and magnetic fields.

∧ **Pellet of plutonium-238 glowing from its own heat. Plutonium-238 is used to fuel space probes.**

C. Accelerate the ions in a cyclotron and smash the calcium ions into a spinning target.

D. Detect the new element and its [5]**disputes** / **attributes**. The first step is to catch everything in a disk.

WORDS IN CONTEXT **B.** Complete the sentences. Circle the correct options.

1. If two friends are having a **dispute**, they are having a *laugh* / *disagreement*.

2. If you **prevail** in a lawsuit, you eventually *win* / *lose*

3. A **counterpart** has a job that *is similar to yours* / *you will likely take over*.

4. If someone is **trustworthy**, you can *never* / *usually* believe what they say.

5. If you **duplicate** something, you *create a copy of* / *destroy* it.

COLLOCATIONS **C.** The verbs in the box are commonly used with the noun **quest**. Complete the sentences using the correct form of the words.

abandon	aid	embark

1. In the 1940s, scientists _____ upon a quest to create new elements.

2. Chemists have not yet _____ their quest to create a long lasting superheavy element.

3. New telescopes have _____ astronomers in their quest to understand the universe.

An artist's impression of a black hole devouring a nearby star

BLACK
HOLES

BEFORE YOU WATCH

DEFINITIONS **A.** Read the information below. The words in **bold** appear in the video. Match each word with its definition.

Black holes are mysterious **entities** that have fascinated scientists for years. The gravitational force of a black hole is so strong that even light cannot escape. Some black holes are formed when massive stars die and collapse. The **matter** that made up the star gets **compressed** to an infinitely **dense** point where space, time, and the laws of physics no longer apply.

1. entity •   • a. to squeeze something so it takes up less space

2. compress •   • b. something that has a clear identity of its own

3. dense •   • c. the substance that makes up any physical object

4. matter •   • d. containing a lot of things in a small space

DISCUSSION **B.** What else do you already know about black holes? Discuss with a partner.

GIST **A.** Watch the video. Note answers to the questions.

1. How big is a stellar black hole? Around how many could there be in our galaxy?

_____

2. How big is a supermassive black hole?

_____

3. What type of black hole is Sagittarius A? Where is it?

_____

4. When was the first black hole discovered?

_____

LABELING **B.** Watch the video again. Match the words in the box to the correct labels on the diagram.

accretion disk	event horizon
singularity	quasar

1 _____

2 _____

3 _____

4 _____

CRITICAL THINKING Inferring Information   The first ever black hole image was revealed in April 2019 (see page 210). Why do you think astronomers felt this was an important achievement? Why do you think there is such an interest in studying black holes? Discuss with a partner.

VOCABULARY REVIEW

Do you remember the meanings of these words? Check (✓) the ones you know. Look back at the unit and review any words you're not sure of.

Reading A

☐ companion ☐ coordinate* ☐ deduce* ☐ distort* ☐ emit

☐ in operation ☐ interpret* ☐ position ☐ precision* ☐ prototype

Reading B

☐ attribute* ☐ bind ☐ charge ☐ collision ☐ counterpart

☐ dispute ☐ duplicate ☐ prevail ☐ quest ☐ trustworthy

* Academic Word List

CULTURAL ENCOUNTERS

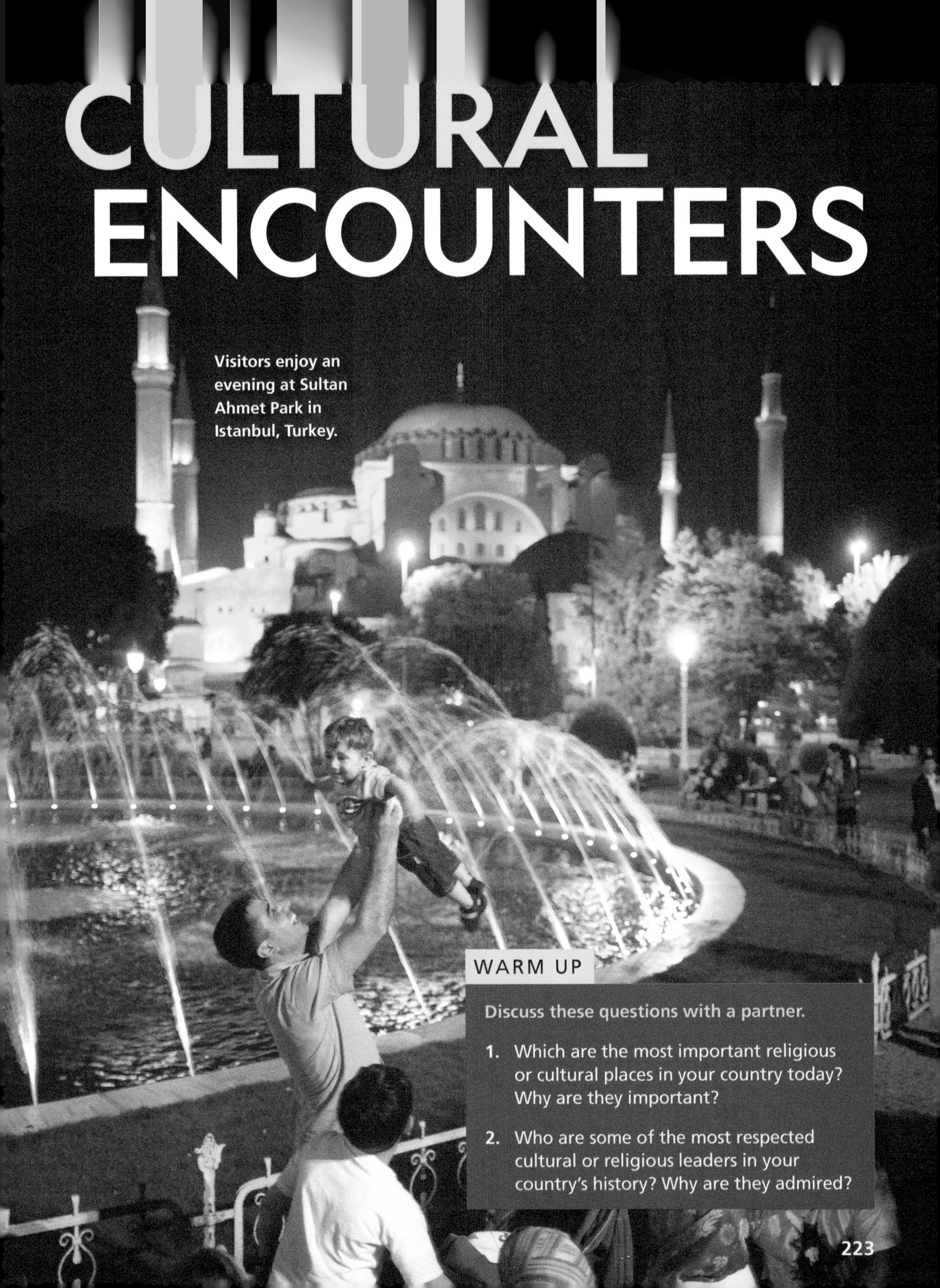

Visitors enjoy an evening at Sultan Ahmet Park in Istanbul, Turkey.

WARM UP

Discuss these questions with a partner.

1. Which are the most important religious or cultural places in your country today? Why are they important?
2. Who are some of the most respected cultural or religious leaders in your country's history? Why are they admired?

BEFORE YOU READ

DISCUSSION **A.** Look at the map on page 226 and discuss these questions with a partner.

1. What modern-day regions did the Ottoman Empire once include?

2. Who was Süleyman the Magnificent and why was he important?

SCANNING **B.** The passage mentions various people associated with Süleyman. Scan and match the people to their descriptions (a–f).

a. Selim	b. Selim II	c. Jean Parisot de la Valette
d. Osman	e. Mehmed the Conqueror	f. Roxelana

1. ___ victor of the siege of Malta   2. ___ Süleyman's father

3. ___ the first Ottoman sultan   4. ___ Süleyman's great-grandfather

5. ___ Süleyman's wife   6. ___ Süleyman's son

> During his reign, Süleyman the Magnificent oversaw some of the greatest architectural achievements in the Islamic world, such as Istanbul's Süleymaniye Mosque.

THE WORLD OF SÜLEYMAN THE MAGNIFICENT

Writer Merle Severy examines the legacy of one of the giant historical figures of the 16th century—a ruler who stood at the crossroads of East and West.

A Near the Hungarian town of Szigetvár, a road sign caught my eye: "Szulimán." It was a dying village, the young having moved away, the old hanging on. "It was named for a sultan who came long ago," a man in his garden told me. I asked what he did there. "I heard that he died here," a woman said. "The old folks would know, but they are all dead now." My curiosity led me to a churchyard in the nearby countryside. On the church facade I saw an Ottoman Turkish inscription. A crescent stood by the wall, bathed in the light of the setting sun. It was at this site, I read, that was buried the heart of Sultan Süleyman.

B The 16th century was an age notable for the overlapping **reigns** of giant historical figures: Spanish Emperor Charles V, protector of the Christian Church; his rival Francis I, King of France; Henry VIII of England; Ivan the Terrible, all-powerful ruler of Russia.

Extent of Ottoman Empire, 1566

✖ Battle site

EMPIRE OF THE OTTOMANS

The Ottoman Empire lasted from the end of the 13th century to the beginning of the 20th—a period of more than 600 years. Occupying a strategic position at the junction of three continents, the empire rose to become a major world power under Süleyman the Magnificent (1494–1566).

From his capital Constantinople (modern-day Istanbul), Süleyman expanded his territory from central Europe to the southern coast of what is now Iraq. He created a powerful navy that secured coastlines along the Red Sea and eastern Mediterranean and brought most of the North African coast under Ottoman control.

C   Yet, even among this **hierarchy** of great leaders, one ruler arguably stood taller than the rest: Süleyman, Commander of the Faithful, Shadow of God on Earth, Protector of the Holy Cities of Mecca, Medina, and Jerusalem, Lord of the Lords of the World, East and West. Revered by his people as "Kanuni," the Lawgiver, and feared and admired by the West as "the Magnificent," Süleyman brought the Ottoman Empire to the peak of its power.

D   Süleyman was born at a time of world war, of East against West, with two superpowers locked in mortal conflict on the lands and seas of three continents. Time and again, Christian and Muslim forces clashed in the seas around the Indian Ocean, the Red Sea, and the Mediterranean, and on land in Europe from Turkey to Austria.

E   Away from what the Ottomans called the Realm of War, the frontier against their unholy enemies, was the Realm of Peace, where races

and religions coexisted with the sultan acting as a great mediator of peoples. At its heart was Constantinople (present-day Istanbul), a cosmopolitan crossroads of continents that grew so large that no other European capital overtook it until the start of the 19th century.

F   It was Süleyman's great-grandfather, Mehmed the Conqueror, who turned Constantinople into the greatest of all European cities. Mehmed was a descendant of nomadic tribesmen from central Asia who became followers of Osman, the first Ottoman sultan, in the 13th century. From these humble origins, Mehmed rose in power, carrying the banner[1] of Islam in a series of conquests through Serbia, Greece, and Eastern Europe; only his death in 1481 prevented him from pressing the conquest of Italy and taking Rhodes, the last Christian stronghold in the east.

---

1 Someone **carrying the banner** of a specific cause or idea stands for that idea.

G Mehmed's dream of building a world empire that brought together East and West would eventually be taken up by his great-grandson, Süleyman. As a young man, the future sultan was educated near the Aegean Sea where he had been assigned as governor. Well-read in history, the Koran, politics, science, astrology, and poetry, and skilled in horsemanship and archery, Süleyman had been carefully prepared for his role as a future world leader.

H On hearing of his father Selim's death in 1520, Süleyman rode for three days until he arrived in Constantinople. As he approached, Süleyman looked at the city that would become his capital: the fortress with its great cannons, the dome of the magnificent Hagia Sophia, the wooden houses sheltering immigrant families. In this crowded city, Spanish Moors and Jews expelled by Ferdinand and Isabella[2] joined with Turks, Greeks, and Armenians in the shops that filled the city's covered bazaar.[3]

I On September 30, eight days after Selim's death, Süleyman took up the sword of Osman in an elaborate ceremony and was declared sultan. From that time on, he held **absolute** power over his people, with the right of instant death over any subject. But as he first rode from his palace, his people gathered to raise their voice in a ritual warning to a new monarch: "Be not proud, my sultan. God is greater than you!"

J Süleyman's first official acts were to order a tomb, mosque, and school built in honor of his father; to free 1,500 Egyptian and Iranian captives; and to pay back merchants for goods that Selim had taken from them. These won him popular approval for piety, magnanimity,[4]

and justice. "It seemed to all men," one observer commented, "that a gentle lamb had succeeded a fierce lion."

K But the lamb proved to be a lion in disguise. A revolt in Syria was put down savagely. Then Süleyman set out to achieve what Mehmed the Conqueror had failed to do. In his first European campaign,[5] the city of Belgrade—the key to Christian defenses in the Balkans—fell after weeks of massed attacks.

L The next summer, in 1522, he besieged[6] Rhodes, which stood between his capital and the ports of Egypt and Arabia, including the Islamic holy city of Mecca. The siege began on July 29 and lasted 145 bloody days, until the knights'[7] desperate defense ended.

M Having brought into submission the strongest fortified city in Christendom, Süleyman offered generous terms: Knights could leave freely within 12 days, and citizens could depart at any time within three years. Again he won admiration for his magnanimity. Little did he realize the price he would pay later for letting the knights go.

N As success followed success in his campaigns, contemporaries wrote with awe of the glories of the sultan's empire. "I know of no state which is happier than this one," reported the Venetian ambassador in 1525. "It is furnished with all God's gifts. It controls war and peace with all; it is rich

> **A portrait of Süleyman the Magnificent**

---

2 **Ferdinand** of Aragon (1452–1516) and **Isabella** of Castile (1451–1504) were rulers of Spain. See Unit 11B reading passage.

3 A **bazaar** is a market area, usually a street of small stalls.

4 **Piety** is dutiful devotion, usually with reference to a particular theology (religion); **magnanimity** is generosity in forgiving an insult or injury.

5 A **campaign** is a series of coordinated activities designed to achieve a goal, such as a military objective.

6 If soldiers **besiege** a place, they surround it in order to stop the people inside from resisting.

7 In medieval times, a **knight** was a man of noble birth who fought for his king or lord.

in gold, in people, in ships, and in obedience; no state can be compared with it. May God long preserve the most just of all emperors."

O The Venetian ambassador's glowing and no doubt **biased** description is perhaps understandable considering the spectacular show that was put on to welcome visitors to the Ottoman capital. A foreign ambassador's reception was carefully designed to show Ottoman grandeur and power at its most impressive.

P On approaching the sultan's Topkapi Palace, the envoy first saw the heads of executed traitors hanging from the Imperial Gate. Passing the executioner's chambers, the envoy entered a shining portico.[8] There he was met on the sultan's behalf by the monarch's vizier, or grand advisor, who, on special occasions, led the envoy past 2,000 bowing officials and heaps of silver coins. The visitor was then offered a "hundred dishes or thereabout, most boiled and roasted."

Q Then on to the sacred inner precincts.[9] The ambassador was robed in gold cloth while his royal presents were inspected, since the sultan was "not to be approached without gifts." At the door of the throne room, two officials held the visitor firmly by the arms. The visitor was led across the room, then forced to subordinate himself by kneeling down and kissing the sultan's foot. He was then raised to deliver his message.

R The sultan, heavy with silk, gold and silver threads, sat on a jewel-studded throne. Süleyman might make a comment or indicate with a nod that the audience was over. The ambassador was then led backwards out of the room, never turning his back on the sultan. The sultan's response might come much later, usually via his advisor.

S The envoys who met Süleyman in this way would scan his features for signs of his health and character. From their descriptions, we

know something of how the great sultan looked and acted, but we know very little of his thoughts, of what really was in the mind of the Lord of Lords.

T What sort of man was Süleyman? Of his private life—his attitudes and his thoughts— we can **infer** very little. His campaign diaries are written in the third person, without emotion. For example, from his third campaign: "The Emperor, seated on a golden throne, receives [his] viziers ... ; massacre of 2,000 prisoners; the rain falls in torrents."

U Glimpses of humanity are rare, but revealing. After the siege of Rhodes, Süleyman **consoles** the knights' leader for his loss, praises his brave defense, then **confides** to a follower: "It is not without regret that I force this brave man from his home in his old age."

V We know that Süleyman showed wisdom as a lawgiver, creating a new code of laws and giving legal protection to minorities. He was also pious, **consulting** theologians on crucial decisions; just, allowing no corruption or injustice to go unpunished; and, usually, fair.

W Ironically, it was an act of generosity that led, years later, to his greatest defeat. As a young man, Jean Parisot de la Valette fought against Süleyman in the siege of Rhodes, but was later released. Just over four decades later, la Valette led the defense of the great Christian stronghold of Malta. The surprise defeat at the hands of the Christian knights marked the beginning of the end of Ottoman domination in the Mediterranean.

X As the siege of Malta ended, Süleyman was entering his 73rd year, making him the longest-reigning of all Ottoman monarchs. During his reign, he had extended his Islamic empire through southeastern Europe, across much of the Middle East, and in North Africa as far west as Algeria. His code of laws, known as the *kanun-i Osmanî* ("Ottoman Laws"), was to last more than 300 years, and he presided over some of the greatest architectural achievements in the Islamic world.

---

8 A **portico** is a porch or covered walkway with columns supporting the roof.

9 **Precincts** are districts, as of a city, or the parts or regions immediately surrounding or within a place.

Y Despite these achievements, Süleyman's mood became increasingly dark. To wipe out the disappointment of Malta, he set out on May 1, 1566, to capture Vienna. The sultan could no longer sit on a horse, so he rode in a carriage, making the journey painfully slow. Suddenly, word came that a Hungarian count[10] had executed one of Süleyman's governors and was now hiding in Szigetvár. In a fury, Süleyman diverted his entire army to avenge the injustice.

Z Even with only 2,500 defenders, Szigetvár held off the Ottomans for a month, until the fortress was finally shattered by explosives. Holding up his jeweled sword in surrender, the count came out with his survivors—but there was no sultan to greet him. Süleyman had died in the night in his tent.

AA Following Süleyman's death, the Ottoman Empire was squeezed by Russian expansion in the east and European domination of southern Asia. Ottoman possessions in the Mediterranean lost their strategic role. Western technology overtook Ottoman military might, and—with no new lands, taxes, or manpower—imperial decline set in. During the 19th century, the empire became known as the "Sick Man of Europe." Nevertheless, when more than a dozen nations emerged from its umbrella in the early 20th century, their languages, religions, and cultures had been largely preserved—a legacy, in part, of Süleyman's tolerance of minorities.

BB Three weeks after the emperor's death, the sultan's **successor** was announced, and Selim, the son of Süleyman and his queen Roxelana, became the new Sultan Selim II. It is believed that Süleyman's heart was buried where he died, and the rest of his remains began the long journey home. When the sultan's body reached the capital, the army fell silent, as did the people who followed behind. Their leader all their lives, he raised their sacred empire to its golden age. Their descendants would look back on it with pride and **nostalgia**—but they would never see his like again.

10 A **count** is a nobleman in European countries.

THE SEARCH FOR THE LOST TOMB OF SÜLEYMAN

After the siege of Szigetvár, Süleyman's body was taken to Constantinople for burial. It was said that his heart remained behind in Hungary, buried in a golden casket beneath the tent where he died, but it has never been found. Professor Norbert Pap from the University of Pécs in Hungary believes he may be getting close. In a settlement near Szigetvár, archeologists have unearthed Ottoman brick and tile, plus 16th-century luxury goods from the East. Pap believes the lost tomb of Süleyman the Magnificent may not be far away.

Yet other scholars believe the entire story was merely a colorful myth made up years later. "All they had to do was bury the body—intact—and exhume it later," says renowned Ottoman scholar Nicholas Vatin. This had been done before, with the body of Selim I in 1520, notes Vatin. Keeping the death of a sultan secret until the successor could be informed was not unusual for the Ottomans in the 16th century. Vatin has concluded that the story was just local folklore. "The romantic story of Süleyman's heart being buried in Hungary, I'm sorry to say, is just a myth."

Statues in the Turkish-Hungarian Friendship Park commemorate the battle at Szigetvár.

A. Choose the best answer for each question.

VOCABULARY

1. In paragraph B, the phrase *overlapping reigns* indicates that the leaders mentioned in this paragraph _____.

    a. were more powerful than kings in previous centuries
    b. ruled their lands during some of the same years
    c. lived longer lives than previous monarchs
    d. ruled during a time of war and trouble

DETAIL

2. Which of the following leaders made Constantinople the most important city in Europe?

    a. Süleyman   b. Osman   c. Mehmed   d. Selim

DETAIL

3. Which of the following is NOT true about Constantinople at the time of Selim's death in 1520?

    a. It contained diverse groups of people.
    b. It was where Süleyman was living.
    c. It was located in the Realm of Peace.
    d. It was the heart of the Ottoman Empire.

PARAPHRASE

4. Choose the sentence that is closest in meaning to this sentence from paragraph K: *But the lamb proved to be a lion in disguise.*

    a. Süleyman was not interested in warfare, only in peace.
    b. Süleyman proved that it was better to be powerful than kind.
    c. Süleyman proved to be much fiercer than people first thought.
    d. Süleyman seemed fierce, but was actually very gentle.

INFERENCE

5. What does the author imply in paragraph M?

    a. The "generous" terms offered were not really very generous.
    b. Although Rhodes was thought to be strong, it fell very easily.
    c. The knights were allowed to become citizens of Rhodes.
    d. Süleyman would later regret treating the knights so liberally.

RHETORICAL PURPOSE

6. Why does the author quote from Süleyman's campaign diaries in paragraph T?

    a. to show his writing revealed little about his true personality
    b. to support the idea that the third campaign was his most important
    c. to demonstrate that he was not only a military genius but also a skillful writer
    d. to point out the impact of bad weather on military operations

DETAIL

7. What does the author say about the siege of Malta?

    a. It was considered Süleyman's most brilliant campaign.
    b. It was the final battle in which Süleyman fought.
    c. The siege did not last as long as Süleyman had predicted.
    d. Jean Parisot de la Valette's victory there was unexpected.

B. Complete the summary of Süleyman's life using no more than three words from the passage in each space.

Süleyman's Youth

Süleyman learned politics and history near [1]_____. He became

proficient at [2]_____. After his [3]_____ in 1520,

Süleyman became sultan. He was known by many names, including "Shadow

of [4]_____."

The Royal Court

A visitor to the Topkapi Palace would walk past thousands of officials and

mountains of [5]_____. The visitor was then required to kiss the

[6]_____.

His Battles

Süleyman's first military objective was to capture Belgrade—critical to

[7]_____ in the Balkans. In 1522, his [8]_____ of

Rhodes lasted nearly four months. Süleyman's final battle in Szigetvár was to

[9]_____ the execution of one his governors.

His Death

Süleyman died in 1566. Some people believe his [10]_____ is buried

in Szigetvár. However, Ottoman scholar Nicholas Vatin says this story is a local

[11]_____.

CRITICAL THINKING Identifying Evidence   The author makes several claims about Süleyman's character as a leader. Note down at least one example or piece of evidence to support each of the claims.

Claim	Evidence
Süleyman was a wise leader.	
He was humane.	
He was known for his piety.	
He was generous.	

Creating a Mental Map of a Text

The text of an article is often divided into sections, each corresponding to an important supporting idea of the whole article. Sometimes each section has its own heading; in other cases, the start of new sections may be indicated by spacing or typography, such as the use of a different font. Section titles usually refer to the overall main idea of the section rather than to a specific detail. Titles and opening lines of sections are useful for creating a mental map of the organization.

CREATING A MENTAL MAP

A. Match the headings (a–h) to the correct sections of the chart. Two headings are extra.

a. Birth of a Leader

b. The End of the Dream

c. The Secret Sultan

d. The Capture of Vienna

e. An Audience with Süleyman

f. The Lamb and the Lion

g. A Dying Village

h. The Lord of Lords

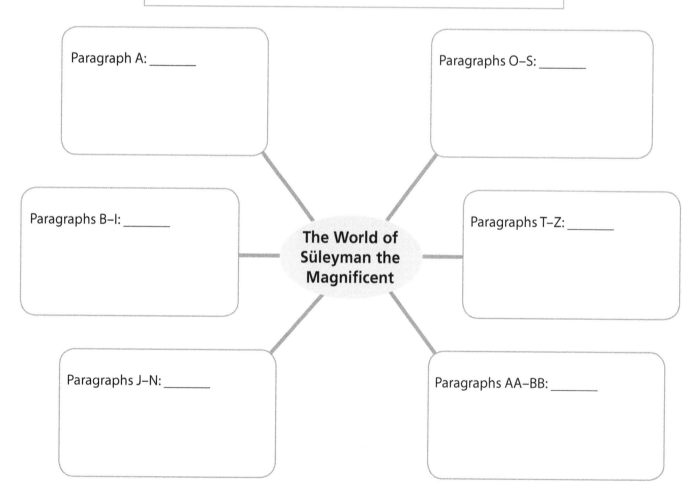

Paragraph A: _____

Paragraphs O–S: _____

Paragraphs B–I: _____

The World of Süleyman the Magnificent

Paragraphs T–Z: _____

Paragraphs J–N: _____

Paragraphs AA–BB: _____

CREATING A MENTAL MAP

B. Add dates, names of places, and other supporting information to each section of the chart in Activity A.

COMPLETION **A.** Complete the information using the correct form of the words in the box. Five words are extra.

absolute	biased	confide	console	consult
hierarchy	infer	nostalgia	reign	successor

During his [1]_____ in the 12th century, Salah al-Din Yūsuf ibn Ayyūb—better known as Saladin—ruled over the lands of Egypt, Syria, Mesopotamia, and Yemen.

Saladin began his life as a soldier, quickly rising up through the military [2]_____. After taking control of Egypt in 1171, he seized power in Syria following the death of its king. Some saw this as an act of treason against the king's son (the intended [3]_____), but Saladin felt his actions were justified. His mission was to defend Muslim lands from the Christian Crusaders arriving from Europe.

∧ **Saladin, leader of the Muslim forces against the Crusaders, was also the first sultan of Egypt and Syria.**

While historical accounts from this period are somewhat unreliable, we can [4]_____ from his actions that Saladin was a fair and generous ruler. For example, he mediated truces between other Muslim leaders, he [5]_____ with his councils on important matters, and he also showed mercy to many of his prisoners.

DEFINITIONS **B.** Complete the definitions using the unused words from the box in Activity A.

1. _____: a sentimental longing for a period in the past

2. _____: to discuss inner thoughts or secrets with someone

3. _____: to comfort (e.g., after a loss)

4. _____: in favor of one group or idea over another

5. _____: complete; without question

WORD USAGE **C.** The adjective **biased** can sometimes be confused with the noun **bias**. Complete each sentence by choosing the correct word.

1. This article is far too *bias / biased* in my opinion.

2. When writing an essay, it's important to give a balanced argument without any *bias / biased*.

3. I thought our team played well, but I'm probably *bias / biased*.

4. The interviewers were careful not to show any *bias / biased* towards a candidate.

BEFORE YOU READ

DEFINITIONS **A.** The following words related to religion and worship appear in the reading passage. Match each word with its definition.

cathedral	clergy	creed	prophet	shrine

1. _____: a set of beliefs, or principles, that strongly influence the way a person lives and works
2. _____: a person who is believed to speak for a divine authority
3. _____: a place of worship associated with a holy person or object
4. _____: the leaders of the religious activities of a group of believers
5. _____: an important church that has a bishop in charge

SKIMMING AND PREDICTING **B.** Quickly skim the passage. Check (✓) the topics you think the author discusses. Then read through the passage to check your ideas.

- ☐ origins of the Moors
- ☐ how the Moors came to Spain
- ☐ Moorish architecture
- ☐ Moorish poetry
- ☐ Moorish paintings
- ☐ how the Moorish era ended

> The Mosque–Cathedral of Córdoba, Spain, is one of the most accomplished examples of Moorish architecture.

WHEN THE MOORS
RULED SPAIN

From the Rock of Gibraltar, writer Thomas J. Abercrombie set out to explore a forgotten corner of Europe's past.

A   "Perfect weather for a morning's sail—or an intercontinental passage," said my Spanish shipmate, Rafa, as I scanned the rising mists ahead. Suddenly a silhouette of our destination appeared above the haze ahead: Gibraltar. "Wow, what a beauty!" Rafa exclaimed.

B   A beacon for mariners since the dawn of seafaring, the famous Rock of Gibraltar was one of the Pillars of Hercules (Jabal Musa, behind us on the northern coast of Africa, formed the other). For ancient Romans and Greeks, the pillars marked the boundary of the known world. For me, the stronghold marked the first stop on a journey into a neglected corner of Europe's history, a distant time when Muslims ruled Spain and Islam had a powerful influence on the West.

C   "Only recently have the Spanish begun to approach their Islamic past," Rafa told me. In recent years, Rafa had presided over a Madrid-based institute that promotes cultural

exchange between Spain and its Muslim neighbors. "We are finding that much of what we think of as 'pure Spanish,' our architecture, our temperament,[1] our poetry and music—even our language—is a blend from a long Arabic heritage."

D Rafa and I were sailing in the wake of Tariq ibn Ziyad, a Muslim general. With soldiers and horses in four boats, he crossed from Ceuta on the African side—as did we—and set up camp on the narrow ledge below, where the town of Gibraltar sits today. In the spring of 711, he marched northward with 12,000 Muslims. At the Rio Barbate, south of Cadiz, the invaders met the hastily assembled forces of Spain's Visigoth[2] king, Roderic. "Before us is the enemy; behind us, the sea," shouted Tariq, drawing his sword and **invoking** Allah for his blessing and support. "We have only one choice: to win!"

E The battle of Barbate proved a mortal wound for the weak Visigoth ruler. King Roderic was slain; his body was never recovered. Whole battalions of soldiers fled, and the Christian army collapsed. The Islamic conquest of Spain had begun.

F The creed of Islam had been revealed to the seventh-century prophet-statesman Muhammad in distant Arabia. It spread swiftly, embracing the entire desert peninsula by the time of his death in 632. Six years later, Syria and Palestine fell to the Muslims, and from their new capital in Damascus, Muslim armies spread eastward through Mesopotamia to India and Central Asia, westward to the Nile and across North Africa. A century after the birth of Islam, its call to prayer rang from minarets[3] all the way from the Atlantic to the outskirts of China, an empire larger than Rome's at its height.

G History named the Muslim conquerors of Spain "Moors," probably because they arrived by way of Morocco, but the Moors themselves never used the term. They were Arabs, from Damascus and Medina, leading armies of North African Berber converts. Most married into Spanish and Visigoth families or took

---

1 Your **temperament** is your basic nature, such as how you react to situations.

2 The **Visigoths** were a tribe who settled in France and Spain in the 4th century A.D.

3 **Minarets** are tall towers attached to mosques. They have projecting balconies from which people are called to prayer.

The Alhambra, palace fortress of the Moors, in Granada, Spain is now one of the country's major tourist attractions.

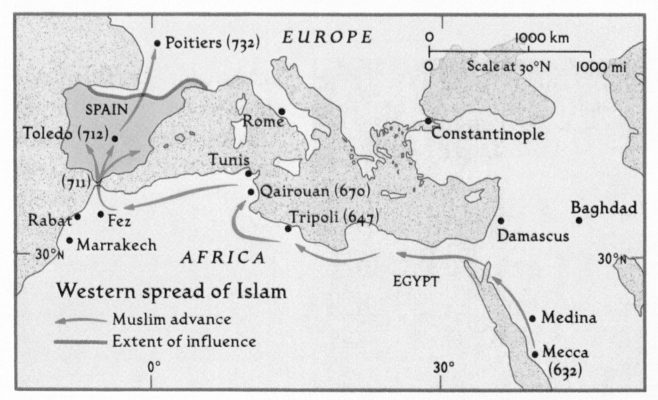

In a mere hundred years, the Prophet Muhammad's followers spread the word of Islam westward from Mecca through northern Africa to Spain and France, where their advance was halted in 732.

fair-skinned Galician[4] slaves as wives. From this mix of race and culture sprang a civilization that would have a major influence on Spain, including its language: the name Gibraltar descends from *Jabal Tariq*, Arabic for "Tariq's mountain."

H From Gibraltar, I followed Tariq's footsteps northward. After the victory at the Rio Barbate, he moved swiftly, with Spanish cities falling to him in quick succession. Early in 712, his soldiers rode through the gates of the Visigoth capital, Toledo, where the remaining Christian armies were forced to retreat to the northernmost mountains of Spain.

I The Moors' hold of Toledo lasted for over 300 years. In 1085, it fell to Alfonso VI of Castile and Leon, who thereby **initiated** the *Reconquista*—the Reconquest of Spain by the Christians. For several centuries after Toledo's recapture, the city remained **liberal**, tolerant, and bilingual. Alfonso X supported an important 13th-century translation school where Christian, Muslim, and Jewish scholars collaborated to translate manuscripts into Latin—works by the Greek scholars Aristotle and Ptolemy; **empirical** studies of algebra and mathematics by al-Khwarizmi;[5] and the Canon of Ibn Sina (Avicenna), which remained Europe's standard medical textbook for 500 years.

J Today, the whole city of Toledo has been declared a national monument, and it remains the country's religious capital. Mosques and synagogues have been restored and **splendid** palaces opened to the public—museums to display Toledo's abundant cultural heritage.

K But there is a dark side, too, to the region's history. In 1469, Prince Ferdinand of Aragon wed Princess Isabella of Castile, uniting Christian Spain under their rule. They waged war against Moorish rulers to the south and **persecuted** Muslims and Jews in their own lands.

---

4 **Galicians** were a race of people who lived in the kingdom of Galicia, in northwest Spain.

5 **Muhammad ibn Musa al-Khwarizmi** was a Muslim scholar who studied at the House of Wisdom in Baghdad.

L In 1480 they established the Spanish Inquisition.[6] Before it was over, three centuries later, thousands of Muslims and Jews had died, and an estimated three million people had been driven into exile. Having lost many of its leading businessmen, artists, and scientists, Spain found itself a victim of its own cruelty.

M From Toledo, a train ride south brought me to Andalucía, a region where Islamic culture sank its deepest roots. Perhaps it is not surprising: Southern Spain, with its warm, gentle landscape, grape vines, and olive and citrus trees, is almost a mirror of parts of Morocco and the eastern Mediterranean. Here the Arabs felt at home.

---

6 The **Spanish Inquisition** was a religious tribunal established by Catholic monarchs Ferdinand of Aragon and Isabella of Castile.

N In 756, Prince Abd-al-Rahman, whose dynasty had been overthrown in Syria, planted his capital at Córdoba in Andalucía's heartland. Under his successors, Córdoba blossomed into a city of half a million people with more than 20 suburbs, 500 mosques, 300 public baths, 70 libraries, and long stretches of paved, lamp-lit streets. The largest city in western Europe, Córdoba rivaled Baghdad and Constantinople as the greatest cultural center of the world.

O The highlight for most visitors to Córdoba is its Mezquita-Catedral, or Mosque-Cathedral, which in 1986 celebrated its 1,200th anniversary. Begun by the first Abd-al-Rahman, it is a shrine that rivals in size Islam's holiest in Mecca, and that still today retains its status as the crown jewel of Moorish architecture.

ˇ **The interior of Cordoba's Mosque-Cathedral is a forest of columns and arches.**

As my eyes grew accustomed to the darkness, I wandered through a forest of more than 800 columns and Moorish arches. My footsteps led me to the mosque's domed *mihrab*, or prayer area. Arabic calligraphy decorated the walls, declaring "... praise to Allah who led us to this place."

P In the dim vastness, I hardly noticed the cathedral. After the Christian Reconquest, Catholics began using the Mezquita as a church and for 300 years held services there. Then the clergy persuaded Emperor Charles V to raise a cathedral in its midst, despite strong protests from city leaders who felt that **amending** the building in this way would **violate** its sanctity.[7] Later, when he inspected the rather banal addition to the extraordinary mosque, Charles confessed disappointment: "By installing something that is commonplace," he declared, "you have destroyed what was once unique."

Q When Córdoba fell to the Christian Reconquest in 1236, and when Seville fell 12 years later, the Moors found themselves confined to a 320-kilometer strip along Spain's southeast coast, curving from Gibraltar to Almería. Here sultans of the Nasrid dynasty ruled from their stronghold at Granada. From 1248 to 1354, they raised their masterpiece, a clay-red palace-fortress known as the Alhambra. I climbed the hill leading to the Alhambra with Professor Miguel José Hagerty, a lecturer on Arabic poetry at the University of Granada.

R "Arab Spain nurtured scores of poets, and many of its rulers—Abd-al-Rahman I, for instance—were poets in their own right," Professor Hagerty said. Strict Islamic tradition discourages the making of "graven images," so painting and sculpture never flourished among the Moors. Instead, they channeled creative energy into language. With its wealth of vocabulary, its distinctive sounds, its flowing calligraphy, Arabic is well suited to the task.

S "Little has been translated," he said, but he quoted some lines that survived the journey into Spanish and English. From Ibn al-Sabuni:
I present you a precious mirror
Behold there the beauty that consumes me
O furtive love, your reflection is more yielding
And better keeps its promises

T The Nasrid rulers' mansions of the Alhambra make up the most visited site in Spain. It is a miracle that they survived the centuries: They have been abused by squatters,[8] eroded by neglect, and suffered various **appendages**, including a massive addition built during the Renaissance by Charles V. The **integrity** of the Alhambra endures nonetheless, a sublime Moorish mix of artifact and nature.

U Here the walls themselves speak—if you know Arabic. We found quotations and poems in the calligraphy of the walls, archways, and fountains. One marble fountain declared:
No greater mansions I see than mine
No equal in East or West.

V I had to agree. Even in the oil-rich Arab countries of today, architects with unlimited budgets have yet to match the Alhambra.

W The marriage of Ferdinand and Isabella sealed the fate of the weakening Granada sultans. In 1492, the same year that they launched Christopher Columbus on his historic voyage across the Atlantic, the king and queen rode into Granada to preside over the abdication[9] of the last Moorish ruler, Muhammad Abu-Abdullah—Boabdil, as the Spanish call him.

X On the way out of Córdoba, I paused at a pass above the city called *Suspiro del Moro*, "the Sigh of the Moor." It was here Boabdil stopped to look back and shed a tear over his lost kingdom. According to legend, his domineering mother, Aisha, berated[10] him for passively allowing his

---

7 If you talk about the **sanctity** of something, you mean that it is very important and should be treated with respect.

8 **Squatters** are people who live in unused buildings without having a legal right to do so.

9 An **abdication** occurs when a person gives up being king or queen.

10 When someone is **berated**, they are scolded angrily.

kingdom to fall: "Fitting you cry like a woman over what you could not defend like a man."

Y The remote villages of the Alpujarras, halfway up the southern slopes of Mulhacén, Spain's highest peak, were the last domains of the Moors in Spain until they were finally driven into exile in 1609. Many towns still wear their Arabic names, as does Mount Mulhacén and the Alpujarras itself. I descended from the mountains via a series of sharp turns to a very different world: Spain's Costa del Sol—tropical, cosmopolitan, and booming. In 2018, 82 million visitors came to Spain, nearly two for every Spaniard. "It's an invasion—but a peaceful one," says Costa del Sol Tourist Board promotion manager Diego Franco.

Z All over the coastal region are signs of modern-day Moors; signs in Arabic script point you to the Lebanese Delicatessen, the Banco Saudi-Espanol, to Arab doctors, a Muslim cemetery ...

AA Near the Andalucía Plaza Casino, I drank coffee with Mokhles "George" El-Khoury, a Christian Arab who moved here from Beirut to run a building-management firm. "[Andalucía] reminds me of Lebanon—without the wars and politics," George said. "You have the mountains, the sea, the fine climate of olives and palm trees. The Spanish are a warm people, not stiff and formal like many Europeans. The food is much like ours, so is the shape of the houses and the towns. To an Arab—well, Andalucía feels like home."

BB Nowhere is this more true than in the old Muslim capital of Córdoba, where I spent my last Spanish days. I was awakened there early one morning by the noise of workmen at the Mezquita across the street. No other artifact more richly evokes the golden age of the Moors, a stormy millennium that brought together two faiths, two cultures, two continents. Throughout, while king and sultan fought bitterly for the hand of Spain, ordinary life prospered as people of different backgrounds worked together to create the

brilliant civilization that helped lead Europe out of the Dark Ages.[11]

CC Ultimately the Moors themselves faded into history, leaving behind their scattered dreams. But Spain and the West stand forever in their debt.

---

11 The **Dark Ages** refers to a period of cultural and economic decline in Western Europe following the end of the Roman Empire.

THE ART OF FLAMENCO

Arabic poetry was crafted, above all, for recital and song. In Morocco and Spain, the soul-stirring music of *cante jondo*, the deep song of flamenco, is still played and sung by descendants of ethnic minorities who survived the Inquisition centuries ago.

Throughout Spain the art of flamenco is threatened by its commercialization in shows called *tablaos*, characterized by dramatic lighting and loud amplifiers. Sacrificed in the process is flamenco's most distinctive aspect, its *duende*: soul. But after midnight, it is still possible to sample flamenco *puro* ("pure Flamenco") in the bars of Granada's Albaicin area, when locals gather to recall the moods and rhythms of a lost age.

A. Choose the best answer for each question.

DETAIL

1. What does the author say about the word *Moors*?

    a. It was applied only to the North African Berber soldiers.

    b. It was probably used because the invaders came to Spain from Morocco.

    c. It was what the Muslim conquerors called themselves.

    d. It was originally applied to the Visigoth conquerors of Spain.

DETAIL

2. The name *Gibraltar* comes from the name of a _____.

    a. Visigoth ruler

    b. Christian king

    c. Moorish war leader

    d. Galician slave

INFERENCE

3. Why was it relatively easy for Tariq ibn Ziya to conquer southern Spain?

    a. Spain's army was not very well prepared.

    b. Southern Spain was less Christian than the north.

    c. Spain's army was not loyal to King Roderic.

    d. Tariq had more soldiers in his army.

INFERENCE

4. From the information in paragraph I, we can infer that _____.

    a. at least some of Toledo's scholars could understand Latin

    b. Alfonso X was the Spanish leader who recaptured Toledo from the Moors

    c. Ibn Sina helped translate his medical textbook from Arabic to Spanish

    d. speaking or writing in Arabic in Toledo after 1085 was forbidden

REFERENCE

5. In paragraph K, the word *their* refers to _____.

    a. Muslims and Jews

    b. Moorish rulers to the south

    c. Ferdinand and Isabella

    d. Spanish Christians

VOCABULARY

6. The word *banal* in paragraph P is closest in meaning to _____.

    a. ordinary and unexciting

    b. small and inconspicuous

    c. strange and unlikely

    d. unholy and insulting

DETAIL

7. Which of these is NOT true about the Alhambra?

    a. Nasrid rulers lived there.

    b. There are quotations and poems in Arabic on the walls.

    c. It is the least visited site in Spain.

    d. It had been vandalized and neglected over the years.

B. Complete the timeline with words and dates from the reading.

632	Islam covers all of [1]_____.
[2]_____	Muslims take over Syria and Palestine.
[3]_____	Tariq ibn Ziyad's army begins attack on southern Spain.
712	Ibn Ziyad takes the city of [4]_____.
756	Prince Abd-al-Rahman makes Córdoba his [5]_____.
1085	Alfonso VI begins the [6]_____ of Spain.
[7]_____	Córdoba is retaken by Spain.
1248	After several defeats, the Moors were restricted to Spain's [8]_____.
1354	The [9]_____ is completed.
1469	Ferdinand and Isabella initiate war against the Moors.
1480	The [10]_____ begins.
[11]_____	The last ruler of the Moors renounces his throne.
[12]_____	The last Moors are forced out of Spain.

CRITICAL THINKING Reflecting

Think of a country or culture that has been strongly influenced by another country or culture. Consider the areas below and note some ideas, then discuss with a partner.

language   food   music   architecture   customs

_____

_____

◄ Crowds in Guardamar del Segura, Spain, take part in a festival commemorating the 13th-century conflict between Moorish and Christian soldiers.

Inferring an Author's Attitude

In many articles, authors commonly reveal their attitudes about the topics with words with positive or negative meanings. Often, these words are adjectives, but other methods—such as metaphoric language—can express positive or negative opinions as well. For example:

We found the service in that restaurant *terrible*, but the food was *exceptionally good*.

Natalie is a *graceful* dancer, but her partner dances like an *awkward elephant*.

INFERRING
ATTITUDE

A. Find the discussion of the topics listed below in the article. Decide if the author's attitude toward the topic is positive (+) or negative (–). Note words or phrases that signal the author's attitude.

Topic	Author's attitude	Words or phrases that indicate the author's attitude
Toledo in the two centuries after its reconquest (paragraphs I–J)		
The rule of Ferdinand and Isabella (paragraphs K–L)		
Andalucía (paragraphs M–N)		
Córdoba (paragraphs N–O)		
The cathedral inside the Mezquita (paragraph P)		
Arabic language and poetry (paragraphs R–S)		
Changes to the Alhambra since its construction (paragraph T)		
Tablaos shows (The Art of Flamenco sidebar)		

INFERRING
ATTITUDE

B. What is the author's overall attitude toward the Moors? Circle the best adjective below. Then discuss your reasons with a partner.

a. questioning   b. neutral   c. critical   d. respectful

COMPLETION **A.** Complete the information using the correct form of the words in the box.

empirical	initiate	liberal	persecute	splendid	violate

The incredible city of Toledo stands as a(n) ¹_____ showcase of Spanish history. From 712, under the rule of the Caliphate of Córdoba, Toledo enjoyed the benefits of a(n) ²_____ society in which Muslims, Jews, and Christians co-existed. During Alfonso VI's reign, Christian, Muslim, and Jewish scholars continued to collaborate, translating Arabic and Hebrew documents into Spanish and Latin. They also ³_____ advancements in education that lasted centuries. These included ⁴_____ studies in science and mathematics. However, in the 1400s, intolerance flared in Toledo. Muslims and Jews were ⁵_____ and their religious rights were ⁶_____. Many were expelled from Spain.

⌃ **El Greco's** *View of Toledo* **is considered among the best-known depictions of the sky in Western art and a masterpiece of the Spanish Renaissance.**

DEFINITIONS **B.** Match each word with its definition.

1. **amend**   •   • a. to refer to something to support an argument
2. **appendage** •   • b. the state of being whole and complete
3. **integrity**   •   • c. to change something
4. **invoke**   •   • d. something attached to a larger object

COLLOCATIONS **C.** The nouns in the box are frequently used with the verb **violate**. Complete the sentences with the correct words.

agreement	law	privacy

1. If you don't pay your taxes, you are violating the _____.
2. Reading someone else's email violates their _____.
3. If you break a contract, you are violating the _____ you signed.

CROSSROADS OF THE WORLD

∨ Istanbul's Bosphorus Strait forms the continental boundary between Europe and Asia.

BEFORE YOU WATCH

DEFINITIONS

A. The words in **bold** appear in the video. Match each one with its definition. Use a dictionary to help.

1. **bustling** •   • a. (n) busy; full of life

2. **contrasting** •   • b. (adj) being the most powerful or influential

3. **divide** •   • c. (n) the joining of two different things

4. **dominating** •   • d. (adj) showing a difference between two or more things

5. **fusion** •   • e. (v) to separate

PREVIEWING

B. Read the excerpts from the video. Complete the sentences using the words in Activity A.

1. "Turkey sits on the border of Europe and Asia, creating a _____ of Eastern and Western culture."

2. "The Bosphorus Strait is a _____ waterway that runs through the center of the city."

3. "The strait forms part of the continental boundary between Europe and Asia and _____ Istanbul in two."

4. "Istanbul's beautiful skyline is a mix of _____ architectural styles."

5. "One of the most _____ sites of the skyline is the Galata Tower."

GIST **A.** Watch the video. Check your answers in Before You Watch B.

DETAILS **B.** Watch the video again. Complete the notes in the chart.

Bosphorus Strait
- runs through the city center
- part of the continental boundary between ¹_____
- get a great view of the city by taking a ²_____

Galata Tower
- dominates skyline
- built in ³_____
- ⁴_____ meters high

Hagia Sophia
- originally built as a ⁵_____
- turned into a ⁶_____ after Ottoman conquest
- became a ⁷_____ in 1935

Sights of Istanbul

Süleymaniye Mosque
- built between ¹¹_____
- grave of ¹²_____ is located in the garden
- showcases the work of Ottoman architect Sinan

Kizkulesi Tower
- located at the entrance to ⁸_____
- originally built as a ⁹_____ for goods
- renovated in 1990s and now a popular site for ¹⁰_____

CRITICAL THINKING Personalizing Design a tour to showcase five or more historical sites of a city or town you know well. Note your ideas and then explain your tour to a partner, giving reasons for your choices.

VOCABULARY REVIEW

Do you remember the meanings of these words? Check (✓) the ones you know. Look back at the unit and review any words you're not sure of.

Reading A

☐ absolute ☐ biased* ☐ confide ☐ console ☐ consult*

☐ hierarchy* ☐ infer* ☐ nostalgia ☐ reign ☐ successor*

Reading B

☐ amend* ☐ appendage ☐ empirical* ☐ initiate* ☐ integrity*

☐ invoke* ☐ liberal* ☐ persecute ☐ splendid ☐ violate*

* Academic Word List

PRECIOUS
RESOURCES

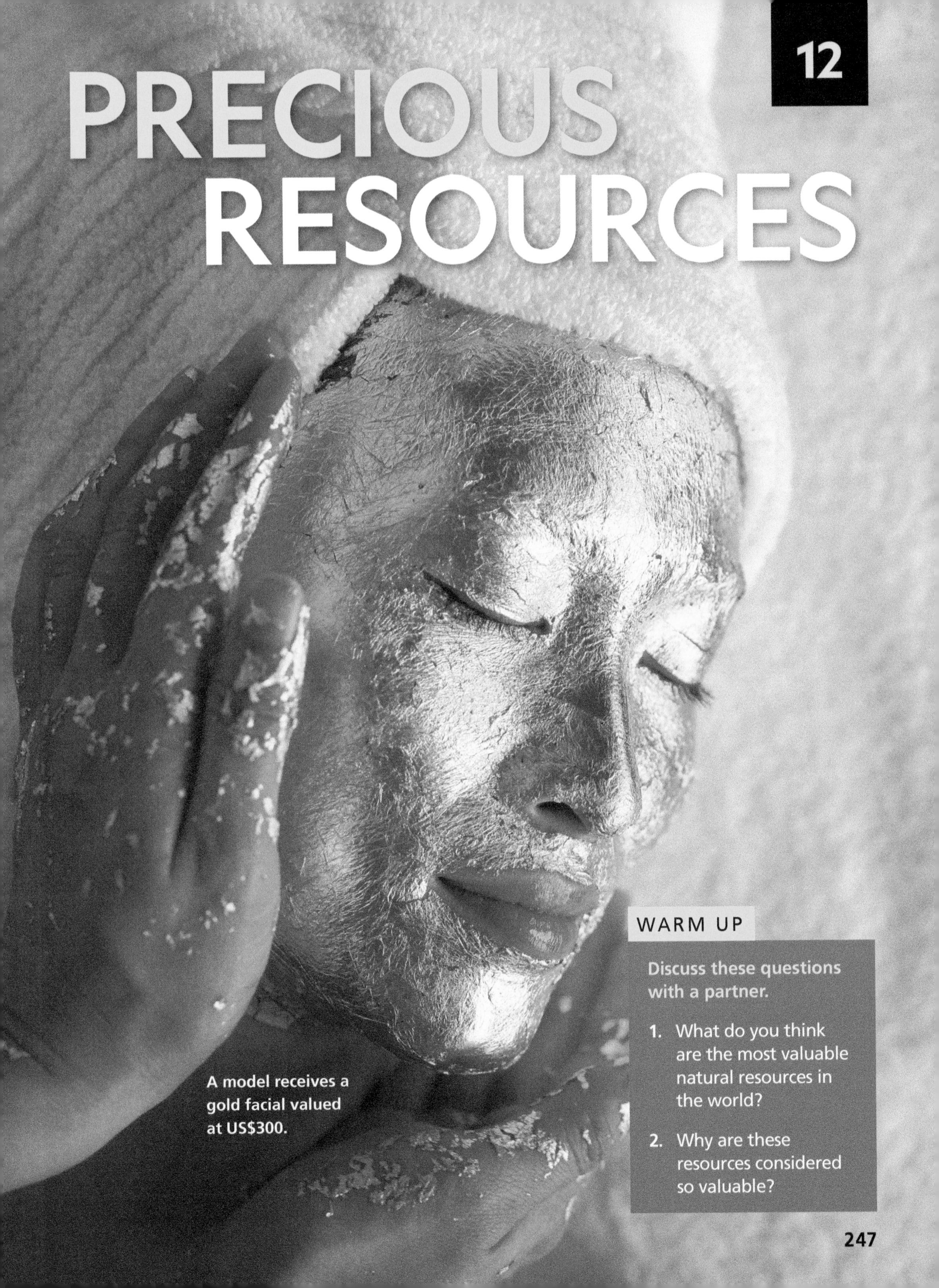

A model receives a
gold facial valued
at US$300.

WARM UP

Discuss these questions
with a partner.

1. What do you think
   are the most valuable
   natural resources in
   the world?

2. Why are these
   resources considered
   so valuable?

> ⌄ Customers purchase discounted gold jewelry at a store in Henan Province, China.

BEFORE YOU READ

DISCUSSION **A.** Look at the photo and read the caption. Apart from jewelry, what else is gold useful for? Share your ideas with a partner.

SKIMMING **B.** Quickly skim the article and match each section (1–5) with its topic (a–e). Then read the passage to check your ideas.

1. Paras A–D •   • a. how big companies are mining the world's gold
2. Paras E–H •   • b. the working life of a female truck driver at a gold mine
3. Paras I–L •   • c. the attraction of gold from ancient to modern times
4. Paras M–S •   • d. how a truck driver feels about her job
5. Paras T–U •   • e. the influence of gold on India's economy and society

GOLD FEVER

From an open mine in an Indonesian rain forest to an elaborate wedding ceremony in southern India, writer Brook Larmer follows the path of humanity's most desired commodity.

A **AS A GIRL GROWING UP** on the remote Indonesian island of Sumbawa, Nur Piah heard tales about vast quantities of gold buried beneath the mountain rain forests. They were legends—until geologists from a U.S. company, Newmont Mining Corporation, discovered a curious green rock near a dormant[1] volcano about 13 kilometers from her home. The rock's mossy color meant it contained copper, an occasional companion to gold, and it wasn't long before Newmont began setting up a mine named Batu Hijau, meaning "green rock."

B Nur Piah, then 24, replied to a Newmont ad seeking "operators," thinking that she might be able to get a job answering phones. When she arrived for training, her boss showed her a different kind of operating booth—the cab of a Caterpillar 793, one of the world's largest trucks. Standing 6 meters tall and 13 meters long, the truck was bigger than her family home. Its wheels alone were double her height. "The truck terrified me," Nur Piah recalls. Another shock soon followed when she saw the mine itself. "They had peeled the skin off the Earth!" she says. "I thought, whatever force can do that must be very powerful."

C Ten years later, Nur Piah, the daughter of a Muslim cleric, is part of that force herself. Pulling a pink head scarf close around her face, she smiles demurely[2] as she starts up the Caterpillar's engine and heads into the pit at Batu Hijau. Her vehicle is part of a fleet of more than a hundred trucks that removes close to a hundred million tons of rock from the ground every year.

D For millions of years, a 550-meter volcano stood here; however today, no hint of it remains. Layers of rock have been removed, and the space the volcano once occupied has been turned into a pit that is 1.6 kilometers wide and reaches more than a hundred meters below sea level. By the time the gold supplies at Batu Hijau have been **depleted**, the pit will be about 450 meters below sea level. The environmental impact doesn't concern Nur Piah anymore. "I only think about getting my salary," she says.

---

1 When a volcano is **dormant**, it is inactive but may become active in the future.
2 If an action is done **demurely**, it is done in a modest and reserved manner.

E THERE IS ONE THING, however, that Nur Piah finds curious: In a decade at Batu Hijau, she has never seen a speck of the gold she has helped mine. The engineers monitoring the process track its presence in the copper compounds that are extracted. And since the gold is shipped out to smelters[3] overseas, nobody on Sumbawa ever sees the hidden treasure that has transformed their island.

F Newmont is one of several giant mining corporations that are pursuing gold to the ends of the Earth, from the lowlands of Ghana to the mountaintops of Peru. Part of the challenge of mining for gold is that there is so little of it: In all of history, only about 190,000 tons of gold have been mined, barely enough to fill two Olympic-size swimming pools. More than two-thirds of that has been extracted since 1950. Now the world's richest deposits—particularly those in the United States, South Africa, and Australia—are fast being depleted, and new discoveries are rare.

G In recent years, attracted by the benefits of operating in the developing world—lower costs, higher yields, fewer regulations—Newmont has generated tens of thousands of jobs in poorer regions of the world. But it has also come under attack from conservationists, who have **filed** complaints about **unrestrained** ecological destruction and the forced relocation of villagers. At Batu Hijau, where Newmont is responsible for the mine's operation, the company has responded by spending more on its community development and environmental programs—and by dismissing its critics.

H "Why is it that activists thousands of miles away are yelling, but nobody around the mine complains?" asks Malik Salim, Batu Hijau's former senior external relations manager. "Gold is what drives everybody crazy."

I GOLD HAS BEEN DRIVING people crazy for millennia. The desire to possess gold has driven people to extremes, fueling wars and conquests, boosting empires and currencies, leveling mountains and forests. Gold is not vital to human existence; it has, in fact, relatively few practical uses. Yet its chief attractions—its unusual density and malleability,[4] along with its imperishable[5] shine—have made it one of the world's most desired commodities, a symbol of beauty, wealth, and immortality. From pharaohs (who chose to be buried in what they called the "flesh of the gods") to financiers (who, following Sir Isaac Newton's advice, made it the foundation of the global economy), nearly every society has invested gold with an almost mythological status.

J Humankind's feverish attachment to gold shouldn't have survived the modern world. Few cultures still believe that gold can give eternal life, and every country in the world—the United States was last, in 1971—has done away with the gold standard,[6] which the economist John Maynard Keynes famously called "a barbarous[7] relic." But gold's appeal not only endures; fueled by global uncertainty, it grows stronger.

K Aside from extravagance,[8] gold is also **reprising** its role as a safe haven in financially unstable times. Gold's recent surges have been amplified by concerns over a looming global recession. In 2007, demand exceeded mine production by 59 percent. "Gold has always had this kind of magic," says Peter L. Bernstein, author of *The Power of Gold*, "but it's never been clear if we have gold—or gold has us."

L While investors flock to gold-backed funds, jewelry still accounts for two-thirds of the demand, generating a record $53.5 billion in worldwide sales in 2007. In the United States, an activist-driven "No Dirty Gold" campaign

---

3 **Smelters** are machines or places that melt ores in order to extract the metals they contain.

4 **Malleability** refers to the ease with which an object can be altered and changed.

5 If a thing is **imperishable**, it never dies out or disappears.

6 **The gold standard** is a monetary system where the value of a country's currency is tied to the value of gold.

7 If something is described as **barbarous**, it is considered primitive and uncivilized.

8 **Extravagance** is the spending of more money than is reasonable or than you can afford.

WHAT IT'S WORTH

In coins and later backing for paper money, the price of gold has fluctuated with world crises and market forces. After 1971, when the dominant U.S. dollar was no longer tied to gold, the metal became a freely traded commodity. It reached US$1,000 per ounce for the first time in March 2008, but in real terms, its actual value was still well below its peak in the early 1980s.

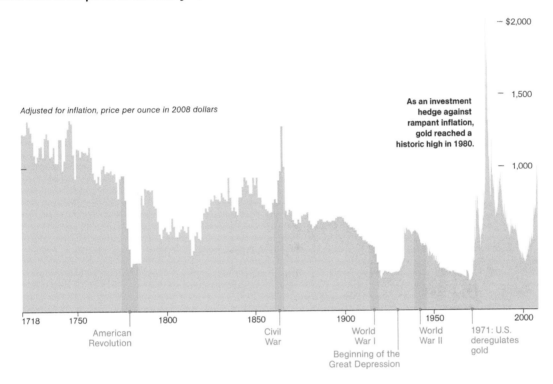

Adjusted for inflation, price per ounce in 2008 dollars

As an investment hedge against rampant inflation, gold reached a historic high in 1980.

1718	1750	1800	1850	1900	1950	2000

American Revolution

Civil War

World War I

Beginning of the Great Depression

World War II

1971: U.S. deregulates gold

HOW IT'S USED

Jewelry dominates gold consumption. The metal is also widely used in electronics as an efficient and reliable conductor of electricity. Gold-backed investment funds (exchange-traded funds, or ETFs) became popular as a "safe option" during the financial crisis beginning in mid-2008.

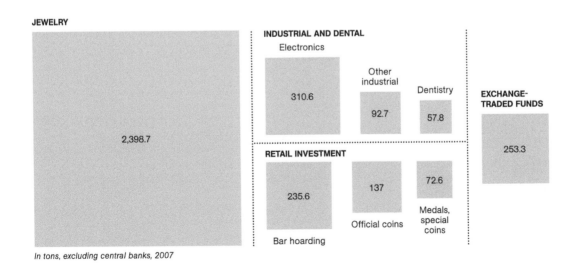

JEWELRY

2,398.7

In tons, excluding central banks, 2007

INDUSTRIAL AND DENTAL

Electronics
310.6

Other industrial
92.7

Dentistry
57.8

RETAIL INVESTMENT

Bar hoarding
235.6

Official coins
137

Medals, special coins
72.6

EXCHANGE-TRADED FUNDS
253.3

has persuaded many top jewelry retailers to stop selling gold from mines that cause severe social or environmental damage. But such concerns have little impact on the biggest consumer nations, namely China and India, which together account for over half the world's gold jewelry sales.

M NOWHERE IS THE GOLD OBSESSION more culturally entrenched[9] than in India. Per capita income in this country of 1.3 billion people is $2,700, but it has been a world leader in gold demand for several decades. In 2017, India consumed 737 tons of gold, about 20 percent of the world gold market, just behind China (955 tons). India produces very little gold of its own, but its citizens have hoarded[10] up to 24,000 tons of the yellow metal—40 times the amount held in the country's central bank.

N India's obsession stems not simply from a love of extravagance, or the rising prosperity of an emerging middle class. For Muslims, Hindus, Sikhs, and Christians alike, gold plays a central role at nearly every turning point in life—most of all when a couple marries. There are some ten million weddings in India every year, and in all but a few, gold is crucial both to the spectacular event itself and to the transaction between families and generations. "It's written into our DNA," says K.A. Babu, a manager at the Alapatt jewelry store in the southwestern city of Kochi. "Gold equals good fortune."

O The importance of gold is most obvious during the springtime festival of Akshaya Tritiya, considered the most **auspicious** day to buy gold according to the Hindu calendar. The quantity of gold jewelry Indians purchase on this day—over 20 tons in 2018—so exceeds the amount bought on any other day of the year throughout the world that it often pushes gold prices higher.

P "We grow up in an atmosphere of gold," says Renjith Leen, a magazine editor based in Kerala, a relatively prosperous state on India's southern tip that claims just 3 percent of the country's population but 7 to 8 percent of its gold market. When a baby is born, a grandmother rubs a gold coin in honey and places a drop of the liquid on the child's tongue for good luck. When the child is three years old, a learned family member takes a gold coin and traces words on the child's tongue to give the gift of eloquence.[11]

Q Aside from its cultural significance, gold is also the bedrock of the Indian economy. "Gold is the basis of our financial system," says K.A. Babu. "People see it as the best form of security, and nothing else lets you get cash as quickly." Hoarding gold as an intergenerational family nest egg[12] is an ancient tradition in India. So, too, is pawning[13] gold jewelry for emergency loans—and then buying it back.

R As the price of the metal goes up, however, poor Indian families are having a harder time raising the gold they need for dowries.[14] Rajam Chidambaram, a 59-year-old widow living in a slum on the outskirts of Kochi, recently found a young man to marry her only daughter, aged 27. The groom's family, however, demanded a dowry far out of her reach: 25 sovereigns, or 200 grams of gold (worth approximately $8,500 today). Chidambaram, a cleaning woman, has only the two earrings she wears; the gold necklace she once owned went to pay off her deceased husband's hospital bills. "I had to agree to the groom's demand," Chidambaram says, wiping away tears. "If I refuse, my daughter will stay home forever."

S In the end, local financiers advanced a loan for her daughter's dowry. Her daughter may now

---

9 If a custom or an idea is **entrenched**, it is firmly established and difficult to change.

10 When something is **hoarded**, it is accumulated and kept hidden away for future use.

11 Someone who has the gift of **eloquence** can write and speak very well.

12 A person's **nest egg** refers to their monetary savings, which have been put aside for later use.

13 **Pawning** is the act of giving or depositing personal property as security for payment of money borrowed.

14 **Dowries** are portions of money or property given by a bride's family to her husband at marriage.

be married, but Chidambaram is now faced with a debt that she may spend the rest of her life trying to repay.

T FOUR THOUSAND KILOMETERS AWAY, in her new house in the village of Jereweh, Nur Piah is focused more on the present than the future. "So many people depend on me," she says. Her husband makes some money as a timber trader, but Nur Piah's salary—about $650 a month—paid for their two-story concrete home. As if in tribute,

she has hung a large painting of the yellow Caterpillar 793 on her wall.

U Nur Piah's job is not without its **hardships**. Maneuvering the enormous truck over a 12-hour shift is especially stressful, she says, when the pit's graded roads are slicked by torrential rains. But now, after a long day, she smiles contentedly as her child, age six, falls asleep on her lap. The girl's middle name is Higrid, the Indonesian approximation of "high-**grade**," the best ore in the mine.

A GOLDEN WEDDING

V The gold ornaments come out of the velvet boxes one after another. They are family treasures that Nagavi, a 23-year-old Indian bride, always knew she would wear on her wedding day. The eldest daughter of a coffee plantation owner in the southern Indian state of Karnataka, Nagavi grew up marveling at the weddings that mark the **merger** of two wealthy Indian families. However, it's not until the morning of her own arranged wedding to the only son of another coffee plantation family that she understands just how beautiful the golden tradition can be.

Henna and gold bracelets adorn the arms and hands of an Indian bride.

W By the time Nagavi is ready for her wedding, the university graduate has been transformed into an Indian princess, covered in gold. An elaborately crafted hairpiece is so heavy—two and a half kilograms—that it pulls her head back. She is also wearing three gold necklaces. Those, and a dozen other pieces of jewelry, act as effective counterweights. As the family members **convene**, Nagavi walks slowly out of her home, trying to keep her balance as she tosses rice over her head in a traditional gesture of farewell.

X The gold treasures Nagavi wears are not a traditional dowry. In this circle of coffee growers around the town of Chikmagalur—unlike in many poorer parts of the country—it is considered inappropriate for a groom's family to make **explicit** demands. "This is seen as my 'share' of the family wealth," says Nagavi, gazing at the millions of dollars of gold jewelry. As with any Indian wedding, the gold also serves to display the value she brings to the union. "With daughters, you have to start saving gold from the day they are born," says Nagavi's father, C.P. Ravi Shankar. "It's important to marry them off well."

A. Choose the best answer for each question.

PURPOSE

1. What is the main purpose of paragraph F?

    a. to show how gold production has decreased in the past 50 years
    b. to emphasize that gold is actually a very rare commodity
    c. to point out how successful giant mining companies have been
    d. to indicate that some rich new gold deposits have been found

COHESION

2. Where would be the best place to insert this sentence in paragraph G?
For example, it stresses its efforts to reclaim the heaps of discarded rock, by covering them with soil and allowing the jungle to grow again.

    a. before the first sentence
    b. after the first sentence
    c. after the second sentence
    d. after the third sentence

INFERENCE

3. The quote from John Maynard Keynes in paragraph J shows that Keynes thought that _____.

    a. the United States should have maintained the gold standard
    b. gold's appeal was about to end
    c. the gold standard was out of date
    d. no one still believed that gold gives eternal life

DETAIL

4. Today, the country that consumes the second largest amount of gold is _____.

    a. China   c. the United States
    b. India   d. Indonesia

APPLICATION

5. Given the information in paragraph M, approximately how many tons of gold are held in the central bank of India?

    a. 410   c. 18,000
    b. 600   d. 95,000

CAUSE AND EFFECT

6. Which of the following causes Nur Piah the most job-related stress?

    a. the difficulty of finding gold
    b. the low wages she receives
    c. driving her truck in bad weather
    d. spending long hours at work

DETAIL

7. Which of the following is true about Nagavi?

    a. Her husband has many brothers.
    b. She got married after she graduated from university.
    c. Her family is from a very poor part of India.
    d. She is her father's only daughter.

B. Complete the sentences about the reading passage and infographic. Use no more than three words from the text for each answer.

1. The trucks at the Batu Hijau mine take away nearly a _____ of rock each year.

2. Despite its popularity—and the fact that it causes conflict and destruction—gold actually has a limited number of _____.

3. The United States was the last country to have its currency tied to the _____.

4. The countries of _____ account for more than 50 percent of gold jewelry sales.

5. Indians bought more than _____ of gold on one day during a popular festival in 2018.

6. In India, gold is used a lot during ceremonies for the approximately _____ held every year.

7. Around two-thirds of all gold mined is used by the _____ industry.

8. In real terms, the price of gold was at its highest in the _____.

9. ETFs were common investments at the time of the _____ in the late 2000s.

CRITICAL THINKING Evaluating Pros and Cons

▶ Imagine a mining company wants to dig for gold at a newly found deposit near your hometown. Work with a partner. List the pros and cons of such a plan.

Pros	Cons

▶ Work with a small group. Debate the issue. One side supports the company's plans, and the other side opposes it. Which side has the most convincing argument?

∨ Trucks are dwarfed by the vast scale of Batu Hijau mine, Indonesia.

Identifying Coherence Devices

Authors use a number of devices to clearly link together ideas within paragraphs and sentences. Here is a summary of the most common coherence devices.

Personal pronouns (*it, he, they,* etc.): Newmont is an American mining company. It is based in Denver, Colorado.

Demonstratives (*this, that, these, those, such*): Only about 190,000 tons of gold have ever been mined. And about half of that has been extracted.

Forms of *other* (*another, other, others*): One place mining companies have looked for gold is in the lowlands of Ghana. Another is in the mountains of Peru.

Signal words (*however, in addition, for example,* etc.): The gold that is found on Sumbawa is shipped overseas. <u>Therefore</u>, no one on the island sees any pure gold.

Synonyms: Aside from its cultural significance, gold is also the <u>bedrock</u> of the Indian economy. "Gold is the <u>basis</u> of our financial system."

UNDERSTANDING COHERENCE DEVICES

A. Scan the passage. Note answers to the questions below.

1. What does *they* refer to in the second sentence of paragraph A?

_____

2. What does *another shock* refer to in paragraph B?

_____

3. What does *those* refer to in paragraph F?

_____

4. What does *it* refer to in the last sentence of paragraph J?

_____

5. What does *such concerns* refer to in paragraph L?

_____

6. What does *those* refer to in paragraph W?

_____

IDENTIFYING SYNONYMS

B. Scan the passage. Note the synonyms used by the author for each word below.

1. *tales* (paragraph A)   _____

2. *truck* (paragraph C)   _____

3. *gold* (paragraph M)   _____

VOCABULARY PRACTICE

COMPLETION   **A. Complete the information using the correct form of the words in the box.**

auspicious	deplete	file	grade	hardship	unrestrained

Mongolia has some of the Earth's largest high-¹_____ gold, copper, and uranium reserves. For many, the current mining boom marks a(n) ²_____ time in the growth of the country's economy. However, the gold rush has also brought problems.

⌃ **A father and son pan for gold in Sharygol, Mongolia.**

Many of the mining sites whose resources have been ³_____ have been taken over by illegal miners known as "ninjas." Their unofficial status has allowed for the ⁴_____ use of mercury in the mines, which pollutes nearby rivers. Environmentalists have ⁵_____ complaints about the issue, as they are concerned about the impact on local habitats and communities. For example, local herders will face additional ⁶_____ since they depend on the land and its waters for their way of life.

COMPLETION   **B. Complete the information. Circle the correct words.**

In India, gold plays an important part in the ¹**merger** / **reprise** of two families through marriage. As part of the wedding transaction, it is common for the groom's family to make ²**convened** / **explicit** requests for the bride to bring gold jewelry into the family. Even relatively poor Indian families are required to provide gold for a daughter's wedding, sometimes ³**reprising** / **depleting** the process if they have more than one daughter. When the families finally ⁴**convene** / **deplete** for the wedding, the gold is worn by the bride to publicly display the value she has brought to the marriage.

WORD LINK   **C. The suffix -ship in hardship has the meaning of "state" or "condition." Add -ship to the words in the box to complete the sentences.**

member	partner	scholar

1. Many clubs require members to pay a _____ fee.
2. Some students receive a _____ to help pay for college fees.
3. The two countries formed a _____ to tackle pollution in the region.

12B

▽ Evaporation pools in Bolivia's Salar de Uyuni are filled with lithium-rich brine pumped from beneath the surface. Bolivia has 17 percent of the world's lithium—a heat-resistant metal capable of storing substantial amounts of energy—and is keen to extract it.

BEFORE YOU READ

DISCUSSION **A.** Look at the photo and read the caption. What do you know about lithium? Why might countries like Bolivia be keen to extract it? Discuss with a partner.

PREDICTING **B.** The following people are mentioned in the reading. How do you think they might feel about lithium mining in Bolivia? Positive? Negative? Discuss ideas with a partner. Then read to check your ideas.

Álvaro García Linera, Bolivia's vice president

Patricio Mendoza, Uyuni's mayor

Miguel Parra, Bolivian chemical engineer

Juan Benavides, Bolivian geologist

THE RUSH FOR WHITE GOLD

A ONE EARLY SATURDAY MORNING IN LA PAZ, Álvaro García Linera—the silver-haired vice president of Bolivia—greets me in the spacious salon outside his office overlooking Plaza Murillo. The politician is known in his country as a Marxist ideologue,[1] but today he presents himself as a capitalist pitchman.[2]

B The pitch in question involves lithium. García Linera speaks of his country's natural resource in a simultaneously factual and awestruck way. Lithium, essential to our battery-fueled world, is also the key to Bolivia's future, the vice president **assures** me. A mere four years from now, he predicts, it will be "the engine of our economy." All Bolivians will benefit, he continues, "taking them out of poverty, guaranteeing their stability in the middle class, and training them in scientific and technological fields so that they become part of the intelligentsia[3] in the global economy."

C But as the vice president knows, no pitch about lithium as Bolivia's economic **salvation** is complete without addressing the source of that lithium: the Salar de Uyuni. The 10,000-square-kilometer salt flat, one of the country's most magnificent landscapes, will almost certainly be altered—if not forever damaged—by mining the resource underneath it.

D "Have you been to the Salar de Uyuni?" García Linera asks. When I reply that I'll be heading there soon, the vice president loses his air of detachment and seems full of nostalgia. "When you go to the Salar," he instructs me, "go there one night. Spread a blanket in the center of the Salar, and turn on some music."

*   *   *

E It takes a day to drive from the world's highest capital city to the world's largest salt flat. The route passes steadily downhill through small villages, until leveling out, at about 3,600 meters, into a mostly vacant stretch of land occasionally animated by llamas.[4] By late afternoon, the salt flat can be seen across the plain.

F I reach the Salar—Spanish for "salt flat"—just before sunset, and for over a kilometer I drive along its smooth and firm surface until it becomes evident that this is the middle of nowhere. The spectacle seems unreal: kilometers of whitewashed level terrain, its starkness perfected by the cloudless blue sky and the Andean peaks in the distance. Motorcycles and 4x4s drive across the roadless surface, destinations unknown. Here and there solitary people wander about, gazing into what the Bolivian vice president calls "the **infinite** table of snowy white."

---

1 An **ideologue** is someone who follows a certain set of political beliefs.

2 A **pitchman** is a person who tries to sell something to someone, especially one who aggressively markets their goods.

3 The **intelligentsia** of a country or community are its most educated people.

4 A **llama** is an animal used to carry loads, especially in South America.

G Somewhere out of sight on infinity's edge, bulldozers are plowing evaporation pools in the Salar—long and precise excavations, like a grid of enormous swimming pools. The bulldozers will be moving this way soon—how soon, no one can say with any certainty.

H Here is what we do know. First, that underneath the world's biggest salt flat lies another wonder: one of the world's greatest lithium deposits—perhaps 17 percent of the planet's total. Second, that by **exploiting** its lithium reserves, the government of Bolivia—where 40 percent of the people live in poverty—envisions a pathway out of its economic misfortune.

I The salt flat had long been regarded by Bolivians as little more than a geographical anomaly.[5] While surrounding mountains are celebrated in indigenous stories, "the Salar has never had cultural significance," says Uyuni's mayor, Patricio Mendoza. "People were afraid that if they took a walk on it, they might get lost and die of thirst or their llamas would damage their hooves on the salt."

J The Salar's fortunes changed in the 1980s, when a La Paz tour operator named Juan Quesada Valda laid eyes on it. Quesada was searching for a tourist destination to **rival** Lake Titicaca.[6] When he beheld the Salar, he experienced a **revelation**, recalls his daughter Lucía: "You can find lakes anywhere," she says, "but you cannot find a salt flat like this anywhere else in the world. He knew he could sell this place."

K An architect by training, Quesada **proceeded to** build the first of several hotels made almost entirely out of blocks of salt in Colchani, a village at the eastern edge of the Salar. Adventurous foreigners began to show up to bask[7] in the great pale desert. Weddings, yoga lessons, and automobile races would eventually be staged

on it. Today the salt hotels are typically full and Uyuni has become a vacationland bustling with college-age backpackers.

L "Maybe 90 percent of our economy is tourism," Mendoza says. All of which is to say that in Bolivia's morose history of economic disappointments, the Salar provides a happy if modest exception. But now comes Bolivia's future, in the form of lithium.

*　　　*　　　*

M What gold meant to earlier eras, and petroleum to the previous century, lithium may eclipse in the coming years. Long used in medication to treat bipolar disorders—and in items as varied as ceramics and nuclear weapons—it has emerged as an essential component for the batteries in computers, cell phones, and other electronic devices.

N The global market's annual consumption of lithium in 2017 was approximately 40,000 metric tons, representing a roughly 10 percent increase year by year since 2015. Meanwhile, in the same period, lithium prices nearly tripled—a clear reflection of how fast demand has been rising.

O That will likely intensify as electric cars become more popular. One **version** of the Tesla Model S runs on a battery pack with about 65 kilograms of lithium compounds—the equivalent of what's in 10,000 cell phones. The investment firm also projects that every time electric-vehicle sales replace a percentage of all vehicles sold, the demand for lithium increases by 70,000 metric tons a year. Given that France and the United Kingdom have already announced that they'll ban the sale of cars running on gas or diesel by 2040, it would seem evident that a country abounding with lithium need never fear poverty.

P However, Bolivia first faces several hurdles, and the most daunting is a scientific one. Producing battery-grade lithium from brine involves separating out sodium chloride, potassium chloride, and magnesium chloride. This last is particularly expensive to remove. Bolivia's lithium

---

5 If something is an **anomaly**, it is different from what is usual or expected.

6 **Lake Titicaca** is a large, high-altitude lake between Bolivia and Peru.

7 If you **bask** in a place, you lie there and enjoy its warmth and sunshine.

CHARGING AHEAD

Lithium's unique chemical properties—it's the lightest of all metals, heat resistant, and capable of storing substantial amounts of energy in batteries—are fueling a global rush to extract it from hard-rock minerals and brines.

WHERE IT IS AND WHERE IT GOES

Lithium deposits around the world are estimated at 53 million metric tons. Australia currently leads in extraction, but South America is the continent with the greatest amount of this valuable resource.

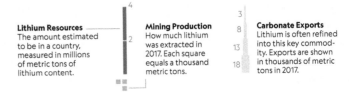

Lithium Resources
The amount estimated to be in a country, measured in millions of metric tons of lithium content.

Mining Production
How much lithium was extracted in 2017. Each square equals a thousand metric tons.

Carbonate Exports
Lithium is often refined into this key commodity. Exports are shown in thousands of metric tons in 2017.

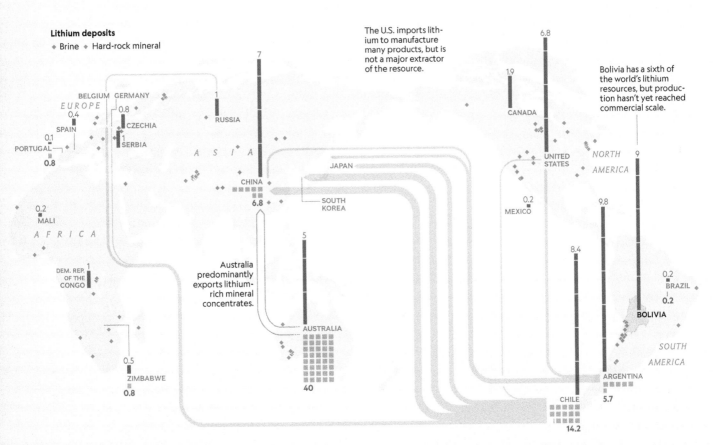

Lithium deposits
• Brine ◆ Hard-rock mineral

The U.S. imports lithium to manufacture many products, but is not a major extractor of the resource.

Bolivia has a sixth of the world's lithium resources, but production hasn't yet reached commercial scale.

Australia predominantly exports lithium-rich mineral concentrates.

EUROPE
BELGIUM GERMANY 0.8
SPAIN 0.4
PORTUGAL 0.1
0.8
CZECHIA
SERBIA 1
RUSSIA 1
ASIA
CHINA 6.8
JAPAN
SOUTH KOREA
MALI 0.2
AFRICA
DEM. REP. OF THE CONGO 1
ZIMBABWE 0.5
0.8
AUSTRALIA 5 / 40
CANADA 1.9
UNITED STATES
MEXICO 0.2
NORTH AMERICA 9
BRAZIL 0.2 / 0.2
BOLIVIA 9.8
SOUTH AMERICA
ARGENTINA 5.7
CHILE 8.4 / 14.2

PRODUCTION INCREASING

Projecting high demand for lithium compounds, mining production outpaced consumption worldwide in 2017, according to estimates.

LITHIUM WORLDWIDE

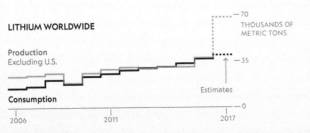

70 THOUSANDS OF METRIC TONS

Production Excluding U.S.

35

Estimates

Consumption

0

2006   2011   2017

BRINE VS. HARD ROCK

Hard-rock minerals were the main source of lithium until the 1990s, when brines, a cheaper source of lithium carbonate, overtook them.

LITHIUM EXTRACTION

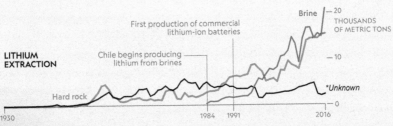

First production of commercial lithium-ion batteries

Chile begins producing lithium from brines

Brine — 20 THOUSANDS OF METRIC TONS

— 10

Hard rock

*Unknown

— 0

1930   1984 1991   2016

"UNKNOWN" INCLUDES LITHIUM DATA FROM THE U.S. (1936–1998) AND CHINA (2000–2017) THAT DOESN'T DISCLOSE THE BREAKDOWN BETWEEN HARD-ROCK AND BRINE SOURCES. MEASUREMENTS ARE IN METRIC TONS (A METRIC TON IS 2,205 POUNDS) OF LITHIUM CONTENT. MANUEL CANALES AND MATTHEW W. CHWASTYK, NGM STAFF; AMANDA HOBBS; RONALD PANIAGUA. SOURCES: BRIAN JASKULA, U.S. GEOLOGICAL SURVEY; BRENT A. ELLIOTT AND RAHUL VERMA, BUREAU OF ECONOMIC GEOLOGY, UNIVERSITY OF TEXAS; BRINE VS. HARD ROCK CHART: S.H. MOHR AND OTHERS, *MINERALS* 2012 (UPDATED USING REFERENCES CITED IN ARTICLE); BATTERIES CHART: ADAPTED WITH PERMISSION FROM *MRS BULLETIN* 40 (2015)

> Salar de Uyuni viewed by satellite. The rectangular patches in the south indicate a large lithium mining area.

deposits have a relatively high magnesium content. "While the ratio of magnesium in Chile is 5 to 1, in Uyuni it's 21 to 1," says Bolivian chemical engineer Miguel Parra, "four times the concentration. So it's a much simpler operation for them. For us, separating magnesium from lithium is the biggest challenge."

Q There are other issues, such as: What does Bolivia intend to do with the heaps of magnesium waste? The Bolivian government claims that it has a unique processing method that will somehow reduce waste, but just how much is speculative. "The environmental impact in Chile and Argentina is low," claims Bolivian geologist Juan Benavides, "but we're not able to extrapolate,[8] really, because the magnesium content in Bolivian lithium is very high. All we know is … that the lithium regulations and laws in Argentina and Chile are more stringent[9] than in Bolivia."

R Among the greatest concerns is how much water will be required to extract the lithium. Two rivers flow into the salt flat. One is thin enough to be a creek; the other, shallow enough to wade across. Both are crucial to the local growers of quinoa,[10] of which Bolivia is the world's second largest supplier, after Peru.

Though the Bolivian government insists that 90 percent of the water it uses will come from salt water rather than underground, some experts are **skeptical**. "Year after year, the water is going to be the major resource that is needed," says Oscar Ballivián Chávez, a Bolivian geologist. "They'll need vast quantities, more than any other mine in Bolivia."

S And finally, there's the unspoiled natural wonder of the Salar itself. Though revered by human visitors for its boundless austerity,[11] it is also a breeding ground for several animal species such as the Chilean flamingo. "Our plant is located far away from these sanctuaries," García Linera says, adding, "This demonstrates our **commitment** to the environment."

T I thought about these unanswered questions as I headed once again through the colorless daydream of the Salar—an illusion of simplicity that apparently goes on forever, but in fact, cannot.

---

8 If you **extrapolate** from facts, you use them as a basis for general statements about a situation.

9 Rules and laws that are **stringent** strictly control something.

10 **Quinoa** is the small seeds of a plant eaten as a grain and popular as a health food.

11 **Austerity** refers to a place having no human warmth or comfort.

READING COMPREHENSION

A. Choose the best answer for each question.

GIST
1. What is the central conflict that is explored in this article?
   a. The conflict between indigenous people and those of European ancestry.
   b. The conflict between the tourist industry and the mining industry.
   c. The conflict between economic development and the environment of the Salar.
   d. The conflict between Bolivia and its neighbors in South America.

REFERENCE
2. The word *it* in the second sentence of paragraph C refers to _____.
   a. lithium
   b. the Salar de Uyuni
   c. mining
   d. the economy

DETAIL
3. The author would probably NOT describe the Salar de Uyuni as _____.
   a. remote
   b. flat
   c. empty
   d. unvisited

DETAIL
4. The main reason the Bolivian government wants to extract lithium in Salar de Uyuni is _____.
   a. to meet the global demand for lithium
   b. to replace the tourism industry
   c. to stimulate their poor economy
   d. because Salar de Uyuni is unpopulated

APPLICATION
5. According to the information in paragraph O, if the percentage of electric vehicles sold goes from 3 percent to 5 percent in one year, the demand for lithium will probably increase by _____ metric tons.
   a. 10,000
   b. 40,000
   c. 70,000
   d. 140,000

VOCABULARY
6. The word *morose* in paragraph L is closest in meaning to _____.
   a. lengthy
   b. tangled
   c. gloomy
   d. infamous

UNDERSTANDING INFOGRAPHICS
7. According to the infographic, the greatest amount of lithium is extracted in _____.
   a. Australia
   b. Bolivia
   c. Chile
   d. Argentina

B. Look again at the infographic Charging Ahead. Note answers to the questions.

1. Which continent has the greatest amount of lithium deposits? _____

2. Which country is the leading exporter of lithium? _____

3. From which source—brine or hard rock—has lithium most commonly been
obtained in recent years? _____

4. In which part of Australia are most of the country's lithium deposits located? _____

C. Which paragraph from the reading passage contains the following information?
Write the appropriate letter.

1. _____ a description of where Bolivia will get the water it needs for the extraction process.

2. _____ an example of an industry that will use a lot of lithium in the future

3. _____ comparison between countries of the environmental effects of magnesium waste

4. _____ a history of the uses of lithium

5. _____ an explanation of why extracting lithium in Bolivia is more expensive than in Chile

6. _____ arguments that local wildlife may not be impacted by lithium extraction

CRITICAL THINKING Evaluating Arguments

▶ The author mentions two main issues Bolivia faces with the process of extracting lithium.
Complete the chart with information from the reading passage.

Issue	Government's view	Expert's view
Dealing with waste		
Lack of water		

▶ Which of the views is more convincing? Discuss your reasons with a partner.

▶ Do you think Bolivia should extract lithium from Salar de Uyuni? Consider the factors below.
Discuss your ideas with a partner.

Bolivia's economy   environmental issues   global growth in lithium usage

costs of extraction   effects on tourism   high poverty levels

Synthesizing Ideas Across Readings

Synthesizing occurs when you think critically about a topic using information from two or more sources. By comparing information, you can gain new ideas or insights into the topic. Synthesizing is an ongoing process that often draws upon other skills, such as summarizing, comparing/contrasting, and evaluating ideas. As you read a text, consider how this new information relates to what you previously read about a similar topic.

COMPARING INFORMATION

A. Do these facts describe gold, lithium, or both? Add the letters (a–j) to the Venn diagram. Use information from Reading A and Reading B

a. has fairly few practical uses
b. is in high demand
c. has been used to treat bipolar disorder
d. is melted using smelters
e. has a market of 40,000 metric tons a year
f. is found in deposits containing magnesium
g. is mined in Peru
h. is used in electronics
i. has recently tripled in price
j. is a symbol of immortality

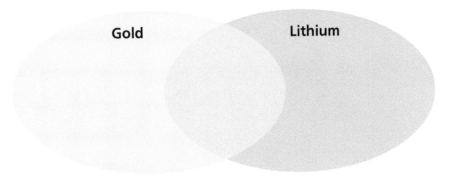

Gold   Lithium

SYNTHESIZING INFORMATION

B. Discuss these questions in a group.

1. Do you think extraction of gold or lithium causes more environmental damage?

2. Do you think the demand for gold or lithium will rise more in the future? Why? What evidence from the reading supports your opinion?

3. Imagine you can invest in either gold or lithium. Which would you choose? Why?

The black dot in this image is a SUV, giving scale to the vast salt flats at Salar de Uyuni.

COMPLETION **A. Complete the information by circling the correct words.**

There are few places that can [1]**assure** / **rival** the beauty of Salar de Uyuni. Stretching out toward a seemingly [2]**skeptical** / **infinite** horizon, it is all that's left of several prehistoric lakes that dried up.

While the lithium at Salar de Uyuni may prove to be Bolivia's economic [3]**salvation** / **version**, this area is also a lucrative extraction site for salt. Workers scrape the salt from the desert floor and place it into small piles where it is left

⋀**Miners dig for salt deposits at Salar de Uyuni.**

to dry. After a few days, the salt is moved to a processing facility, where it is heated to dry it further. Factory workers [4]**proceed** / **assure** to add iodine and the product is sealed into bags as table salt.

Despite having this incredible natural resource, it is not fully [5]**exploited** / **skeptical**. Only a few families have a [6]**version** / **commitment** to working the salt flats. In fact, Bolivia actually imports salt because most people prefer sea salt.

WORDS IN CONTEXT **B. Complete the sentences. Circle the correct options.**

1. A **revelation** is a(n) *unsurprising and known* / *surprising and unknown* fact.

2. If you **assure** someone, you cause them to be *certain* / *uncertain* about something.

3. A **version** of something is a particular form that *cannot be fully understood by anyone* / *varies from other forms of the same thing*.

4. If you are **skeptical** about something, you *fully agree with* / *have doubts about* it.

WORD LINK **C. The word root *vers* in version means "turned." Match the words to their definitions. Use a dictionary to help.**

1. reverse •   • a. act of straying from a course

2. averse •   • b. acting against

3. adverse •   • c. to move backward

4. diversion •   • d. having a strong dislike of something

A lithium battery manufacturing plant for automotive use in Tangshan, China

THE LURE OF LITHIUM

BEFORE YOU WATCH

DEFINITIONS **A.** Read the excerpts from the video. Match each word in **bold** with its definition.

"Ever since its discovery, lithium has been found to be incredibly **versatile**, including strengthening glass and **refining** metal **alloys**."

"The versatility of lithium has helped **catapult** many technological developments, largely due to the metal's unique chemical properties."

"Such a rare commodity has become the **bedrock** of industry and may be the key to the future of civilization."

1. versatile • • a. a substance made from one or more metals

2. refine • • b. capable of being used for many purposes

3. alloy • • c. to make minor changes to improve something

4. catapult • • d. the basis on which something is built

5. bedrock • • e. to launch something quickly

DISCUSSION **B.** You are going to watch a video about lithium. What do you already know about lithium from Reading B? Discuss with a partner.

GIST   **A.** Watch the video. Check (✓) the information that is true about lithium.

- ☐ **1.** Lithium makes up about 2% of the Earth's crust.
- ☐ **2.** Lithium is the lightest element in the universe.
- ☐ **3.** The most popular use of lithium is in batteries.
- ☐ **4.** Lithium melts at a very high temperature.
- ☐ **5.** Lithium is capable of storing large amounts of energy.

COMPLETION   **B.** Watch the video again. Complete the notes

Element	Lithium
Discovery	Year: [1]_____ ; named after Greek word for: [2]_____
Classification	Alkali [3]_____
Uses	Batteries in [4]_____, [5]_____, or electric vehicles
Properties	Heat- [6]_____; highly [7]_____; can store large amounts of [8]_____
Sources	Hard-rock minerals, [9]_____, or saltwater reservoirs called [10]_____

CRITICAL THINKING Synthesizing Ideas   Discuss these questions with a partner.

▶ Gold and lithium are examples of limited resources. What are some other limited non-renewable resources that are important to the world economy?

▶ How long do you think each resource will last? Which would have the greatest impact on the world economy if it runs out?

VOCABULARY REVIEW

Do you remember the meanings of these words? Check (✓) the ones you know. Look back at the unit and review any words you're not sure of.

Reading A

☐ auspicious	☐ convene*	☐ deplete	☐ explicit*	☐ file*
☐ grade*	☐ hardship	☐ merger	☐ reprise	☐ unrestrained*

Reading B

☐ assure*	☐ commitment*	☐ exploit*	☐ infinite*	☐ proceed (to)*
☐ revelation*	☐ rival	☐ salvation	☐ skeptical	☐ version*

*Academic Word List

Photo and Illustration Credits

Cover, 3 Overview, Source imagery © DigitalGlobe Inc., A Maxar Company, 2019, **4–5** Babak Tafreshi/NGIC, **7** Mexico Shoots/Moment/Getty Images, **8–9** Paul Nicklen/NGIC, **10** NG MAPS/NGIC, **12–13** Hernan Canellas/NGIC, **14** Paul Nicklen/NGIC, **15** © f9photos/Shutterstock.com, **17** RapidEye/E+/Getty Images, **18–19** Paul Chesley/NGIC, **20–21** goikmitl/iStock/Getty Images, **23** David Alan Harvey/NGIC, **24** Tom Roche/Shutterstock.com, **26** Pete Mcbride/NGIC, **27** Stephen Alvarez/NGIC, **29** Jimmy Chin/NGIC, **30–31** National Geographic, **32–33** Andrew Wrighting/Alamy Stock Photo, **34** Richard Bull, **36** Design Pics Inc/NGIC, **38** Jeff Pachoud/AFP/Getty Images, **39** Raul Touzon/NGIC, **40–41** Jimmy Chin/NGIC, **43** Daisy Chung/NGIC, **44** Jimmy Chin/NGIC, **46** Jimmy Chin/NGIC, **49** Corey Rich/Aurora/Getty Images, **51** Ciril Jazbec/NGIC, **52–53** Nicholas Kamm/AFP/Getty Images, **55** Library of Congress, **56** Dror Yaron/Center for PostNatural History, **59** NurPhoto/Contributor/Getty Images, **61** NASA, **62–63** Handout/Getty Images Publicity/Getty Images, **64** Cengage, **65** Cengage, **66** Sustainable Development Goals, **68** William Campbell/Corbis Historical/Getty Images, **71** Mark Thiessen/NGIC, **73** Tyrone Turner/NGIC, **74–75** Cristiano Fronteddu/Alamy Stock Photo, **76** Jodi Cobb/NGIC, **78–79** Fernando G. Baptista/NGIC, **81** Neale Clark/robertharding/Getty Images Plus, **83** Arnd Wiegmann/Reuters, **84–85** Michael Orso/Moment/Getty Images, **86** Parker/Lawson/NGIC, **87** Ryan Morris/NGIC, **88** Xavier Testelin/Gamma-Rapho/Getty Images, **90** Andrew Burton/Getty Images News/Getty Images, **92** Daniella Nowitz/NGIC, **93** Warren Faidley/Corbis/Getty Images, **95** Luca Locatelli/NGIC, **96–97** Tyrone Turner/NGIC, **99** Tyrone Turner/NGIC, **101** Alvaro Valino/NGIC, **103** ZUMA Press Inc/Alamy Stock Photo, **105** Boston Globe/Contributor/Getty Images, **106** Michael Melford/NGIC, **108** B. O'Kane/Alamy Stock Photo, **110** Jason Treat/NGIC, **112** Bloomberg/Contributor/Getty Images, **114** Look/Alamy Stock Photo, **115** Eco Images/Universal Images Group/Getty Images, **117** Joel Sartore/NGIC, **118–119** Brian Skerry/NGIC, **120–121** Fernando G. Baptista/NGIC, **122** Brian Skerry/NGIC, **123** Ryan Morris/NGIC, **125** Brian Skerry/NGIC, **127** Brian Skerry/NGIC, **128–129** Mark Kolbe/Getty Images News/Getty Images, **131** Sebastien Bozon/AFP/Getty Images, **132** Joel Sartore/NGIC, **134** (l) Joel Sartore/National Geographic Photo Ark/NGIC, **134** (r) Joel Sartore/NGIC, **136** Mark Bowler/Nature Picture Library, **137** AP Images/Evan Vucci, **139** South_agency/E+/Getty Images, **140–141** Robert Clark/NGIC, **142–143** Alfred Pasieka/Science Photo Library/Getty Images, **144** BSIP/Contributor/Universal Images Group/Getty Images, **146** The Asahi Shimbun/Getty Images, **148** Mohd Rasfan/AFP/Getty Images, **149** Mark Thiessen/NGIC, **151** Bryan Christie Design/NGIC, **153** Mark Thiessen/NGIC, **154** Mark Thiessen/NGIC, **156** Mark Thiessen/NGIC, **157** BSIP, **159** Daniel J. Cox/Oxford Scientific/Getty Images, **160–161** Mike Theiss/NGIC, **162** Peter Essick/NGIC, **164** Mariel Furlong/NGIC, **166** Mint Images/Mint Images RF/Getty Images, **168** Michael Melford/The Image Bank/Getty Images, **169** Frans Lanting/NGIC, **170** Bence Mate/Nature Picture Library, **174** Mikhail Metzel/TASS/Getty Images, **176** Ranulph Thorpe/Alamy Stock Photo, **177** Joel Sartore/NGIC, **178** Joel Sartore, National Geographic Photo Ark/NGIC, **179** Dave Yoder/NGIC, **180–181** Todd Anderson/Alamy Stock Photo, **183** GraphicaArtis/Archive Photos/Getty Images, **184–185** Fernando G. Baptista/NGIC, **187** NGIC, **189** Chesnot/Getty Images Entertainment/Getty Images, **190–191** Michael Melford/NGIC, **192–193** Fred De Noyelle/Godong/Corbis Documentary/Getty Images, **194** Aflo Co. Ltd./Alamy Stock Photo, **196** Boston Globe/Contributor/Getty Images, **198** Michael DeFreitas South America/Alamy Stock Photo, **199** VCG/Contributor/Getty Images, **200** Jeremy Sutton-Hibbert/Getty Images News/Getty Images, **201** NASA/JPL, **202–203** Babak Tafreshi/NGIC, **204** Dave Yoder/NGIC, **206–207** Jason Treat/NGIC, **209** Markus Thomenius/Alamy Stock Photo, **210** Handout/Getty Images News/Getty Images, **211** European Space Agency/NASA, C. Gunn/Science Source, **212** Mulrooney Oxford UK/Alamy Stock Photo, **214–215** John Tomanio/NGIC, **217** Max Aguilera-Hellweg/NGIC, **218** Baron/Hulton Archive/Getty Images, **220** Scientifica/Corbis NX/Getty Images Plus, **221** Mark Garlick/Science Photo Library/Getty Images, **222** Bill Heinsohn/The Image Bank/Getty Images, **223** Dave Yoder/NGIC, **224–225** Raul Touzon/NGIC, **226** Lisa Bignzoli/NGIC, **227** Suleiman II (oil on canvas), Italian School, (16th century)/Kunsthistorisches Museum, Vienna, Austria/Bridgeman Images, **229** Attila Kisbenedek/AFP/Getty Images, **233** age fotostock/Alamy Stock Photo, **234–235** Geography Photos/Universal Images Group/Getty Images, **236** David Pegzlz/Shutterstock.com, **237** NGM MAPS/NGIC, **238** Design Pics Inc/NGIC, **240** Andrea Pistolesi/Stone/Getty Images, **242** Kevin Wheal Spain/Alamy Stock Photo, **244** View of Toledo, c.1597–99 (oil on canvas), Greco, El (Domenico Theotocopuli) (1541–1614)/Metropolitan Museum of Art, New York, USA/Bridgeman Images, **245** CasarsaGuru/E+/Getty Images, **247** Robert Clark/NGIC, **248–249** VCG/Getty Images, **251** Blow.Charlesw M/NGIC, **253** William Albert Allard/NGIC, **255** Randy Olson/NGIC, **257** Jonas Gratzer/LightRocket/Getty Images, **258–259** Cedric Gerbehaye/NGIC, **261** Manuel Canales/NGIC, **262** ESA/eyevine/Redux Pictures, **265** Mike Theiss/NGIC, **266** Kimberly Sue Walker/age fotostock/Getty Images Plus, **267** Xinhua/Xinhua News Agency/eyevine/Redux Pictures

NGIC = National Geographic Image Collection

Text Credits

9–13 Adapted from "Secrets of the Maya Otherworld," by Alma Guillermoprieto: NGM, August 2013, **19–22** Adapted from "Divining Angkor," by Richard Stone: NGM, July 2009, **30–34** Adapted from "This Woman is Your Adventurer of the Year," by Mary Anne Potts: nationalgeographic.com, **41–44** Adapted from "How Alex Honnold Made 'the Ultimate Climb'—Without a Rope," by Mark Synnott: NGM, Feb 2019, **53–57** Adapted from "Why Do Many Reasonable People Doubt Science?" by Joel Achenbach: NGM, Mar 2015, **63–66** Adapted from "Gates Report Shows 'Mind-Blowing' Progress—and Work to Do," by Susan Goldberg: NGM, Nov 2018, **75–79** Adapted from "Vanishing Venice," by Cathy Newman: NGM, Aug 2009, **85–88** Adapted from "Rising Seas," by Tim Folger: NGM, Sep 2013, **97–101** Adapted from "It Starts at Home," by Peter Miller: NGM, Mar 2009, **107–110** Adapted from "Plugging Into the Sun," by George Johnson: NGM, Sep 2009, **119–123** Adapted from "Quicksilver," by Kenneth Brower: NGM, Mar 2014, **129–132** Adapted from "Building the Ark," by Elizabeth Kolbert: NGM, Oct 2013, **141–144** Adapted from "Brain Science," by Carl Zimmer: NGM, Feb 2014, **150–152** Adapted from "bi-on-ics," by Josh Fischman: NGM, Jan 2010, **161–164** Adapted from "The Genius of Swarms," by Peter Miller: NGM, July 2007, **170–172** Adapted from "Edward O. Wilson: From Ants, Onward," by Tim Appenzeller: NGM, May 2006, **181–185** Adapted from "A Man for All Ages," by Kenneth MacLeish: NGM, Sep 1977, **191–194** Adapted from "The Power of Writing," by Joel L. Swerdlow: NGM, Aug 1999, **203–207** Adapted from "Cosmic Dawn," by Yudhijit Bhattacharjee: NGM, Apr 2014, **215–218** Adapted from "Element Hunters," by Rob Dunn: NGM, May 2013, **225–229** Adapted from "The World of Süleyman the Magnificent," by Merle Severy: NGM, Nov 1987, **235–240** Adapted from "When the Moors Ruled Spain," by Thomas J. Abercrombie: NGM, July 1988, **249–253** Adapted from "The Real Price of Gold," by Brook Larmer: NGM, Jan 2009, **261–265** Adapted from "This Metal Is Powering Today's Technology—at What Price?" by Robert Draper: NGM, Feb 2019

NGM = National Geographic Magazine

Acknowledgments

The Authors and Publisher would like to thank the following teaching professionals for their valuable feedback during the development of the series.

Akiko Hagiwara, Tokyo University of Pharmacy and Life Sciences; **Albert Lehner**, University of Fukui; **Alexander Cameron**, Kyushu Sangyo University; **Amira Traish**, University of Sharjah; **Andrés López**, Colégio José Max León; **Andrew Gallacher**, Kyushu Sangyo University; **Angelica Hernandez**, Liceo San Agustin; **Angus Painter**, Fukuoka University; **Anouchka Rachelson**, Miami Dade College; **Ari Hayakawa**, Aoyama Gakuin University; **Atsuko Otsuki**, Senshu University; **Ayako Hisatsune**, Kanazawa Institute of Technology; **Bogdan Pavliy**, Toyama University of International Studies; **Braden Chase**, The Braden Chase Company; **Brian J. Damm**, Kanda Institute of Foreign Languages; **Carol Friend**, Mercer County Community College; **Catherine Yu**, CNC Language School; **Chad Godfrey**, Saitama Medical University; **Chen, I-Ching**, Wenzao Ursuline University of Languages; **Cheng-hao Weng**, SMIC Private School; **Chisako Nakamura**, Ryukoku University; **Chiyo Myojin**, Kochi University of Technology; **Chris Valvona**, Okinawa Christian College; **Claire DeFord**, Olympic College; **Davi Sukses**, Sutomo 1; **David Farnell**, Fukuoka University; **David Johnson**, Kyushu Sangyo University; **Debbie Sou**, Kwong Tai Middle School; **Devin Ferreira**, University of Central Florida; **Eden Kaiser**, Framingham State University; **Ellie Park**, CNC Language School; **Elvis Bartra García**, Corporación Educativa Continental; **Emiko Yamada**, Westgate Corporation; **Eri Tamura**, Ishikawa Prefectural University; **Fadwa Sleiman**, University of Sharjah; **Frank Gutsche**, Tohoku University; **Frank Lin**, Guangzhou Tufu Culture; **Gavin Young**, Iwate University; **Gerry Landers**, GA Tech Language Institute; **Ghada Ahmed**, University of Bahrain; **Grace Choi**, Grace English School; **Greg Bevan**, Fukuoka University; **Gregg McNabb**, Shizuoka Institute of Science and Technology; **Helen Roland**, Miami Dade College; **Hersong Tang**, Shih Chien University; **Hiroshi Ohashi**, Kyushu University; **Hiroyo Yoshida**, Toyo University; **Hojin Song**, GloLink Education; **HuangFu Yen-Fang**, Tainan University of Technology; **Huey-Jye You**, NTUST; **Jackie Bae**, Plato Language School; **Jade Wong**, Belilios Public School; **James McCarron**, Chiba University; **Jane Kirsch**, INTO George Mason University; **Jenay Seymore**, Hong Ik University; **Joanne Reid**, Shin Min Senior High School; **John Appleby**, Kanda Institute of Foreign Languages; **John Nevara**, Kagoshima University; **Jonathan Bronson**, Approach International Student Center; **Joseph Zhou**, UUabc; **Josh Brunotte**, Aichi Prefectural University; **Junjun Zhou**, Menaul School; **Kaori Yamamoto**; **Katarina Zorkic**, Rosemead College; **Keiko Miyagawa**, Meiji University; **Kevin Tang**, Ritsumeikan Asia Pacific University; **Kieran Julian**, Kanda Institute of Foreign Languages; **Kim Kawashima**, Olympic College; **Kyle Kumataka**, Ritsumeikan Asia Pacific University; **Kyosuke Shimamura**, Kurume University; **Lance Stilp**, Ritsumeikan Asia Pacific University; **Li Zhaoli**, Weifang No.7 Middle School; **Lichu Lin**, NCCU; **Liza Armstrong**, University of Missouri; **Lucas Pignolet**, Ritsumeikan Asia Pacific University; **Luke Harrington**, Chiba University; **M. Lee**, KCC; **Maiko Berger**, Ritsumeikan Asia Pacific University; **Mandy Kan**, CNEC Christian College; **Mari Nakamura**, English Square; **Masako Kikukawa**, Doshisha University; **Matthew Fraser**, Westgate Corporation; **Mayuko Matsunuma**, Seijo University; **Mei-ho Chiu**, Soochow University; **Melissa Potts**, ELS Berkeley; **Michiko Imai**, Aichi University; **Monica Espinoza**, Torrance Adult School; **Ms. Manassara Riensumettharadol**, Kasetsart University; **My Uyen Tran**, Ho Chi Minh City University of Foreign Languages and Information Technology; **Nae-Dong Yang**, NTU; **Narahiko Inoue**, Kyushu University; **Neil Witkin**, Kyushu Sangyo University; **Noriko Tomioka**, Kwansei University; **Olesya Shatunova**, Kanagawa University; **Patricia Fiene**, Midwestern Career College; **Patricia Nation**, Miami Dade College; **Patrick John Johnston**, Ritsumeikan Asia Pacific University; **Paul Hansen**, Hokkaido University; **Paula Snyder**, University of Missouri-Columbia; **Ping Zhang**, Beijing Royal School; **Reiko Kachi**, Aichi University / Chukyo University; **Robert Dykes**, Jin-ai University; **Rosanna Bird**, Approach International Student Center; **Ryo Takahira**, Kurume Fusetsu High School; **Sadie Wang**, Feng Chia University; **Samuel Taylor**, Kyushu Sangyo University; **Sandra Stein**, American University of Kuwait; **Sanooch Nathalang**, Thammasat University; **Sara Sulko**, University of Missouri; **Serena Lo**, Wong Shiu Chi Secondary School; **Shih-Sheng Kuo**, NPUST; **Shin Okada**, Osaka University; **Silvana Carlini**, Colégio Agostiniano Mendel; **Silvia Yafai**, ADVETI: Applied Tech High School; **Stella Millikan**, Fukuoka Women's University; **Summer Webb**, University of Colorado Boulder; **Susumu Hiramatsu**, Okayama University; **Suzanne Littlewood**, Zayed University; **Takako Kuwayama**, Kansai University; **Takashi Urabe**, Aoyama-Gakuin University; **Teo Kim**, OROMedu; **Tim Chambers**; **Toshiya Tanaka**, Kyushu University; **Trevor Holster**, Fukuoka University; **Wakako Takinami**, Tottori University; **Wayne Malcolm**, Fukui University of Technology; **Wendy Wish**, Valencia College; **Xiaoying Zhan**, Beijing Royal Foreign Language School; **Xingwu Chen**, Xueersi-TAL; **Yin Wang**, TAL Education Group; **Yohei Murayama**, Kagoshima University; **Yoko Sakurai**, Aichi University; **Yoko Sato**, Tokyo University of Agriculture and Technology; **Yoon-Ji Ahn**, Daks Education; **Yu-Lim Im**, Daks Education; **Yuriko Ueda**, Ryukoku University; **Yvonne Hodnett**, Australian College of Kuwait; **Yvonne Johnson**, UWCSEA Dover; **Zhang Lianzhong**, Beijing Foreign Studies University

Special thanks to **Tom Jefferies** for all his contributions throughout the development of the series.

GLOSSARY

These words are used in *Reading Explorer* to describe various reading and critical thinking skills.

Analyze	to study a text in detail, e.g., to identify key points, similarities, and differences
Apply	to think about how an idea might be useful in other ways, e.g., solutions to a problem
Classify	to arrange things in groups or categories, based on their characteristics
Evaluate	to examine different sides of an issue, e.g., reasons for and against something
Infer	to "read between the lines"—information the writer expresses indirectly
Interpret	to think about what a writer means by a certain phrase or expression
Justify	to give reasons for a personal opinion, belief, or decision
Rank	to put things in order based on criteria, e.g., size or importance
Reflect	to think deeply about what a writer is saying and how it compares with your own views
Relate	to consider how ideas in a text connect with your own personal experience
Scan	to look through a text to find particular words or information
Skim	to look at a text quickly to get an overall understanding of its main idea
Summarize	to give a brief statement of the main points of a text
Synthesize	to use information from more than one source to make a judgment or comparison

INDEX OF EXAM QUESTION TYPES

The activities in *Reading Explorer, Third Edition* provide comprehensive practice of several question types that feature in standardized tests such as TOEFL® and IELTS.

Common Question Types	IELTS	TOEFL®	Pages
Multiple choice (gist, main idea, detail, reference, inference, vocabulary, paraphrasing)	✓	✓	14, 35, 58, 67, 80, 102, 111, 124, 133, 145, 153, 165, 173, 186, 195, 208, 217, 230, 241, 254, 263
Completion (notes, diagram, chart)	✓		16, 28, 59, 104, 113, 197, 242, 246
Completion (sentence, summary)	✓	✓	36, 94, 103, 134, 138, 146, 154, 187, 231, 255, 268
Short answer	✓		50, 72, 116, 125, 178, 222, 256
Matching headings / information	✓		15, 25, 112, 232, 264
Categorizing (matching features)	✓	✓	59, 134, 265
True / False / Not Given	✓		16, 68, 174
Rhetorical purpose		✓	23, 47, 80, 89, 90, 124, 165, 173, 208, 230, 254

The following tips will help you become a more successful reader.

1 Preview the text

Before you start reading a text, it's important to have some idea of the overall topic. Look at the title, photos, captions, and any maps or infographics. Skim the text quickly, and scan for any key words before reading in detail.

2 Use vocabulary strategies

Here are some strategies to use if you find a word or phrase you're not sure of:

- **Look for definitions** of new words within the reading passage itself.
- **Identify the part of speech and use context** to guess the meaning of homonyms and new words or idioms (see pages 37 and 126).
- **Identify the word roots and affixes** (if any) of new words (see page 135).
- **Use a dictionary** if you need, but be careful to identify the correct definition.

3 Take notes

Note-taking helps you identify the main ideas and details within a text. It also helps you stay focused while reading. Try different ways of organizing your notes, and decide on a method that best suits you. (see page 28)

4 Infer information

Not everything is stated directly within a text. Use your own knowledge, and clues in the text, to make your own inferences and "read between the lines" (see pages 69 and 167).

5 Make connections

As you read, look for words that help you understand how different ideas connect. For example:

- words that signal **cause and effect**
- words that indicate **sequence**
- words that indicate a **speculation or theory** (see page 155)

6 Read critically

Ask yourself questions as you read a text. For example, if the author presents a point of view, are enough supporting reasons or examples provided? Is the evidence reliable? Does the author give a balanced argument? (see pages 25 and 91)

7 Create a summary

Creating a summary is a great way to check your understanding of a text. It also makes it easier to remember the main points. You can summarize in different ways based on the type of text. For example:

- **timelines or flow charts** (see page 197)
- **T-charts** (see page 255)
- **concept maps** (see page 232)
- **outline summaries** (see page 197)